HUMAN SECURITY REPORT 2005

WAR AND PEACE IN THE 21ST CENTURY

PUBLISHED FOR THE

UNIVERSITY OF BRITISH COLUMBIA, CANADA

NEW YORK • OXFORD
OXFORD UNIVERSITY PRESS
2005

Oxford University Press

Oxford University Press, Inc., publishes works that further Oxford University's objective of excellence in research, scholarship, and education.

Oxford New York

Auckland Cape Town Dar es Salaam Hong Kong Karachi
Kuala Lumpur Madrid Melbourne Mexico City Nairobi
New Delhi Shanghai Taipei Toronto

With offices in

Argentina Austria Brazil Chile Czech Republic France Greece
Guatemala Hungary Italy Japan Poland Portugal Singapore
South Korea Switzerland Thailand Turkey Ukraine Vietnam

Published by Oxford University Press, Inc.
198 Madison Avenue, New York, New York 10016
www.oup.com

ISSN 1557-914X

ISBN 13 978-0-19-530739-9

ISBN 0-19-530739-9

---

1 3 5 7 9 8 6 4 2

Printed in Canada on acid-free paper
Cover design: Digitopolis Media Corporation
Cover photo: Frits Meyst / Panos Pictures

FOREWORD

In a world where war, terrorism and humanitarian crises can seem all-pervasive, the *Human Security Report* offers a rare message of hope.

Drawing on research from around the world, this far-ranging study reveals that for more than three decades positive changes have been quietly taking place.

Over the past 30 years the collapse of some 60 dictatorships has freed countless millions of people from repressive rule. The number of democracies has soared, interstate wars have become increasingly rare, and all wars have become less deadly.

In the early 1990s the number of civil wars began to drop as well—a decline that has continued to this day.

And it's not just wars that are in decline—notwithstanding Rwanda, Srebrenica and Darfur—the number of genocides and other mass killings is also dramatically down worldwide.

The fact that wars have been getting less frequent and less deadly is good news for the developing world, where most armed conflicts now take place.

The *Human Security Report* argues that peace and development are two sides of the same coin—that equitable development helps build security, while war is 'development in reverse'.

Building inclusive democracies and creating more effective development strategies are both highly effective long-term security policies. But as the *Report* shows, the big decline in warfare in the 1990s is due primarily to the dramatic UN-led post–Cold War upsurge in peacekeeping, peacebuilding and conflict prevention. It turns out that co-operative multilateral security strategies are far more effective than the UN's critics allow.

The *Human Security Report 2005* tracks and examines the extraordinary changes in global security that have taken place since the end of World War II. The data are revelatory, the analyses are compelling, and the case for a new approach to securing peace is persuasive.

That new approach is 'human security'.

Human security privileges people over states, reconciliation over revenge, diplomacy over deterrence, and multilateral engagement over coercive unilateralism.

But human security's aspirations and reality do not always coincide. Hundreds of millions of people continue to live in countries wracked by violence and poverty. And human security policies—from preventive diplomacy to post-conflict peacebuilding—are frequently underfunded, lacking in political support and flawed in execution.

The *Human Security Report* provides the data and analysis that show how extraordinary progress has been made despite these limitations.

Archbishop Desmond Tutu
The Desmond Tutu Peace Centre www.tutu.org
June 21, 2005

ACKNOWLEDGEMENTS

Team for the *Human Security Report 2005*
Andrew Mack, director and editor-in-chief
Zoe Nielsen, deputy director

In-house team:
Todd Martin, information officer; Eric Nicholls, program officer (data management); Federico Velasquez, program officer (manuscript coordination); Robert Hartfiel, program officer (coordinator, Human Security Gateway); Leslie Lehman, administrator; Nathan Lepp, program officer; Michael Eddy, research assistant (part-time); Elim Ng, research assistant (part-time)

Consultants:
Jon Tinker, Panos Institute of Canada; Ruth Wilson, West Coast Editorial Associates; Barbara Tomlin, West Coast Editorial Associates; Georgia Dahle, Method Events; Suzy Hainsworth, Maullin Consulting; Ruder Finn Inc.

Design and layout:
Digitopolis Media Corporation

Former members of the in-house team:
Pat Leidl, editorial director; Malcolm MacLachlan, managing editor; Mary Rose MacLachlan, managing editor; Angela Blake, research assistant; Marko Pajalic, research assistant; Jennifer Quirt, research assistant; Sarah Louw, research assistant (part-time); Kristin van der Leest, research assistant (part-time)

Special thanks:
The *Human Security Report* team extends special thanks to the Uppsala Conflict Data Program, Sweden; the International Peace Research Institute, Oslo (PRIO); Linda Cornett and Mark Gibney of the University of North Carolina, Asheville; and Ted Gurr and Monty Marshall of the Center for International Development and Conflict Management at the University of Maryland.

Special thanks also to our funders: the Canadian International Development Agency; Department of Foreign Affairs and International Trade (Canada); the Norwegian Royal Ministry of Foreign Affairs; the Swedish International Development Cooperation Agency; the Swiss Agency for Development Cooperation; the Swiss Federal Department of Foreign Affairs; the Department for International Development (United Kingdom) and the Rockefeller Foundation.

Contributors:
The following individuals provided text, background papers and/or data that were used in the preparation of this report:

Linda Cornett, University of North Carolina, Asheville; Sunil Dasgupta, Georgetown University; Luke Dowdney, ISER/Viva Rio; Kristine Eck, Uppsala University; Epicentre/ Médecins Sans Frontières; Martin Foreman; Faten Ghosn, Pennsylvania State University; Mark Gibney, University of North Carolina, Asheville; Nils Petter Gleditsch, International Peace Research Institute, Oslo (PRIO); Tedd Gurr, University of Maryland; Lotta Harbom, Uppsala University; Barbara Harff, US Naval College; Håvard Hegre, International Peace Research Institute, Oslo (PRIO); Don Hubert, Department of Foreign Affairs and International Trade (Canada); Joakim Kreutz, Uppsala University; Bethany Lacina, Stanford University; Mary Louise Leidl; Monty Marshall, George Mason University; Graeme Newman, State University of New York, Albany; Phil Orchard, University of British Columbia; Glenn Palmer, Pennsylvania State University; Alicia Priest; Les Roberts, Johns Hopkins University; Richard Rose, University of Strathclyde; Bruce Russett, Yale University; Peter Singer, The Brookings Institution; Stephen Stedman, Stanford University; Håvard Strand, International Peace Research Institute, Oslo (PRIO); Fred Tanner, Geneva Centre for Security Policy; Kathy Vandergrift, World Vision; Peter Wallensteen, Uppsala University; Lars Wilhelmsen, International Peace Research Institute, Oslo (PRIO).

Reviewers:
The following individuals reviewed material for this report:

Elissa Goldberg, Department of Foreign Affairs and International Trade (Canada); Peter Grabowsky, Australian National University; Priscilla Hayner, International Center for Transitional Justice; Don Hubert, Department of Foreign Affairs and International Trade (Canada); Macartan Humphreys, Columbia University; Felicity Hill, Uppsala University; LaShawn Jefferson, Human Rights Watch; Mohamed Mattar, Johns Hopkins University; Les Roberts, Johns Hopkins University; Clifford Shearing, Australian National University; Michael Small, Department of Foreign Affairs and International Trade (Canada); Shana Swiss, Women's Rights International; Jon Tinker, Panos Institute of Canada; Kathy Vandergrift, World Vision.

The *Human Security Report* team is deeply grateful to the many other individuals who are not listed above, but who gave generously of both their time and expertise during the preparation of this report.

The Human Security Centre team takes full responsibility for the content of this report.

ABOUT THE HUMAN SECURITY CENTRE

The *Human Security Report* is produced by the Human Security Centre. The centre, which is based at the Liu Institute for Global Issues at the University of British Columbia, was established in 2002 by the Honourable Lloyd Axworthy, former Canadian minister for foreign affairs and then-Director of the Liu Institute. Dr. Axworthy had promoted the concept of human security vigorously while in office and continues to do so in his current position as president and vice-chancellor of the University of Winnipeg.

The Human Security Centre's mission is to make human security-related research more accessible to the policy and research communities, the media, educators and the public. The centre undertakes independent research and works with a large network of collaborators in research institutions around the world.

The Human Security Centre's flagship publication, the annual *Human Security Report,* is complemented by the Human Security Gateway, an online database of human security resources, and two online bulletins, *Human Security News* and *Human Security Research.*

Human Security Gateway (www.humansecuritygateway.info)
The Gateway is a rapidly expanding searchable online database of human security-related resources, including reports, journal articles, news items and fact sheets. The Gateway was developed in collaboration with the Canadian Consortium on Human Security.

Human Security Research (www.humansecuritycentre.org)
Human Security Research is an online monthly compilation of new human security-related research published by university research institutes, think-tanks, governments, IGOs and NGOs.

Human Security News (www.humansecuritycentre.org)
Human Security News is an online daily roundup of the latest human security-related news stories from around the world. It is published on weekday mornings.

All of these e-resources are available free of charge.

PREFACE

The genesis of the *Human Security Report* dates back to the end of the 1990s when I was working as Director of the Strategic Planning Unit in UN Secretary-General Kofi Annan's Executive Office.

Shortly after arriving in New York I was surprised to find that the UN had no way of determining whether wars, mass slaughters of civilians or core human rights abuses were increasing or decreasing around the world.

The fact that there has been a dramatic global decline in political violence since the end of the Cold War was, even then, evident to many conflict researchers. But it had gone largely unnoticed by officials and the public alike—and even some scholars working in the field.

In a sense this wasn't surprising. The global media gave front-page coverage to new wars, but mostly ignored the larger number of existing conflicts that quietly ended. And neither the UN nor any other international organisation collected data on wars, genocides, terrorism and violent abuses of human rights. This is still the case more than five years later.

Without access to reliable data on global and regional trends in political violence, the UN, regional organisations and donor governments had no way of determining whether *in general* their conflict prevention, peacebuilding or human rights promotion policies were effective.

Security issues are extremely sensitive for member states of the UN and all attempts to create a substantial in-house research capacity in the Secretariat that could collate data and examine sensitive security issues have been frustrated.

Fortunately, the scholarly community has produced a wealth of relevant data that to a degree make up for the absence of official statistics. Although much of this material is highly technical and inaccessible to non-specialists, it has provided a solid base for the *Human Security Report 2005*.

The challenge has been to make sense of the mass of often contested data and analysis available in the research community around the world and to commission new material where necessary. Last but not least, the findings had to be integrated into a comprehensive package that was accessible to policymakers and other non-specialists.

This task has proven far more time-consuming than any of us could have imagined.

We owe our funders—the governments of Canada, Norway, Sweden, Switzerland and the United Kingdom—a deep debt of gratitude for their patience.

Finally, we have almost certainly missed some critical new findings that would throw further light on the changes that this report chronicles. We hope that where this is the case readers will let us know so new findings can be included in future volumes.

Andrew Mack
Director
Human Security Centre
Liu Institute for Global Issues
University of British Columbia
June 2005

WHAT IS HUMAN SECURITY?

The traditional goal of 'national security' has been the defence of the *state* from external threats. The focus of human security, by contrast, is the protection of *individiuals*.

Human security is a relatively new concept, now widely used to describe the complex of interrelated threats associated with civil war, genocide and the displacement of populations.

Human security and national security should be—and often are—mutually reinforcing. But secure states do not automatically mean secure peoples. Protecting citizens from foreign attack may be a necessary condition for the security of individuals, but it is certainly not a sufficient one. Indeed, during the last 100 years far more people have been killed by their own governments than by foreign armies.

A new approach to security is needed because the analytic frameworks that have traditionally explained wars between states—and prescribed policies to prevent them—are largely irrelevant to violent conflicts *within* states. The latter now make up more than 95% of armed conflicts.

All proponents of human security agree that its primary goal is the protection of individuals. However, consensus breaks down over precisely what threats individuals should be protected from. Proponents of the 'narrow' concept of human security focus on violent threats to individuals or, as UN Secretary-General Kofi Annan puts it, 'the protection of communities and individuals from internal violence'.

Proponents of the 'broad' concept of human security argue that the threat agenda should include hunger, disease and natural disasters because these kill far more people than war, genocide and terrorism combined. Human security policy, they argue, should seek to protect people from these threats as well as from violence. In its broadest formulations the human security agenda also encompasses economic insecurity and 'threats to human dignity'.

The broader view of human security has many adherents—and it is easy to see why. Few would dispute the desirability of protecting people from malnutrition, disease and natural disasters as well as from violence. Moreover there is considerable evidence to suggest that all of these societal threats are interrelated in the mostly poor countries in which they are concentrated.

While still subject to lively debate, the two approaches to human security are complementary rather than contradictory.

For both pragmatic and methodological reasons, however, the *Human Security Report* uses the narrow concept.

The pragmatic rationale is simple. There are already several annual reports that describe and analyse trends in global poverty, disease, malnutrition and ecological devastation: the threats embraced by the broad concept of human security. There would be little point in duplicating the data and analysis that such reports provide. But no annual publication maps the trends in the incidence, severity, causes and consequences of global violence as comprehensively as the *Human Security Report*.

The methodological rationale is also simple. A concept that lumps together threats as diverse as genocide and affronts to personal dignity may be useful for advocacy, but it has limited utility for policy analysis. It is no accident that the broad conception of human security articulated by the UN Development Programme in its much-cited 1994 *Human Development Report* has rarely been used to guide research programs.

Scholarly debate is a normal part of the evolution of new concepts, but it is of little interest to policymakers. The policy community is, however, increasingly using the concept of human security because it speaks to the interrelatedness of security, development and the protection of civilians.

CONTENTS

List of boxes

List of figures

Sven Torfinn / Magnum Photos

WAR AND PEACE IN THE 21ST CENTURY

Introduction

The first *Human Security Report* presents a comprehensive and evidence-based portrait of global security. It identifies and examines major trends in global political violence, asks what factors drive these trends and examines some of the consequences. It poses major challenges to conventional wisdom.

Over the past dozen years, the global security climate has changed in dramatic, positive, but largely unheralded ways. Civil wars, genocides and international crises have all declined sharply. International wars, now only a small minority of all conflicts, have been in steady decline for a much longer period, as have military coups and the average number of people killed per conflict per year.[1]

> The number of genocides and politicides plummeted by 80% between 1988 and 2001.

The wars that dominated the headlines of the 1990s were real—and brutal—enough. But the global media have largely ignored the 100-odd conflicts that have quietly ended since 1988. During this period, more wars stopped than started.

The extent of the change in global security following the end of the Cold War has been remarkable:

- The number of armed conflicts around the world has declined by more than 40% since the early 1990s (see Figure 1.1 in Part I).[2]
- Between 1991 (the high point for the post–World War II period) and 2004, 28 armed struggles for self-determination started or restarted, while 43 were contained or ended. There were just 25 armed secessionist conflicts under way in 2004, the lowest number since 1976.[3]
- Notwithstanding the horrors of Rwanda, Srebrenica and elsewhere, the number of genocides and politicides plummeted by 80% between the 1988 high point and 2001 (Figure 1.11).
- International crises, often harbingers of war, declined by more than 70% between 1981 and 2001 (Figure 1.5).
- The dollar value of major international arms transfers fell by 33% between 1990 and 2003 (Figure 1.10). Global military expenditure and troop numbers declined sharply in the 1990s as well.
- The number of refugees dropped by some 45% between 1992 and 2003, as more and more wars came to an end (Figure 3.1).[4]

- Five out of six regions in the developing world saw a net decrease in core human rights abuses between 1994 and 2003 (Figures 2.6 and 2.7).

The positive changes noted above date from the end of the Cold War. Other changes can be traced back to the 1950s:

- The average number of battle-deaths per conflict per year—the best measure of the deadliness of warfare—has been falling dramatically but unevenly since the 1950s. In 1950, for example, the average armed conflict killed 38,000 people; in 2002 the figure was 600, a 98% decline.
- The period since the end of World War II is the longest interval of uninterrupted peace between the major powers in hundreds of years.[5]
- The number of actual and attempted military coups has been declining for more than 40 years. In 1963 there were 25 coups and attempted coups around the world, the highest number in the post–World War II period. In 2004 there were only 10 coup attempts—a 60% decline. All of them failed.[6]

International terrorism is the only form of political violence that appears to be getting worse, but the data are contested. Although some datasets have shown an overall decline in international terrorist incidents since the early 1980s (Figure 1.12), the most recent data suggest a dramatic increase in the number of high-casualty attacks since the September 11 attacks on the US in 2001.

Myths and misunderstandings

Public understanding of global security is hampered by many myths and misunderstandings about its nature. Some of these are originated in the media; others were propagated, or reiterated by, international organisations and NGOs. Such myths include claims that:

- The number of armed conflicts is increasing.
- Wars are getting deadlier.
- The number of genocides is increasing.
- The gravest threat to human security is international terrorism.
- 90% of those killed in today's wars are civilians.[7]
- 5 million people were killed in wars in the 1990s.
- 2 million children were killed in wars during the last decade.
- 80% of refugees are women and children.
- Women are the primary victims of war.
- There are 300,000 child soldiers serving around the world today.

Not one of these claims is based on reliable data. All are suspect; some are demonstrably false. Yet they are widely believed because they reinforce popular assumptions. They flourish in the absence of official figures to contradict them and conjure a picture of global security trends that is grossly distorted. And they often drive political agendas.

A consistent theme in the *Human Security Report 2005* is the inadequacy of available data, especially comparable year-on-year data that can be used to document and measure national, regional and global trends. In some cases, data are simply non-existent.

> International terrorism is the only form of political violence that appears to be getting worse, but the data are contested.

To address these challenges when preparing this report, the Human Security Centre has drawn on a variety of data compiled by research institutions around the world and commissioned a major public opinion poll on popular attitudes to security in 11 countries. The Human Security Centre also commissioned a new dataset from Uppsala University's Conflict Data Program. The Uppsala/Human Security Centre dataset is the most comprehensive yet created on political violence around the world. Its findings, the first of which are published in this report, will provide key trend data for future editions of the *Human Security Report*.

Structure and contents

The *Human Security Report 2005* has a five-part structure:

- **Part I: The changing face of global violence** looks mainly at long-term global and regional trends in political violence.
- **Part II: The human security audit** presents the findings of the new dataset on political violence around the world. It also examines other threats to human security.
- **Part III: Assault on the vulnerable** explores the impact of political violence on refugees, women and children.
- **Part IV: Counting the indirect costs of war** examines some of the long-term, indirect effects of war.
- **Part V: Why the dramatic decline in armed conflict?** examines the major drivers of the radical improvement in global security since the end of the Cold War.

> The period following the end of World War II was the longest interval in many centuries without a war between the major powers.

The following discussion briefly outlines the main themes of the report and reviews some key findings from the various sections.

War trends

In the early 1990s, at precisely the point that media commentators in the West began to fret about a worldwide explosion in ethnic violence, the number of armed conflicts began to drop (Figure 1.1). This little-noticed decline, which has been carefully tracked by the research community, has continued ever since.

The five-decade period following the end of World War II was the longest interval in many centuries without a war between the major powers, and scholars sometimes refer to it as the 'Long Peace'. This description is deeply misleading. Although no wars between the major powers took place in this period, every decade saw sharp increases in political violence in the rest of the world.

Between 1946 and 1991 the number of state-based armed conflicts being fought worldwide trebled (Figure 1.2), with most of the killing taking place in poor countries (Figure 1.9).

Moreover, although it is true that the major powers did not fight each other during this period, their post–World War II history has been anything but peaceful. Indeed, the UK, France, the US and the Soviet Union/Russia top the list of countries involved in international wars in the last 60 years (Figure 1.3).

> The end of the Cold War brought remarkable changes to the global security climate.

'Realist' scholars attributed the Long Peace between the major powers to the security-enhancing effect of a bipolar security system underpinned by mutual nuclear deterrence. Many worried that the end of the Cold War would usher in a new era of severe crises, even wars, between the major powers.[8] But today, 15 years after the end of the Cold War, the number of international crises is just a small fraction of the 1981 high-point (Figure 1.5) and the prospect of war between the major powers has never seemed more remote.

The end of the Cold War brought remarkable changes to the global security climate. Security pessimists saw the upsurge of secessionist violence in the former Soviet Union, the dissolution of the Yugoslav federation, genocide in Rwanda and other ethnic confrontations as portents of an increasingly violent future.

This pessimism was quite unfounded. Between 1992 and 2003, the last year for which complete data are currently available, the number of armed conflicts (Figure 1.2) dropped by 40%. The number of wars—the most deadly category of armed conflict—declined even more sharply.

In most parts of the world the drop in conflict numbers started after the end of the Cold War (Figure 1.2). But in two important regions the decline started earlier. In the

Middle East and North Africa, political violence began to decrease at the beginning of the 1980s. In part this was because the front-line Arab states recognised that fighting wars with a conventionally superior and nuclear-armed Israel was a fruitless endeavour, and in part because ruthless state repression was succeeding in crushing domestic insurgencies.

In East Asia, Southeast Asia and Oceania the decline in both the number and deadliness of armed conflicts started in the mid-1970s (Figures 1.2 and 1.9). This was a period in which massive external involvement in the region's conflicts was rapidly winding down, and in which countries in the region were experiencing the highest rates of economic growth in the world. As Part V of this report shows, the probability of war decreases as national income, and hence state capacity, increases (Figure 5.4).

The challenge of Africa

Most of the world's armed conflicts now take place in sub-Saharan Africa (Figure 1.2). At the turn of the 21st century more people were being killed in wars in this region than in the rest of the world combined (Figure 1.9).

> Violent conflict exacerbates the conditions that gave rise to it in the first place, creating a 'conflict trap' from which escape is extraordinarily difficult.

Almost every country across the broad middle belt of the continent—from Somalia in the east to Sierra Leone in the west, from Sudan in the north to Angola in the south—remains trapped in a volatile mix of poverty, crime, unstable and inequitable political institutions, ethnic discrimination, low state capacity and the 'bad neighbourhoods' of other crisis-ridden states—all factors associated with increased risk of armed conflict.[9]

The combination of pervasive poverty, declining GDP per capita, poor infrastructure, weak administration, external intervention and an abundance of cheap weapons, plus the effects of a major decline in per capita foreign assistance for much of the 1990s, mean that armed conflicts in these countries are difficult to avoid, contain or end.

Moreover, violent conflict exacerbates the very conditions that gave rise to it in the first place, creating a classic 'conflict trap' from which escape is extraordinarily difficult. Unsurprisingly, sustaining peace settlements is a major challenge in many of the continent's post-conflict countries.

Yet even in Africa there are signs of hope. The new Uppsala/Human Security Centre dataset shows that the number of conflicts in Africa in which a government was one of the warring parties declined from 15 to 10 between 2002 and 2003 (Figure 2.1). The number of cases of 'one-sided' violence—defined as the slaughter of at least 25 civilians in the course of a year and called one-sided because the victims can't fight back—declined from 17 to 11 (Figure 2.1), a drop of 35%. Meanwhile, reported fatalities from all forms of political violence were down by more than 24% (Figure 2.4).

These changes reflect the increased involvement of the international community and African regional organisations in conflict resolution and post-conflict reconstruction, rather than major changes in the underlying risk factors. Africa remains the world's most conflict-prone continent.

Wars have fewer victims today

The decline in the numbers killed in wars has been even more dramatic than the drop in the number of conflicts, although it has taken place over a much longer period and for quite different reasons.

The *Human Security Report 2005* draws on a new dataset on battle-deaths that occurred between 1946 and 2002 in conflicts where a government was one of the warring parties. As Figure 1.6 shows, nearly 700,000 people were killed in the wars of 1950, while in 2002 the figure was just 20,000.

This substantial long-term decline in battle-deaths is due primarily to a radical shift in modes of warfare.

The wars of the 1950s, 1960s and 1970s, and to a lesser degree the 1980s, were characterised by major battles fought by large armies armed with heavy conventional weapons and supported by one or other superpower.

Today most wars are fought in poor countries with armies that lack heavy conventional weapons—or superpower patrons. In a typical low-intensity conflict weak government forces confront small, ill-trained rebel forces equipped with small arms and light weapons. Skirmishes and attacks on civilians are preferred to major engagements. Although these conflicts often involve gross human rights abuses, they kill relatively few people compared with the major wars of 20 or more years ago.

In addition to low-intensity conflicts, a small number of high-tech wars have been fought by the US and its allies since the end of the Cold War. In the Gulf War, Kosovo and Afghanistan, the huge military advantage enjoyed by coalition forces, plus increased use of precision-guided munitions, meant that victory on the battlefield was gained quickly and with relatively few battle-deaths.

The current conflict in Iraq is the exception: while the conventional war that began in 2003 was over quickly and with relatively few casualties, tens of thousands have been killed in the subsequent—and ongoing—urban insurgency.

The battle-death data also demonstrate how the world's deadliest killing zones have shifted locale over time (Figure 1.9):

- From the end of World War II to the mid-1970s, by far the greatest numbers of battle-deaths were in East Asia, Southeast Asia and Oceania.
- In the 1980s, most of the killing took place in the Middle East and North Africa, Central and South Asia, and in sub-Saharan Africa.
- By the turn of the 21st century, sub-Saharan Africa had become the world's most violent region, experiencing more battle-deaths than all other regions combined.

Refugees and displaced persons

While the major wars of the 1950s, 1960s and 1970s were associated with very high death tolls, the available data suggest that these wars did not generate commensurately large flows of displaced people.[10] In fact, the figures indicate that the really big increases in people fleeing their homes in fear of their lives did not start until the 1980s.

Between 1980 and 1992 the total number of people estimated to have been displaced increased from 16 million to more than 40 million. While the data, especially on internally displaced persons, are questionable, there is little doubt about the remarkable upward trend during this period.

Increased targeting of civilians appears to be a major reason for the huge increase. As one UN report put it, 'Refugee movements are no longer side effects of conflict, but in many cases are central to the objectives and tactics of war.'[11]

The battle-death data demonstrate how the world's deadliest killing zones have shifted locale over time.

While displacement is a humanitarian tragedy and puts people at greater risk of succumbing to disease and malnutrition, it also prevents many violent deaths. Indeed, had the millions of people displaced in the 1980s and early 1990s *not* fled their homes, hundreds of thousands, possibly more, would likely have been killed. So the massive displacement in this period is likely part of the reason for the declining number of battle-deaths.

Genocide

Genocides and other deliberate slaughters of civilians are usually counted separately from armed conflicts, on the grounds that the killing of unarmed innocents does not constitute warfare.

Such killings usually—but not always—take place within the context of a war. So if wars decline, we would expect that cases involving the slaughter of civilians would decline as well. This is precisely what has happened, but the 80% decline in the number of genocides (Figure 1.11) since the end of the Cold War has been twice as great as the drop in the number of conflicts

Until now there has been no systematic annual reporting of the death tolls from such one-sided violence. This omission is addressed by the new Uppsala/Human Security Centre dataset discussed in Part II of this report. The data for 2002 and 2003 suggest that cases of one-sided violence are as common as cases of state-based armed conflict, but that one-sided violence kills far fewer people.[12]

Terrorism

Like genocide, terrorism is directed primarily against civilians. But although the focus of enormous attention, international terrorism has killed fewer than 1000 people a year, on average, over the past 30 years.

The trends in international terrorism have been the subject of considerable recent controversy. The US State Department has published data on international terrorist incidents around the world for more than 20 years—a rare exception to the general rule that governments do not collect statistics on trends in political violence.

> International terrorism is a development issue for the global South, as well as being a vital security issue for both the North and South.

The State Department's data for 2003 (Figure 1.12) showed a 60% decline in the number of international terrorist attacks since the early 1980s, and in 2004 the Bush administration cited this finding to support its claim that the US was winning the 'war on terror'. But these data were profoundly misleading—they conflated relatively trivial incidents with 'significant' attacks. The former have indeed decreased, but the latter have shot up more than *eightfold* since the early 1980s (Figure 1.13).

In April 2005 the Bush administration published new data showing a dramatic increase in 'significant' international terrorist attacks in 2004.

Despite the relatively low death toll resulting from international terrorism, it is still a major human security concern for several reasons:

- First, the war on terror has provided a large part of the rationale for major wars in Afghanistan and Iraq.
- Second, as recent opinion survey data show, the US-led counterterror campaign has been associated with extraordinarily high levels of anti-Americanism in the Muslim world.[13] This has almost certainly increased the number of potential terrorist recruits.
- Third—and perhaps most important—terrorists may at some stage acquire and use weapons of mass destruction (WMD). This prospect is of particular concern because terrorists, unlike states, cannot be deterred by threats of nuclear retaliation.

Much of the attention paid to possible WMD attacks has focused on the threat posed to the US and other Western countries. But mass-casualty terror attacks also pose a major threat to poor countries—even when they are not directly targeted.

The likely consequence of a successful high-casualty WMD attack against the US, for example, would be a major downturn in the global economy. According to the World Bank, the September 11 attacks on the US in 2001 pushed millions of people in the developing world into poverty, and likely killed tens of thousands of under-five-year-olds—a far greater toll than the total number of deaths directly caused by the attack.

International terrorism is thus a development issue for the global South, as well being a vital security issue for both the North and the South.

Human rights abuse

The Political Terror Scale (PTS) database, which is maintained by researchers at the University of North Carolina, Asheville, records global and regional trend data on human rights abuse in the developing world. It uses a composite indicator that captures such core human rights abuses as torture, extrajudicial executions, the 'disappearance' of dissidents and officially backed death squads.[14] Drawing on information compiled by Amnesty International and the US State Department, it ranks each country on a five-point scale every year.

Some 20 years of these data are shown in Figures 2.6 and 2.7. Half the regions of the developing world saw the level of state repression increase somewhat between 1980 and 1994, while five out of the six regions discussed showed a modest decrease from 1994 to 2003. Under-reporting and different coding standards in the 1980s likely mean that the reduction in core human rights violations is greater than the trend data suggest.

There has been a dramatic world-wide decline in authoritarianism over the past quarter century.

The most insidious forms of repression occur where the coercive power of the state is so pervasive that actual physical repression rarely has to be used. What might be called 'rule by fear' is most prevalent in highly authoritarian states.

However, there is room for optimism here too, since there has been a substantial worldwide decline in authoritarianism over the past quarter century (Figure 5.3).

Indirect deaths

Many of the costs of war are obvious—battle-deaths, displaced people, flattened cities, destroyed infrastructure, capital flight and slashed living standards. Less obvious are the high numbers of 'indirect' or 'excess' deaths—non-violent deaths that would not have occurred had there been no fighting. In most of today's armed conflicts, war-exacerbated disease and malnutrition kill far more people than missiles, bombs and bullets.

It is no surprise that poor countries suffer most from these indirect deaths. As Part IV of this report demonstrates, these countries experience the most wars, their citizens are more susceptible to disease and malnutrition to begin with, their health systems are fragile and under-funded, and the humanitarian assistance they receive is often too little and too late.

Indirect deaths receive little attention in the media because it is almost impossible to distinguish them from 'normal' deaths caused by malnutrition and disease. Few outsiders notice a statistical increase in already high mortality rates—even though the number of additional deaths is likely to be many times greater than the number of battle-deaths. In some cases the ratio of 'indirect' to 'direct' deaths exceeds 10:1.

Yet only when the death rate from malnutrition and disease escalates suddenly—as has recently happened in Sudan's Darfur region—do indirect deaths engage the attention of the media and generate pressure for action.

The indirect costs of warfare will be a central theme of the *Human Security Report 2006*. Ignorance of the scope and impact of these costs hampers effective planning for humanitarian assistance and post-conflict reconstruction programs. Donor governments, international agencies and NGOs often complain about the lack of information, but few do much to address the problem.

Then, there is the issue of accountability. Neither governments nor rebels are normally held legally or morally responsible for the indirect deaths caused by their actions, in part because the linkage between war, disease and malnutrition is not well understood.

A government or rebel group that slaughters hundreds of civilians in wartime can, in principle, be brought to justice before the International Criminal Court. But if the same government or rebel group acts in a knowingly reckless and negligent manner, and in so doing causes tens or even hundreds of thousands to perish from disease and hunger, it is unlikely ever to be charged with a crime, let alone be successfully prosecuted.

Violent crime

While violent crime is clearly a threat to human security, attempts to track global and regional trends in criminal violence are hampered by lack of data, under-reporting and under-recording, conflicting definitions and, in some cases, the reporting of war deaths as homicides.

Part II includes a review of the available data on global trends in homicide (Figure 2.9) and rape (Figure 2.10). But the discussion is in part an exercise in demonstrating how little we know. The rape data are particularly problematic. It is impossible, for example, to determine whether the increase in rape rates in many regions is a function of increased rape, increased reporting, or both.

> Between 1946 and 1991 there was a twelvefold rise in the number of civil wars—the greatest jump in 200 years.

The extent of rape in war is examined in Part III, but here, too, the discussion is hampered by the absence of reliable cross-national data. However, a major recent case study in Sierra Leone found a clear association between displacement and being a victim of sexual violence. Displaced women were twice as likely to be raped as those who remained in their homes.

Case study evidence indicates that this association may exist in other conflict zones as well. If so, then it is reasonable to assume that the fourfold increase in displacement between the early 1970s and the early 1990s (Figure 3.1) was associated with a major increase in the incidence of sexual violence.

The causes of peace

Over the past three decades two epochal changes in international politics have had a huge but little analysed impact on global security. These changes help explain both the increase in armed conflict around the world from the end of World War II to the early 1990s and its subsequent sharp decline.

Between 1946 and 1991 there was a twelvefold rise in the number of civil wars—the greatest jump in 200 years.[15] The data suggest that anti-colonialism and the geopolitics of the Cold War were the major determinants of this increase (Figure 5.2).

By the early 1980s the wars of liberation from colonial rule, which had accounted for 60% to 100% of all international wars fought since the early 1950s, had virtually ended. With the demise of colonialism, a major driver of warfare around the world—one that had caused 81 wars since 1816—simply ceased to exist.

Then, in the late 1980s, the Cold War, which had driven approximately one-third of all wars (civil as well as international) in the post–World War II period, also came to an end. This not only removed the only risk of violent conflict between the major powers and their allies, it also meant that Washington and Moscow stopped supporting their erstwhile allies in many so-called proxy wars in the developing world. Denied external support, many of these conflicts quietly ground to a halt.

With the colonial era and then the Cold War over, global warfare began to decline rapidly in the early 1990s. Between 1992 and 2002 the number of civil wars being fought each year plummeted by 80%. The decline in all armed conflicts—that is, wars plus minor armed conflicts—was 40%.

The end of the Cold War not only removed a major source of conflict from the international system, it also allowed the UN to begin to play the security-enhancing role that its founders had intended, but which the organisation had long been prevented from pursuing.

> With the colonial era and then the Cold War over, the number of armed conflicts began to decline rapidly in the early 1990s.

With the Security Council no longer paralysed by Cold War politics, the UN spearheaded a veritable explosion of conflict prevention, peacemaking and post-conflict peacebuilding activities in the early 1990s. Part V of this report describes the extent of this unprecedented surge in activism, which included:

- A sixfold increase in the number of preventive diplomacy missions (those that seek to stop wars from starting) mounted by the UN between 1990 and 2002.
- A fourfold increase in peacemaking activites (those that seek to stop ongoing conflicts) over the same period (Figure 5.5).
- A sevenfold increase in the number of 'Friends of the Secretary-General', 'Contact Groups' and other government-initiated mechanisms to support peacemaking and peacebuilding missions between 1990 and 2003.
- An elevenfold increase in the number of economic sanctions in place against regimes around the world between 1989 and 2001.
- A fourfold increase in the number of UN peacekeeping operations between 1987 and 1999 (Figure 5.6). The increase in numbers was not the only change. The new missions were, on average, far larger and more complex than those of the Cold War era and they have been relatively successful in sustaining the peace. With 40% of post-conflict countries relapsing into war again within five years, the importance of preventing wars from restarting is obvious.

The UN did not act alone, of course; the World Bank, donor states, a number of regional organisations and thousands of NGOs worked closely with UN agencies and often played independent conflict prevention, conflict mitigation and peacebuilding roles of their own. Prior to the end of the Cold War there had been little sustained activity in any of these areas.

Not one of the peacebuilding and conflict prevention programs *on its own* had much of an impact on global security in this period. Taken together, however, their effect has been profound.

As the upsurge of international activism grew in scope and intensity through the 1990s, the number of crises, wars and genocides declined. Correlation does not prove cause, of course, and Part V reviews other possible explanations for the dramatic decline in political violence in the post–Cold War era.

Over the long term the evidence suggests that the risk of civil war is reduced by equitable economic growth, increased state capacity and inclusive democracy. Development is a necessary condition for security—and vice versa.

But Part V demonstrates that none of these factors can account for the sharp decline in political violence around the world that started in the early 1990s and has continued ever since. It argues that the single most compelling explanation for this decline is the upsurge of international activism described briefly above and in more detail in Part V.

As the upsurge of international activism grew through the 1990s, the number of crises, wars and genocides declined.

The *Human Security Report 2006* will include a more detailed examination of the debates that continue to divide the scholarly community about the causes of peace.

No grounds for complacency

The dramatic improvements in global security documented in this first *Human Security Report* are real and important. But they are no cause for complacency. Some 60 wars are still being fought around the world and the post–Cold War years have also been marked by major humanitarian emergencies, gross abuses of human rights, war crimes, and ever-deadlier acts of terrorism. But the conflicts that remain—in Iraq, Darfur and elsewhere—continue to exact a deadly toll.

Moreover, the fact that wars come to an end does not necessarily mean that their underlying causes have been addressed. Indeed, a recent UK government report argues that much of the decrease in armed conflict is due, in fact, to its 'suppression or containment, rather than resolution'.[16] In addition to creating a legacy of bitter hostility that hampers reconciliation, armed conflicts invariably exacerbate the structural conditions that led to their outbreak in the first place. This is why the greatest single risk factor for armed conflict is a recent history of political violence.

Some current developments suggest that the progress of the past dozen years now may be at risk. In May 2005 the International Crisis Group reported that ten conflict situations around the world had deteriorated in the previous month; only five had improved.[17] In June 2005 the influential *Peace and Conflict 2005* report noted that 'risks of future genocides and political mass murder remain high in a half-dozen countries and a significant possibility in a dozen others.'[18]

The risk of new wars breaking out—or old ones resuming—is very real in the absence of a sustained and strengthened commitment to conflict prevention and post-conflict peacebuilding. The post–Cold War decline in conflict numbers was not inevitable—and it is certainly not irreversible.

But while there is no room for complacency, nor is there any cause for pessimism. The international community's successes in reducing armed conflict worldwide in the post–Cold War era have been achieved despite inadequate resources, ad hoc planning, inappropriate mandates (in the case of UN peace operations) and lack of support from the countries most able to help. With additional resources, more appropriate mandates, and a greater commitment to conflict prevention and peacebuilding, far more could be achieved.

Effective policy doesn't just need extra resources and greater political commitment. It also requires a better understanding of global and regional security trends—and of why some conflict prevention and mitigation strategies succeed while others fail.

Providing the data and analysis to further such an understanding is the central goal of the *Human Security Report.*

OVERVIEW

ENDNOTES

1. References for all statistics in the Overview are found in the main body of the *Report* unless otherwise noted.
2. The data cited here refer to conflicts in which a state is one of the warring parties. Until 2002 no data were collected for armed conflicts in which a state was *not* a party.
3. This finding—from Monty G. Marshall and Ted Robert Gurr, *Peace and Conflict 2005*, Center for International Development and Conflict Management (College Park, MD: University of Maryland, May 2005)—is not discussed in the *Human Security Report 2005* because *Peace and Conflict 2005* was published after the relevant section of this report was written.
4. There was no comparably sustained decrease in the number of internally displaced persons—that is, those who had fled their homes but had not crossed into another country and become refugees.
5. John Mueller, *Retreat from Doomsday: The Obsolescence of Major War* (New York: Basic Books, 1989).
6. Heidelberg Institute on International Conflict Research, *Conflict Barometer 2004* (Heidelberg: Insitute on International Conflict Research, University of Heidelberg, 2005), www.hiik.de/en/ConflictBarometer_2004.pdf (accessed 31 May 2005). These findings will be discussed in detail in the *Human Security Report 2006*.
7. Note that this claim refers to people killed in *fighting*, not those who die of war-induced disease and/or malnutrition.
8. See John J. Mearsheimer, 'Why We Will Soon Miss the Cold War', August 1990, http://teachingamericanhistory.org/library/index.asp?document=713 (accessed 31 May 2005).
9. The discussion on Africa draws on a paper prepared for this report by Monty G. Marshall and Ted Robert Gurr and on their *Peace and Conflict 2005*.
10. While the UN was collecting refugee data during this period, little effort was made to collect data on internally displaced persons (IDPs). The IDP data, which are now collected by independent organisations such as the Global IDP Project, almost certainly underestimate the true number of people displaced within their own borders between the 1960s and the beginning of the 1980s.
11. UN High Commissioner for Refugees, *The State of the World's Refugees: Fifty Years of Humanitarian Action* (Oxford: Oxford University Press, 2000).
12. This is not always the case, of course. More people were killed in the Rwandan genocide in 1994 than on all the world's battlefields in 1950, the year with the highest battle-death toll in the post–World War II era.
13. Pew Research Center, 'A Year After Iraq: Mistrust of America in Europe Ever Higher, Muslim Anger Persists', Survey Reports, Pew Research Center website, http://people-press.org/reports/display.php3?PageID=796 (accessed 15 August 2005).
14. The central focus of the Political Terror Scale is state repression; however, the identity of the perpetrators of human rights abuses is not always clear, so some of the violence that is recorded may be perpetrated by non-state groups.
15. Note that civil wars are defined here as conflicts that have incurred at least 1000 battle-deaths. Only armed conflicts in which a government was one of the warring parties are discussed.
16. Prime Minister's Strategy Unit, 'Investing in Prevention: an International Strategy to Manage Risks of Instability and Improve Crisis Response', The Challenges of Instability: Overview of Instability, http://www.strategy.gov.uk/downloads/work_areas/countries_at_risk/report/chapter1.htm (accessed 30 August 2005).
17. International Crisis Group, 'Crisis Watch', no. 21, 1 May 2005, International Crisis Group website, www.crisisgroup.org/home/index.cfm?l=1&id=3399 (accessed 31 May 2005).
18. Monty G. Marshall and Ted Robert Gurr, *Peace and Conflict 2005*.

Heidi Bradner / Panos Pictures

PART I

THE CHANGING FACE OF GLOBAL VIOLENCE

Part I of this report describes global and regional trends in contemporary political violence around the world. Examining the period since the end of World War II, it focuses on armed conflicts, genocides and international terrorism. In the absence of official data it draws on research from universities, think-tanks and NGOs. Its findings challenge conventional wisdom.

PART I

THE CHANGING FACE OF GLOBAL VIOLENCE

Heidi Bradner / Panos Pictures

Introduction

The opening words of the United Nations charter signed in 1945 contained a pledge 'to save succeeding generations from the scourge of war'.

In the past decade and a half, the UN has been more successful in reaching this goal than many critics allow. Since the end of the Cold War, armed conflicts around the world have declined dramatically. But the steep drop in the number of wars and international crises, the even steeper decline in the number of genocides and other mass slaughters, and the longer-term decline in battle-death rates have passed largely unnoticed by policymakers, the media and the public alike.

Part I of this report reviews trends in armed conflicts, battle-deaths and genocides in the post–World War II era, and the dramatic changes in the nature of warfare and military organisation that have accompanied these trends. It also examines changing patterns in international terrorist attacks and core human rights violations, and concludes with a review of public opinion poll findings on security fears around the world.

Part I begins with an analysis of the reasons why so few people realise that there has been a radical decline, not just in the numbers of wars, but in other assaults on human security as well. The absence of official statistics on global security trends provides a major part of the explanation.

The review of armed conflict trends that follows is based on data from Uppsala University's Conflict Data Program and the International Peace Research Institute, Oslo (PRIO). It tracks the post–World War II rise in the number of armed conflicts and the subsequent decline following the end of the Cold War. The data also show that the overwhelming majority of today's armed conflicts are fought within, not between, states and that most take place in the poorest parts of the world.

> The steep drop in the number of wars has passed largely unnoticed by policymakers, the media and the public alike.

Civil war is extraordinarily rare in the industrialised world, but the major powers have been involved in a large number of armed conflicts overseas since World War II—almost all in the developing world. The UK, France and the

US have the dubious distinction of having fought more international wars since World War II than any other countries.

Warfare in the 21st century is far less deadly than it was half a century ago. A new dataset created by Bethany Lacina and Nils Petter Gleditsch reveals that the steep but uneven decline in battle-deaths began at the beginning of the 1950s.

> Genocides increased steadily from the 1960s until the 1980s, but have since declined dramatically.

Why have wars become so dramatically less deadly? The key lies in the changing nature of warfare: from the huge, externally supported conventional wars of the 1950s, 1960s and 1970s, to today's predominantly low-intensity conflicts. The discussion of the profound changes in the character of war draws on research by Peter W. Singer and Sunil Dasgupta. These changes include a greatly increased reliance on child soldiers and a growth in paramilitary organisations and private military firms.

Political violence encompasses more than simply warfare. It also includes genocide and international terrorism. A comprehensive dataset created by Barbara Harff shows that genocides and other cases of mass murder increased steadily in number from the 1960s until the end of the 1980s, but have since declined dramatically, notwithstanding the atrocities in Rwanda and the Balkans.

The trend in international terrorist attacks is much less clear. Several datasets suggest that the number of terrorist attacks of all kinds has declined over the past 20 years, but the most recent data from the US government indicate a significant increase in both the number of attacks and casualties in 2004.

Part I concludes with an examination of how people around the world perceive security both at the international level and at home. It includes an analysis by Don Hubert of the importance of determining popular perceptions of security and draws on recent global opinion surveys, including a major poll commissioned especially for this report.

The survey data reveal that people are more worried by violent crime than by warfare, and more scared by terrorism than its limited incidence warrants. But these fears can drive political responses.

Teun Voeten / Panos Pictures

Getting it wrong about war trends

Since the end of the Cold War, there has been a dramatic and sustained decline in the number of armed conflicts. And an uneven but equally dramatic decline in battle-deaths has been under way for more than half a century. Yet these facts remain largely unknown, in part because there are no reliable, official global statistics.

Most people believe that the number of armed conflicts has risen over the past decade, not that it has declined radically. They are wrong.

This misperception is not restricted to the media or the general public. A surprising number of government officials and scholars are also unaware of the decline. Some, indeed, believe that political violence has increased.[1]

In fact, in terms of battle-deaths, the 1990s was the least violent decade since the end of World War II. By the beginning of the 21st century, the probability of any country being embroiled in an armed conflict was lower than at any time since the early 1950s.

Why has this dramatic and sustained global decline in the number and deadliness of armed conflicts received so little attention? There are several reasons:

- First, the world's media pay more attention to new eruptions of political violence than to wars that end quietly. Between 1989 and 2002, some 100 armed conflicts came to an end.[2] Very few of these endings were widely reported.
- Second, new conflicts broke out in a number of post-communist states in the 1990s, especially in the Balkans and the Caucasus. They attracted widespread media attention because they were associated with the dramatic collapse of the Soviet Union, and because the fighting took place on the borders of Western Europe. Other conflicts—Iraq, Somalia, Afghanistan—involved the United States, a fact that alone ensured massive coverage by the US-dominated global media. The media focused on the new wars—largely ignoring those that were ending.
- Third, and most important, *official* statistics on global armed conflict trends do not exist.

Why has this dramatic and sustained decline in the number and deadliness of armed conflicts received so little attention?

Why no official data?

The contrast with data collection and analysis on other major global issues could hardly be greater. Every year, tens of thousands of government officials around the world collect economic, health, education and environmental data that are forwarded for collation and analysis to the relevant international organisations.

Nationally, regionally and globally, these collated data provide information that help governments and international organisations formulate and evaluate policy.[3] It would be inconceivable for the World Bank to make broad policy recommendations that were not backed by official cross-national trend data. Yet the UN, the international organisation charged with protecting and enhancing global security, has no comparable data on armed conflict to help it formulate and evaluate its security policies.

A huge collaborative project involving the UN, the World Bank, and other international organisations, with governments from around the world, is currently collating data to measure progress toward meeting the Millennium Development Goals—which include the target of halving global poverty by 2015. But no data are being collected on armed conflicts—even though war is a major driver of poverty in many parts of the world.

The political constraints

Why are there no official datasets on armed conflicts, genocides or core human rights abuse? The short answer is politics (See 'Why there are no official statistics on political violence'.)

> The UN has no data on armed conflict to help it formulate and evaluate its security policies.

In the last decade, 95% of armed conflicts have taken place within states, not between them. And few governments are anxious to divulge details of violent conflicts within their own borders. Intent on denying their violent political adversaries any legitimacy, many governments label them as criminals—and criminal violence is not warfare, of course. Political leaders invoke national security and sovereignty to justify non-disclosure. But the real cause of their reluctance is often a desire to avoid domestic and external criticism.

> Policymakers have missed the dramatic downturn in political violence.

The existing unofficial datasets on war and genocide are compiled by a handful of modestly funded research institutes and individual scholars. Only a fraction of them—in Sweden, Germany, Canada and the United States—update and publish their data regularly.

Lacking outreach budgets or official status, these research institutes are unable to attract much attention to their findings. The fact that they mostly write in the technical language of the social sciences and publish in little-read scholarly journals does little to help them gain a wider audience.

For all these reasons, it is not surprising that so many policymakers, focused of necessity on the crises of the day, should have missed the dramatic downturn in political violence described in this report. The media and the public are even less well informed.

What to measure?

Measuring armed conflict is a complex and often contested business. Definitions of what constitutes a conflict vary widely, as do data collection methods, accuracy and coding rules. Few of the existing datasets are kept up-to-date. Many are one-offs, created for a specific project and then allowed to languish; none has any official status.

Some data projects count only wars: usually defined as high-intensity conflicts with more than 1000 battle-related deaths per year. The difficulty with this approach, long used by the influential Correlates of War (COW) project to count civil wars, is that some notable armed conflicts such as that

WHY THERE ARE NO OFFICIAL STATISTICS ON POLITICAL VIOLENCE

International organisations collect statistics from governments on health, education, development and the environment. But there are no official data on armed conflicts or human rights abuse.

It is a little known fact that no international organisation collects data on regional or global political violence trends. The contrast with the international efforts now being made to track global progress toward development and ecological sustainability goals could not be greater.

Five years ago at the United Nations Millennium Summit, world leaders committed themselves to achieving eight Millennium Development Goals (MDGs) by 2015.[4] The ambitious targets included the eradication of extreme poverty and hunger and the achievement of universal primary education.

In order to track global, regional and national progress toward the MDGs, a huge international monitoring effort has been created that draws on the expertise of the UN and its many agencies, the World Bank, the International Monetary Fund and the Organization for Economic Cooperation and Development. But no effort was made to track the incidence and severity of armed conflicts, even though war clearly threatens the achievement of the MDGs.

In fact, the threat that armed conflicts poses to the MDGs was completely ignored in the UN's Millennium Declaration, despite the fact (1) that reducing the incidence and costs of armed conflict is clearly a development as well as a security priority, (2) that war, in the words of the World Bank, is 'development in reverse', and (3) that the average civil war costs some $54 billion.[5]

Why didn't the international community also set numerical targets for major reductions in political violence along with the targets for poverty reduction in 2000? Member states of the UN cannot agree on what constitutes terrorism, human rights abuse or even armed conflict. In many parts of the world, the claim that 'one man's terrorist is another man's freedom fighter' still resonates. And defining armed conflict can be just as controversial. Some governments argue that violent political opposition to their rule is simply criminal violence.

It is impossible to *count* events if there is no agreement on how to *define* them. It is also impossible to create official conflict datasets without the cooperation of governments. And governments, particularly in the developing world, have made it clear that such cooperation will not be forthcoming. Various proposals to create a professional in-house analytic and data collection capacity in the UN Secretariat that would focus on security issues have been repeatedly blocked by member states in the General Assembly.

The World Bank, the World Health Organization and other international agencies can draw on a wealth of official data to track global and regional trends, formulate evidence-based policies and evaluate their outcomes. It is ironic that the United Nations, the international organisation charged with preventing 'the scourge of war', has no comparable data to draw on.

in Northern Ireland never get counted at all because they fail to reach the 1000-deaths-a-year threshold. Moreover, if the number of deaths in an ongoing civil war dips below 1000 a year, the conflict ceases to exist according to the COW methodology. If a year later the number of deaths climbs back above the 1000 threshold, a new conflict is recorded when in fact the original conflict never ended.

Other projects measure different *types* of political violence. The Political Instability Task Force (formerly called the State Failure Task Force), for example, divides political violence into revolutionary wars, ethnic conflicts and genocides.

Individual researchers often modify existing datasets to suit their current research purposes—or because they disagree with the coding rules of the original data compilers. There may well be good reasons for doing this, but the consequence is that there is great disparity between the different datasets. Policymakers have good reason to feel confused.

Simply counting the number of conflicts is relatively straightforward. It is generally not that difficult to establish whether a threshold number of battle-related deaths has been crossed. Arriving at accurate figures of total battle-related deaths is far more difficult for several reasons.

First, those who collate battle-death data can only record those events that are reported—and many are not. This is particularly true in conflicts such as Chechnya, where journalists are denied access to the war zone. The result is that death rates in some conflicts will be considerably under-reported. Such problems are generally more serious in developing countries than in developed ones, and in authoritarian states as opposed to democracies.

Second, government and rebel forces often exaggerate the death tolls they claim to have inflicted on their adversaries, creating the possibility of over-counting.

Third, different counting methods can produce quite different estimates of death tolls. These issues are discussed in more detail in Part II of this report.

One way to minimise these problems—they can never be completely resolved—is to collect as many different accounts of battle fatalities as possible. Technology can help here. Researchers at Uppsala University's Conflict Data Program, for example, cull conflict data from many sources, including the 9000 news outlets in the electronic Factiva news database. Factiva is scanned automatically, and the violent incidents that are tagged are then reviewed by the researchers, coded and entered into the database.

Defining armed conflict

One of the primary sources of the *Human Security Report*'s armed conflict data is the dataset created jointly by the Uppsala University's Conflict Data Program and the International Peace Research Institute, Oslo (PRIO). The main Uppsala/PRIO dataset now covers the entire period from 1946 to 2003.

The Uppsala/PRIO dataset was selected for a number of reasons.

- Unlike other datasets, it is updated annually.
- It is widely used within the research community.
- It is becoming increasingly recognised in the policy community.
- It relies on more sources than other data collection projects.
- Its definitions are precise and coding of conflict events can be checked by other researchers. (This is not the case in some conflict datasets.)
- With the new data commissioned for the Human Security Report (see Part II), the Uppsala/PRIO dataset is the most comprehensive single source of information on contemporary global political violence.

The Uppsala/PRIO dataset has traditionally counted only 'state-based' conflicts: armed disputes in which control over government and/or territory is contested, in which at least one of the warring parties is a state, and which result in at least 25 battle-related deaths in a year.[6] The category 'battle-related deaths' includes not only combatants but also civilians caught in the crossfire. The data on most conflicts do not permit distinctions between civilian and combatant deaths to be made consistently.

Conflicts are also categorised according to their intensity. 'Conflicts' have at least 25 battle-related deaths per year; 'wars' have at least 1000 battle-related deaths per year.

Finally, the Uppsala/PRIO dataset divides conflicts into four types. The two primary categories—*interstate* and *intrastate* (civil)—are self-explanatory.

The third type is *extrastate,* a conflict between a state and a non-state group outside of the state's own territory. This definition applies primarily to wars fought to gain independence from colonial rule.

The last category used by Uppsala/PRIO is *internationalised internal conflict.* This type of conflict is essentially an intrastate conflict in which the government, the opposition, or both, receive military support from another government or governments, and where the foreign troops actively participate in the conflict.[7] The war in the Democratic Republic of the Congo, in which a number of foreign military forces were operating within the country, is a recent example. Internationalised internal disputes rarely make up much more than 10% of the total number of conflicts worldwide.

New data, new questions

The definition of armed conflict that Uppsala and PRIO have traditionally used excludes conflicts waged exclusively between non-state actors—such as violent clashes between warlords or intercommunal conflicts between religious or ethnic groups. Uppsala calls these 'non-state conflicts'.

> There were more non-state conflicts in both 2002 and 2003 than state-based conflicts—though the non-state conflicts involved considerably fewer casualties.

Since it was unclear how many of these conflicts were taking place, or how deadly they were, the Human Security Centre commissioned Uppsala to collect data on non-state conflicts for 2002 and 2003. To be counted as a non-state conflict, fighting between non-state actors had to cause at least 25 battle-related deaths within a year.

The new data proved instructive. There were actually more non-state conflicts in both 2002 and 2003 than state-based conflicts—though the non-state conflicts involved considerably fewer fatalities.

The fact that the Uppsala/PRIO dataset had never previously recorded non-state conflicts raised an obvious question: If a major category of political violence had not been counted before, how could anyone be sure that armed conflicts overall had indeed declined during the 1990s? This question is addressed in Part II of this report, where the findings of the new Uppsala/Human Security Centre dataset are presented.

Uppsala's traditional definition of conflict also excluded genocides and massacres—what Uppsala calls 'one-sided violence'. However, the Uppsala/Human Security Centre dataset includes data on the number of cases of one-sided violence in 2002 and 2003 as well as the numbers killed.

Martin Adler / Panos Pictures

Fewer wars, fewer deaths

During the 1990s, after four decades of steady increase, the number of wars being fought around the world suddenly declined. Wars have also become progressively less deadly since the 1950s.

A number of scholars have claimed that the Cold War—the period from the late 1940s to the late 1980s—was one of unprecedented stability. Some even called it the 'Long Peace'.[8]

By century's end, the world was indeed experiencing the longest period of uninterrupted peace between the traditional 'great powers' in hundreds of years. But this welcome trend did not reflect reality in the developing world.

From the beginning of the Cold War to the early 1990s, the number of armed conflicts in developing countries rose inexorably.[9] Every decade witnessed more wars than its predecessor. For the global South, the Cold War was anything but a Long Peace.

In 1992 the number of conflicts worldwide rose to a post–World War II high, as a series of short-lived wars flared in the former Soviet Union. Then something remarkable happened. Just as the Western media started to worry about a worldwide epidemic of ethnic violence, the number of armed conflicts began to drop rapidly.

Today that decline continues. In 1992, more than 50 armed conflicts involving a government were being waged worldwide; by 2003 that number had dropped to 29. Battle-deaths have declined even more steeply, though the trend here is very uneven and has been going on for a much longer time.

In the developing world, the end of the Cold War played a critical role in the decline in armed conflict. It removed a major source of ideological polarisation. It also staunched the flow of resources to warring parties in the South. And it allowed the UN to begin to play the global security role that its founders had originally intended.

Analysing the trends

Figure 1.1 shows the global trend in three types of armed conflict: interstate, intrastate (civil wars) and extrastate (overwhelmingly colonial wars).

> In the developing world the end of the Cold War played a critical role in the decline in armed conflict.

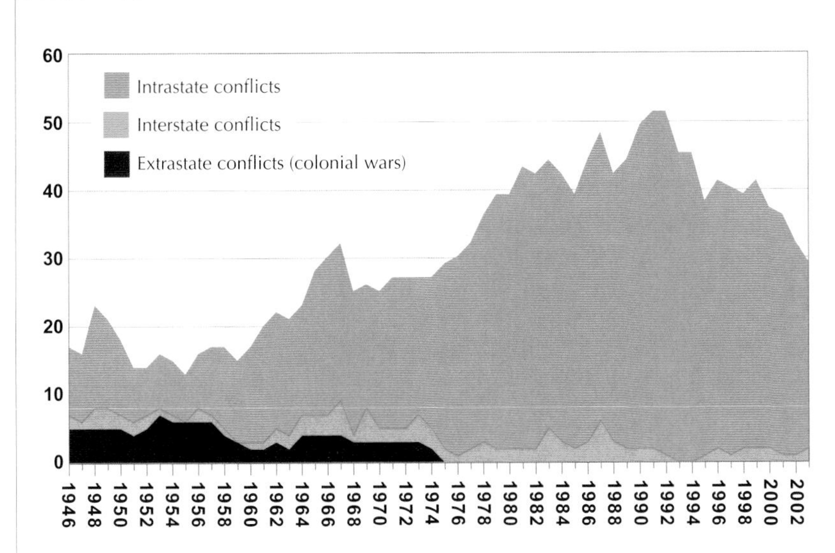

Figure 1.1 A less violent world: Numbers of conflicts, 1946–2003

Since World War II, the number of interstate wars has remained relatively low. Colonial (extrastate) wars had disappeared by the mid-1970s, but civil (intrastate) conflicts rose steadily until 1992, after which they declined steeply.

Source: Uppsala/PRIO, 2004[10]

The conflicts shown in Figure 1.1 resulted in at least 25 battle-related deaths a year. They are of three types: interstate (fought between states), extrastate (colonial wars) and intrastate (civil wars). In all cases one of the warring parties was a state. The graph does not include ethnic or other conflicts where neither warring party was a state, nor does it include cases of 'one-sided' violence such as genocide.
Figure 1.1 is a 'stacked graph', meaning that the number of conflicts in each category is indicated by the depth of the band of colour. The top line indicates the total of number of conflicts of all types in each year. Thus in 1946 there were 5 extrastate conflicts, 2 interstate conflicts, 10 intrastate conflicts and 17 conflicts in total.

It reveals that the number of armed conflicts increased steadily decade by decade throughout the Cold War. Then, in the early 1990s, a steep decline started that continues to this day.

The threefold rise in the overall number of armed conflicts between 1946 and the ending of the Cold War at the beginning of the 1990s is almost all accounted for by a dramatic increase in conflicts *within* states. These now make up more than 95% of all conflicts.

An entire category of armed conflict—extrastate or colonial wars—had virtually ceased to exist by the mid-1970s. Like the end of the Cold War, the end of colonialism eradicated an important global driver of armed conflict.

Figure 1.1 also shows that the number of interstate wars has remained low since the end of World War II. But they include the deadliest wars in this period: the Korean War, the Vietnam War and the Iran-Iraq War, each of which claimed more than a million lives on the battlefield.

In fact the *risk* of interstate war has declined even more than the low absolute numbers in Figure 1.1 suggest. The number of states in the international system has trebled since the end of World War II, increasing the number of potential warring parties. If the average risk of war had remained the same there should have been a commensurate increase in the number of wars. But since the number of wars did not increase, it follows that the average risk of conflict has declined.

Part V of this report briefly reviews the explanations for the decline in the risk of interstate war. Few of these explanations apply to civil wars, which is one reason why civil wars are today the dominant form of armed conflict.

Like the end of the Cold War, the end of colonialism eradicated an important driver of armed conflict.

Figure 1.2 shows that the pattern of decline in armed conflicts is different from region to region and that most armed conflicts throughout the post–World War II period have taken place in the less-developed regions of the world.

FIGURE 1.2

Numbers of armed conflicts, 1946–2003: Global and regional breakdown

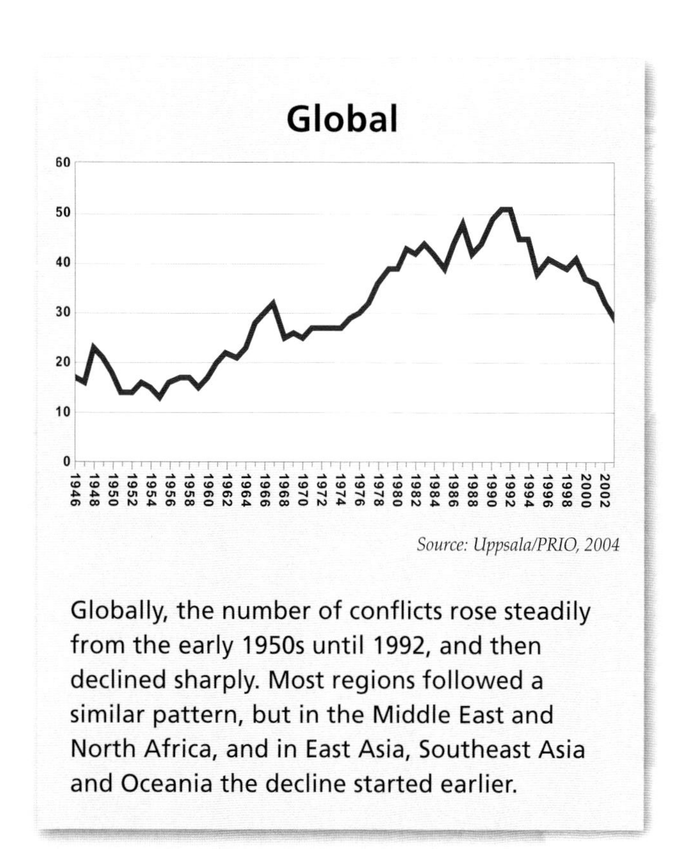

Source: Uppsala/PRIO, 2004

Globally, the number of conflicts rose steadily from the early 1950s until 1992, and then declined sharply. Most regions followed a similar pattern, but in the Middle East and North Africa, and in East Asia, Southeast Asia and Oceania the decline started earlier.

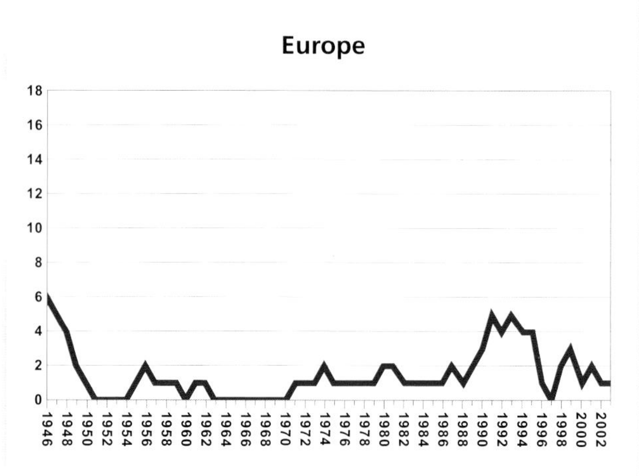

After four decades of relative peace, a series of ethnonationalist wars flared in the Balkans in the 1990s.

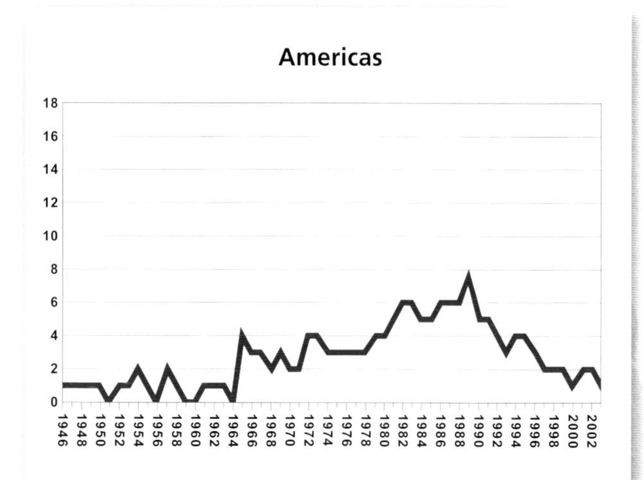

From the 1960s to the 1990s, the number of conflicts, driven in part by Cold War politics, increased steadily. The end of the Cold War saw a dramatic decline in political violence throughout the region.

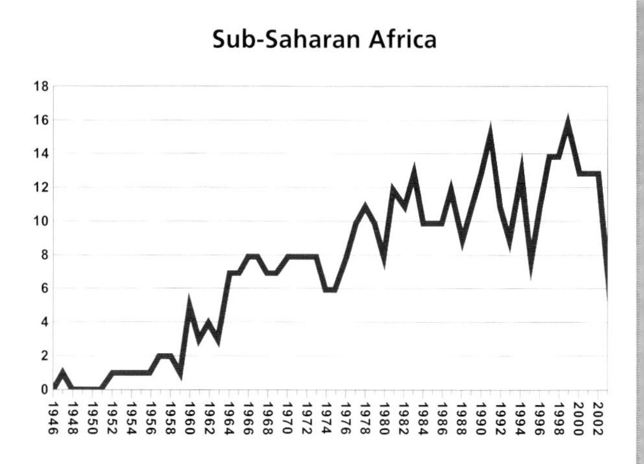

The number of conflicts increased steadily from World War II to 1991, despite the ending of colonial wars. They remained high until 2002, but now seem to be falling.

Middle East and North Africa

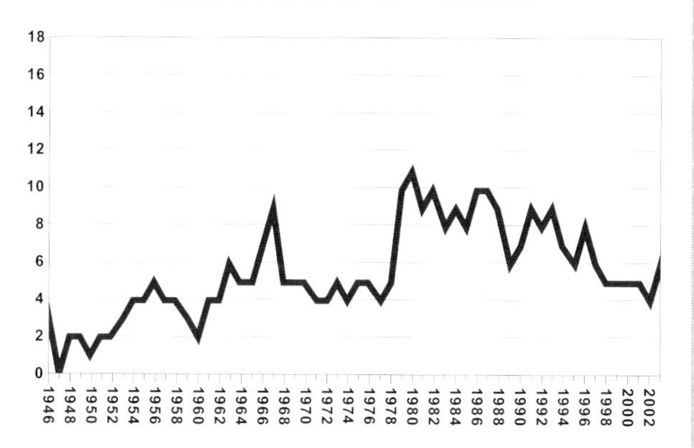

The number of armed conflicts increased steadily from the 1940s to 1980, and has since declined by nearly half.

East Asia, Southeast Asia and Oceania

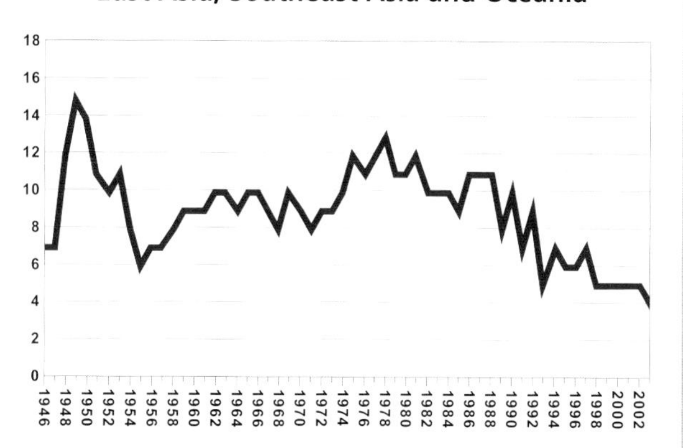

In 2003 there were fewer than one-third as many armed conflicts as in 1978. Since 1978 the decline has been associated with rising prosperity, democratisation and the ending of large-scale foreign intervention.

Central and South Asia

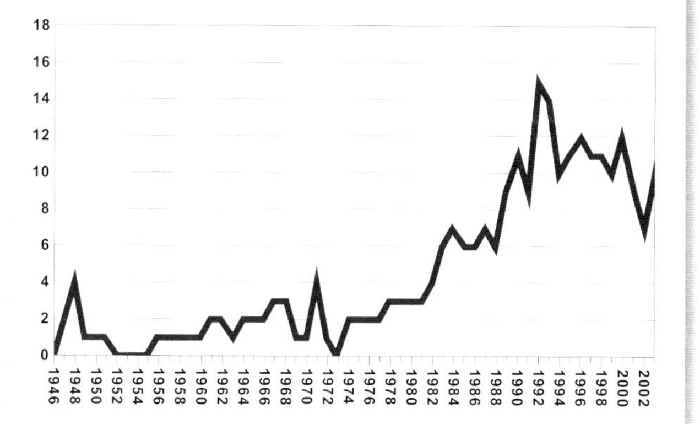

Until the 1970s, conflicts were concentrated in South Asia. The breakup of the Soviet Union in 1991 triggered many new conflicts in Central Asia (including the Caucasus).

These graphs show the total number of conflicts per year, and count only those conflicts with at least 25 battle-related deaths in that year. They include interstate wars, extrastate wars (colonial wars) and intrastate wars (civil wars) where one of the parties was a state. They do not include ethnic or religious conflicts where neither party was a state, or cases of one-sided violence such as genocide.

The world's most war-prone countries

Which countries have fought the most wars in the past half-century?

- Figure 1.3 shows the countries that have fought the most international armed conflicts, either in another country or against a foreign army on their own soil, between 1946 and 2003.[12]
- Figure 1.4 shows the countries that have experienced the most 'conflict-years' between 1946 and 2003. A conflict-year is a calendar year in which a country has been involved in a state-based armed conflict of any type. Because a country can experience several different armed conflicts at the same time, it can experience two or more conflict-years within a single calendar year.[13]

The UK and France, the two states that had the largest colonial empires, have fought the most international wars, as shown in Figure 1.3. Other colonial powers, the Netherlands, Spain and Portugal, also make it into the top 25 in this category. However, only a minority of the wars that these states waged were against anti-colonial independence movements—most were either interstate conflicts or interventions in intrastate wars.

The US ranks third, with most of its wars, like those of the next-in-line Russia, being fought over Cold War issues. US allies Australia, Canada, Italy, New Zealand and Turkey also make the list.

Eight Middle Eastern countries, led by Israel and Egypt, are among the top 25, reflecting that region's violent post–World War II history. They are joined by three countries in East Asia—China, Vietnam (both before and after reunification) and Thailand. In Latin America and Africa, most armed conflicts have been fought within rather than between states. As a consequence, no Latin American countries and only two sub-Saharan African countries, Chad and Ethiopia, are on this list.

Figure 1.3 The countries that have experienced the highest number of international armed conflicts, 1946–2003

Number of wars	Country	Number of wars	Country
21	United Kingdom	5	Portugal
19	France	5	Canada
16	United States of America	4	Vietnam, Republic of
9	Russia (Soviet Union)	4	Chad
7	Australia	4	Libya
7	Netherlands	4	Spain
6	Israel	4	Syria
6	Egypt	4	New Zealand
6	China	4	Italy
6	Thailand	4	Iran
5	Vietnam, Democratic Republic of	4	Ethiopia
5	Turkey	4	Iraq
5	Jordan		

Source: PRIO, 2004[14]

This table shows the countries that have fought the most international wars. The states that head this list are former colonial powers, and the two Cold War superpowers.

Figure 1.4 The most conflict-prone countries, 1946–2003

Conflict years	Country	Conflict years	Country
232	Burma (Myanmar)	40	Chad
156	India	40	South Africa
88	Ethiopia	40	Indonesia
86	Philippines	38	Portugal
79	Israel	36	Cambodia
77	United Kingdom	36	Vietnam, Republic of
66	France	35	Thailand
60	Iraq	34	Sudan
60	Vietnam, Democratic Republic of	33	Guatemala
51	Russia (Soviet Union)	31	Uganda
49	United States of America	31	Libya
48	Iran	31	Turkey
44	Angola	31	Australia
42	Colombia		

Source: PRIO, 2004

This table shows the countries that have experienced the greatest number of conflict-years. By this measure, Burma (Myanmar) and then India are the two most conflict-prone countries.

As explained above, it is possible for a country to be involved in two or more state-based armed conflicts in a given year and thus accumulate more than one conflict-year for each calendar year.

This is why Burma, which in the early 1960s was embroiled in six different intrastate conflicts, tops the list in Figure 1.4 with 232 conflict-years between 1946 and 2003. India's many long-running intrastate conflicts, plus its wars with neighbouring states, ensured its second place with 156 conflict-years.

Had the measure simply been the number of years a state has been involved in any conflict between 1946 and 2003, as against the number of conflict–years, then Israel would have been at the top of the list.

Former colonial powers, the UK, France, Russia/Soviet Union, the US and Portugal, are high on the list primarily because of their involvement in colonial and interstate wars. Australia, a US ally, also makes it onto the list.

East Asia's long post–World War II history of both civil and interstate war is evident in the inclusion of the Philippines, Vietnam (before and after reunification), Indonesia, Cambodia and Thailand.

Burma, which in the early 1990s was embroiled in six different intrastate conflicts, is the world's most conflict-prone country.

In the conflict-prone Middle East, Israel, Iraq, Iran, Libya and Turkey make it onto the list, as do two Latin American countries, Colombia and Guatemala.

Sub-Saharan Africa has six countries on the list: Ethiopia, Angola, Chad, South Africa, Sudan and Uganda.

International crises decline

Wars are rarely unexpected bolts-from-the-blue: interstate wars are nearly always preceded by serious international disputes and crises. What is the long-term trend in such crises?

The International Crisis Behavior Project at the University of Maryland has been tracking international crises for many years. It defines crises as situations in which leaders perceive a heightened probability of military hostilities, a grave threat to national values, and a shortened and finite time within which to make decisions. Figure 1.5 uses data from the Maryland project.

Figure 1.5 International crises plummet, 1946–2001

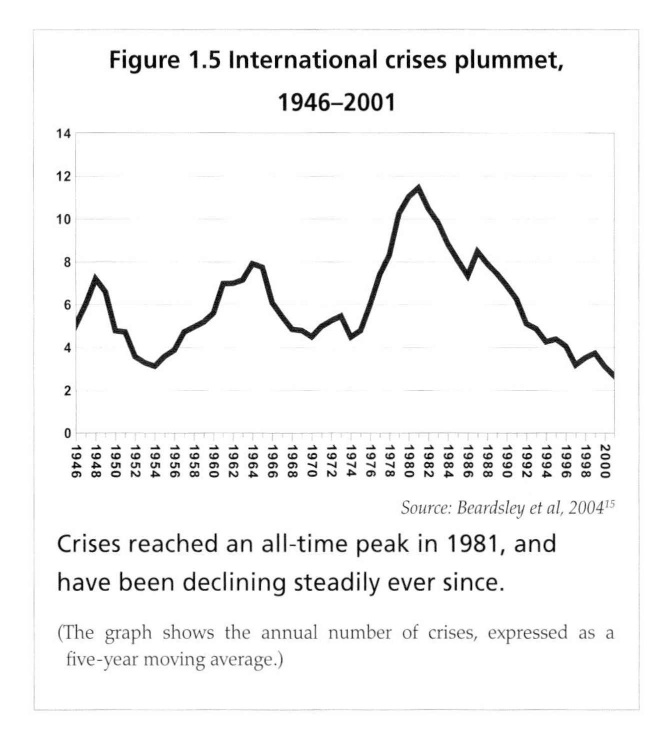

Source: Beardsley et al, 2004[15]

Crises reached an all-time peak in 1981, and have been declining steadily ever since.

(The graph shows the annual number of crises, expressed as a five-year moving average.)

The trend line shows an uneven increase in international crises until the 1980s, and then, as the Cold War wound down, a very steep decline. By 2001 the rate at which international crises were occurring was just one-quarter of that in 1981.

In a study commissioned by the Human Security Centre for the *Human Security Report*, Faten Ghosn and Glenn Palmer of Pennsylvania State University examine recent trends in what are called Militarised International Disputes.[16] This category includes militarised conflict behaviour that falls short of war—threats to use force and displays of force—as well as actual resort to force.

Andrew Testa / Panos Pictures

Trying to stop crises becoming armed conflicts: NATO Secretary-General George Robertson and EU special envoy Javier Solana in Macedonia.

Like international crises, militarised disputes have the potential to escalate into full-scale wars. Most wars are preceded by threats to use force, so other things being equal, the greater the number of militarised disputes between countries the greater the probability that some will escalate into full-scale war.

Ghosn and Palmer found that the frequency of militarised disputes has not changed significantly since the late 1950s, that the severity of militarised disputes appears to have decreased slightly in the past decade, and that the probability that disputes will escalate has declined somewhat too.[17]

The finding that not much has changed with respect to the numbers of militarised disputes might seem to contradict the picture presented here of a marked recent improvement in global security. But, as noted, the number of independent states in the international system has increased threefold since World War II.

If the number of militarised disputes changes little over time, while the number of states has tripled, the average risk to any state of becoming embroiled in such disputes will have decreased quite significantly.

Warfare becomes less deadly

The 20th century saw dramatic changes in the number of people killed on the world's battlefields.

The two world wars accounted for a large majority of all battle-deaths in this period, with Europe being the major killing ground.

> In the second half of the century most of the killing took place in the developing world, especially in Asia.

World War I killed 1 to 3 million people a year on the battlefield. World War II was far more deadly, with an average 3 to 4 million battle-deaths a year. Since the Korean War ended in 1953, the annual global battle toll has never again reached even half a million a year.

In the second half of the century, which is the focus of this report, most of the killing took place not in Europe but in the developing world, especially in Asia.

Figure 1.6 shows the global trend in battle-deaths from 1946 to 2002; battle-deaths include civilians killed in the fighting. These death tolls are from conflicts in which a state is one of the warring parties and do not include deaths from intercommunal and other non-state conflicts. Nor do they include deaths from massacres or genocides, which is why Figure 1.6 does not show a major spike in 1994, the year of the genocide in Rwanda.

Figure 1.6 War becomes less deadly: Battle-deaths, 1946–2002

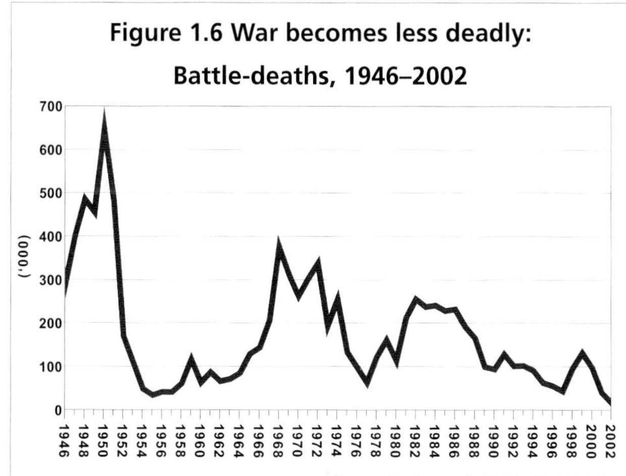

Source: Lacina and Gleditsch, 2004 [18]

Since the end of the Korean War in 1953, there has been a clear but uneven decline in battle-deaths around the world.

There was a marked but uneven downward trend in global battle-deaths during the second half of the 20th century. Figure 1.6 shows absolute figures: the total number of deaths per year. But it does not take into account the fact that the world population more than doubled between 1950 and 2000.

Figure 1.8, in contrast, presents a decade-by-decade picture of global battle-deaths per thousand of the world's population. Using death rates per thousand rather than absolute numbers gives a better picture of the declining deadliness of warfare. The battle-death rate in the 1990s was only one-third that of the 1970s.

Figure 1.8 is based on a different dataset to Figure 1.6, and counts only those conflicts in which there were at least 1000 battle-deaths in a year. Since it averages deaths across each decade, the trend in Figure 1.8 looks somewhat different than that in Figure 1.6.

> From 1946 to 2002 a mere five wars accounted for more than half of all battle-deaths.

The single most important reason for the decline in battle-deaths over the past 50 years is the changing nature of warfare.

From 1946 to 2002 a mere five wars together accounted for more than half of all battle deaths. They were the Chinese Civil War (1946–49), the Korean War (1950–53), the Vietnam War (1955–75), the Iran-Iraq War (1980–88) and the wars in Afghanistan (1978–2002). All involved huge armies and heavy conventional weapons, while today's wars are predominantly low-intensity conflicts.

WHO'S WAR DEATH DATA AND THE *HUMAN SECURITY REPORT*

The World Health Organization is the only international agency that has published data on war death numbers. Its death toll estimates, for the years 1998 to 2002, were far higher than those of other datasets.

In the Overview we noted that neither governments nor international organisations publish annual counts of the number or the human cost of armed conflicts. There is one partial exception to this rule. The World Health Organisation (WHO) provided estimates of global and regional war deaths from 1998 to 2002 in the *World Health Report*. The dataset used for these reports also disaggregated war deaths on the basis of age and gender, something that no other datasets have done.

The *Human Security Report* does not use WHO data for two reasons.

First, WHO war death data cover only five years—1998 to 2002—in contrast to the 57-year period—1946 to 2002—covered by the Lacina and Gleditsch battle-death data. A five-year time series obviously cannot describe long-term trends, nor is it very useful for statistical analysis.

Second, we have concerns about the methodology WHO used to determine war deaths.

The *World Health Report* findings do, however, pose a challenge to the Lacina and Gleditsch dataset on which the *Human Security Report* relies. The global war death totals from violence that WHO reports are from two to nine times greater than the battle-deaths reported by Lacina and Gleditsch, and the WHO's data bear little relationship to any other dataset.[19]

WHO researchers have stressed the uncertainty that surrounds their estimates, and they define war deaths somewhat more widely than Lacina and Gleditsch. But WHO's more inclusive definition of 'collective violence' cannot possibly account for the huge disparity between its death toll totals and those of the Lacina and Gleditsch dataset.

WHO reports provide little information on how the war death data are estimated, other than to say that they were obtained from a variety of published and unpublished war mortality databases, including the Project Ploughshares *Armed Conflict Report* for 2001 and 2002.[21]

Project Ploughshares is a widely respected Canadian NGO that estimates ranges of battle-death numbers each year for countries in conflict. Its estimates are somewhat higher than those of Lacina and Gleditsch, in part because it defines conflicts differently. But Project Ploughshares' estimates are much lower than the WHO war death estimates.

WHO vets its death data from its 'primary source', Project Ploughshares, 'against the historical and current estimates of other research groups'.[22] But the disparity between the Lacina and Gleditsch data and the WHO data is striking. Figure 1.7 illustrates the differences.

It seems likely that WHO estimates are higher than those of other datasets because WHO researchers take median estimates of deaths from other sources and then multiply them by an 'adjustment factor'. It is not clear what that factor is, how it is determined, why it should differ from year to year, and what the rationale behind it is. Nor is it clear how WHO establishes the global and regional gender and age breakdowns for their war death data.

In 2002 WHO revised the death total for 2000 from 310,000 down to 235,000. The *World Health Report* no longer includes war death data.

	Lacina and Gleditsch	WHO
1998	97,893	588,000
1999	134,242	269,000
2000	99,536	235,000
2001	42,068	230,000
2002	19,368[20]	172,000

Figure 1.7 War death estimates compared

WHO war death figures are many times greater than the Lacina and Gleditsch figures. It is not clear why.

Source: Human Security Centre, 2005

Figure 1.8 War death rates by decade, 1950–1997

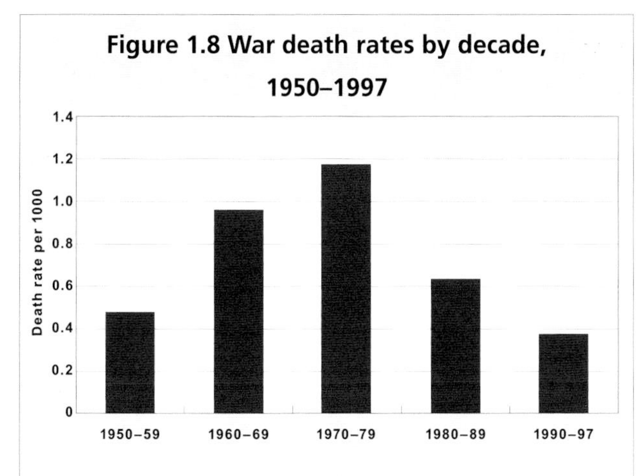

Source: Human Security Centre 2004[25]

When global battlefield deaths are measured not in absolute numbers but per thousand of the world's population per decade, it becomes clear that war in the 1990s was only one-third as deadly as in the 1970s.

As Bethany Lacina and Nils Petter Gleditsch point out in the most comprehensive recent analysis of post-World War II battle-deaths, 'the most cataclysmic battles of the past half century were related to the now defunct ideological polarization between East and West'.[23] The fact that conflicts are no longer exacerbated by the imperatives of Cold War geopolitics means that one of the major drivers of high battle-death rates has also ceased to exist.

The best single indicator of the deadliness of wars is the average number of battle-deaths per conflict per year. In 1950 there were more than 38,000 deaths per conflict; in 2002 there were just 600—an extraordinary change.[24]

Battle-deaths by region

Against this remarkable worldwide decline in the deadliness of warfare, what has been the regional picture? Figure 1.9 provides a breakdown of battle-death tolls in each of the world's major regions.

- From 1946 to the mid-1970s by far the highest battle-death tolls were on the battlefields of East Asia, Southeast Asia and Oceania.
- By the 1980s the focus of global warfare had shifted and the Middle East and North Africa, sub-Saharan Africa, and Central and South Asia were experiencing the highest number of battle-deaths.
- In the 1990s wars in the Balkans hit a continent that had not seen significant fighting since the aftermath of World War II.
- At the beginning of the new millennium the battle-death toll in sub-Saharan Africa was greater than the toll in all other regions combined.

Beyond battle-deaths

Battle-deaths are an important measure of the human costs of war, but they do not provide the whole picture. As Lacina and Gleditsch put it: 'The number of battle-deaths provides an exhaustive measure of how many have died in combat operations. But it does not provide a remotely adequate account of the true human costs of conflict. War kills people in less direct (but highly predictable) ways, especially when it causes the collapse of a society's economy, infrastructure of health and human services, and public safety systems.'[26]

The number of battle-deaths does not provide a remotely adequate account of the true human costs of conflict.

There are no global trend data on indirect deaths—those caused by war-induced malnutrition and disease. Indirect deaths are examined in Part IV of this report.

FIGURE 1.9

Numbers of battle-deaths, 1946–2002: Global and regional breakdowns

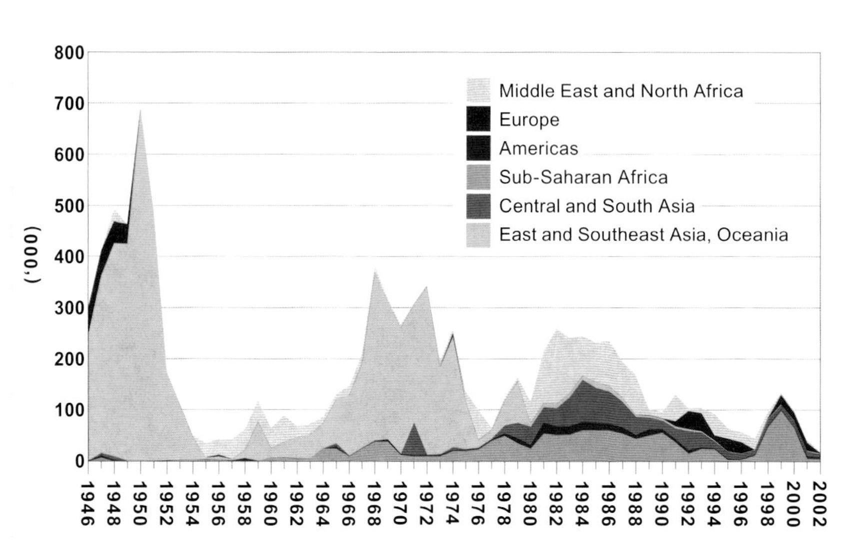

The regional focus of battle-deaths has shifted from decade to decade. In this 'stacked graph', the number of deaths in each region each year is indicated by the depth of the band of colour, and the total number of deaths is indicated by the top line on the graph.

Source: Lacina and Gleditsch, 2004

Americas

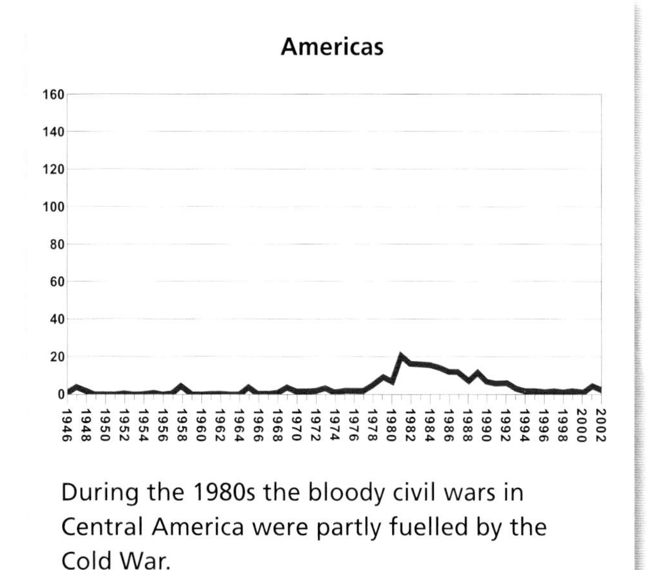

During the 1980s the bloody civil wars in Central America were partly fuelled by the Cold War.

Sub-Saharan Africa

Battle-deaths in sub-Saharan Africa rose from almost zero in 1950 to about 100,000 in 2000.

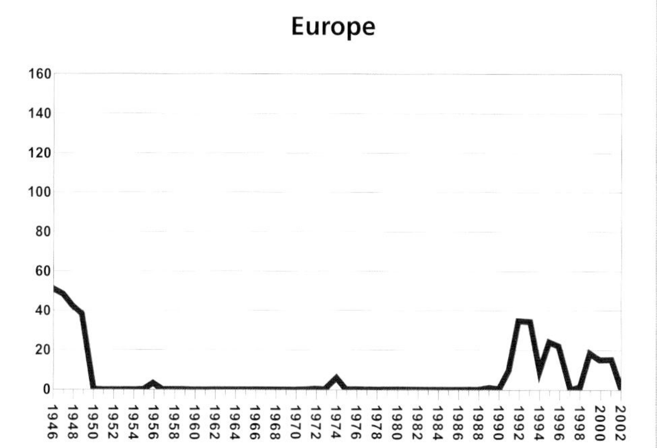

Following the aftermath of World War II, Europe was largely peaceful until the collapse of the Soviet Union.

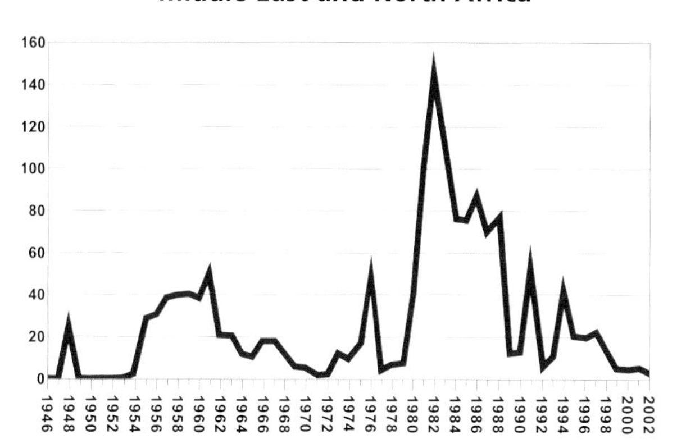

In the first half of the period most battle-deaths were associated with Algeria's bloody war for independence; in the second half it was the Iran-Iraq War.

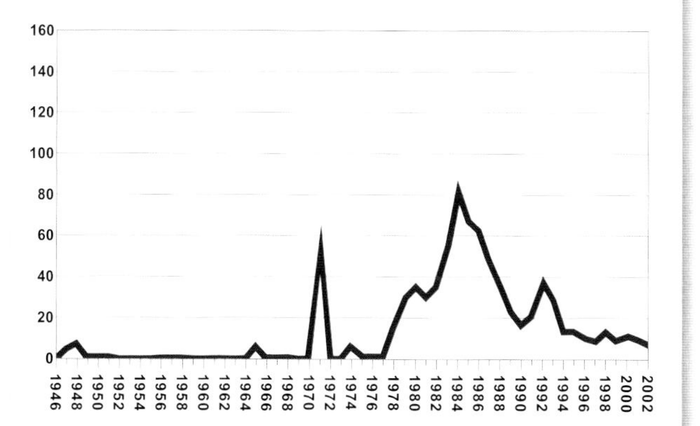

The first three peaks represent the wars between India and Pakistan in 1947–48, 1965–66 and 1971. Later peaks are mainly due to the long-running conflict in Afghanistan, and to the civil war in Sri Lanka.

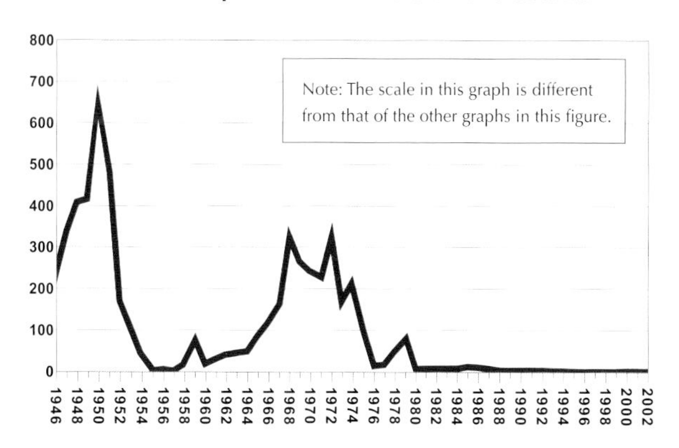

After accounting for most of the world's battle-deaths from 1946 to the mid-1970s, the region has been free of major conflict since the fighting in Cambodia and Vietnam came to an end.

David Rose / Panos Pictures

The changing nature of warfare

Today's conflicts tend to be low-intensity civil wars, or 'asymmetric' wars in which high-tech forces fight poorly armed opponents. The world's armies are changing too, relying more on child soldiers, paramilitary forces and private military firms.

Warfare has evolved dramatically in the last few decades. The major wars of the 1950s, 1960s and 1970s—the Chinese Civil War, the Korean War and the wars in Indochina—involved huge armies that deployed heavy conventional weapons and engaged in major battles. The warring parties were sustained by the superpowers, and the death tolls were high.

> Low-intensity conflicts kill few people compared with conventional wars.

By the end of the century the nature of armed conflict had changed radically.

Most of today's armed conflicts fall into one of two categories. The vast majority are so-called 'low-intensity' civil wars, almost all of which take place in the developing world. They are typically fought by relatively small, ill-trained, lightly armed forces that avoid major military engagements but frequently target civilians.

While often conducted with great brutality, these low-intensity conflicts kill relatively few people compared with major conventional wars.

Wars in the second category are very different. Often called 'asymmetric' conflicts, they involve US-led 'coalitions of the willing', using high-tech weaponry against far weaker opponents who have few or no allies. The Gulf War, Kosovo, and the ongoing conflicts in Iraq and Afghanistan fall into this category.

Due to the extreme power imbalances that favour the US-led coalitions, the battle phase of these wars usually ends quickly—within weeks rather than years—and with relatively few combat deaths compared with the major wars of the Cold War period.

Changes in the scope and deadliness of armed conflicts have been paralleled by other global shifts in military recruitment and organisation. These have been driven in part by economic imperatives and in part by political changes. This section examines three such changes: a reliance on child soldiers, the increasing use of paramilitary forces and the privatisation of warfare.

Child soldiers

The deployment of children in war is hardly a new phenomenon, but it is widely believed to be a rapidly growing one. It is also illegal. Recruitment of children (persons under 18) into military forces is prohibited by the UN's 2000 Convention on the Rights of the Child, while the 1998 Rome Statute of the International Criminal Court defines conscripting children under 15, or deploying them in battle, as a war crime.[27]

> Children have been used for terrorist missions in Northern Ireland, Colombia and Sri Lanka.

According to Brookings Institution analyst Peter Singer, the use of child soldiers has become so common that it can be thought of as 'a new phenomenon of warfare'.[28] Children fight in almost 75% of today's armed conflicts and the numbers serving in—or recently demobilised from—government and rebel forces engaged in war have been estimated at 300,000.[29] A further half-million are thought to be serving in militaries that are not at war.[30]

Nearly a third of the militaries that use child soldiers include girls in their ranks.'Underage girls have been present in the armed forces of 55 countries; in 27 of those countries, girls were abducted to serve and in 34 of them, the girls saw combat.'[31]

Children have been used for terrorist missions in Northern Ireland, Colombia and Sri Lanka. Children as young as 13 have been recruited by the Palestinian Islamic Jihad and Hamas organisations for suicide operations.[32]

The recruitment of children is driven by a number of factors. First, the ready availability of cheap, easy-to-use light weapons such as the AK-47 more than offsets children's major drawback as fighters in earlier eras: their lack of physical strength. Now that many weapons are 'child-portable', children can often be as effective as adults on the battlefield.

Second, in the less-developed countries where most wars now take place, burgeoning youth unemployment creates a pool of potential recruits who may have few other survival options. Military recruiters, particularly those who work for rebel groups, see children as both cheap and expendable.

Third, the 'otherwise unpopular armies and rebel groups have been able to field far greater forces than they would otherwise, through strategies of abduction or indoctrination.'[33]

Despite increasingly active NGO campaigns against the recruitment and use of child soldiers, and some rhetorical support for action at the UN Security Council, this abuse continues—and has in some cases increased.

The impact of recruitment and military service on children is examined in more depth in Part III.

The rise of paramilitaries

Usually more heavily armed than the police, though more lightly armed than the military, paramilitaries can be disciplined forces under effective government control—or private armies operating outside legal constraints, responsible only to themselves, and operating death squads and torture camps.

Like child soldiers, paramilitaries are inexpensive to arm, quick to train and require little logistical support. Their rapid recent growth has been driven in part by the same economic imperatives that have swelled the ranks of child soldiers.

The term paramilitary embraces a wide variety of organisations: armed police, border guards, counter-insurgency specialists, internal security forces, riot squads, intelligence agencies, militias and even privatised armies. Most exist outside regular police or traditional military command structures—and almost all fall into one of three broad categories:

- Militarised police forces (such as China's People's Armed Police).
- Militias (such as Colombia's self-defence groups).
- Intelligence agencies (such as the former Soviet Union's KGB and Pakistan's Inter Service Intelligence).

THE ARMS TRADE, DEFENCE BUDGETS AND TROOP STRENGTHS

With the end of the Cold War in the 1990s, international arms transfers, world military expenditures and troop numbers all declined.

According to the Stockholm International Peace Research Institute's *SIPRI Yearbook 2004*, the annual value of major arms transfers worldwide in 2003 was approximately half that of 1987—although there has been a modest increase since 2000. Russia was the major exporter in 2003, responsible for almost 37% of all weapons deliveries. The United States came second with almost 24%. Asia, led by India, was the major recipient region.[34] (SIPRI uses the term 'arms transfers' rather than 'arms trade' because some major transfers of arms are in effect gifts, or are made on terms that are not strictly trade.)

Figure 1.10 shows only transfers of major conventional weapons—tanks, aircraft, ships—not transfers of the small arms and light weapons that kill most people in most of today's wars. There are no good data on transfers of small arms, but according to Peter Batchelor (formerly of the Small Arms Survey), 'the value and the volume of the legal international trade [in small arms] has appeared to decline since the 1990s. This has been led by a dramatic fall in the trade of military weapons, and also certain categories of civilian firearms.' Speaking in 2003, Batchelor added that the illicit trade is believed to be worth about $1 billion, some 20% of the legal trade in small arms.[35]

NGO campaigns to staunch the flow of these smaller weapons to conflict zones have had only modest success. And even if the transfer of these weapons could be cut back radically, this would not reduce the number of small arms and light weapons already out there. A 2003 estimate suggested that there were 639 million small arms and light weapons in circulation around the world—238 to 276 million of them in the United States.[36]

World military spending in the 1990s followed the same trend as global arms transfers. According to the US State Department, it dropped from $254 for every man, woman and child on the planet in 1989, to $142 per person in 1999, a decline of 43%. As a share of world GDP it fell from 4.1% to 2.7% in the same period. Eastern Europe and the former Soviet Union's share of global military spending fell by 34%, while East Asia's share more than doubled. Numbers serving in armed forces around the world dropped some 26%, from 28.6 million to 21.3 million.[37]

In the new century, global arms spending has again been heading up, led by the United States. Washington requested $420.7 billion for fiscal 2005, an 8% increase—and plans to spend $2.2 trillion over the next five years. China and Russia each spent around $50 billion in 2003, Japan and the UK $41 billion each.[38]

The UN, by contrast, currently spends some $4.47 billion a year for all its worldwide peacekeeping operations.[39] This compares with the $5.6 billion *a month* that the US is spending on the occupation in Iraq.[40]

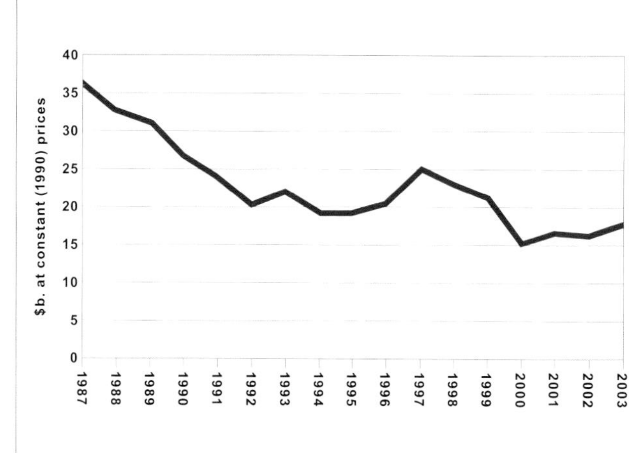

Figure 1.10 Major arms transfers, 1987–2003

International transfers of major conventional weapons fell steadily after the end of the Cold War, though they have been rising again since 2000.

Source: SIPRI 2004[41]

The growth of paramilitary forces is one of the most significant recent changes in the global security landscape. In Russia, China and India—three of the five countries with the largest armed forces in the world—paramilitary forces now account for between one-third and one-half of total military personnel.[42]

A 1999 study of Asian militaries found that between 1975 and 1996 the ratio of security forces to population had risen by 29% in Thailand, by 42% in Burma, by 63% in China, by 64% in Pakistan, by 71% in India, and by 81% in Sri Lanka.[43] Most of these increases were the result of a build-up of paramilitary forces.

Many paramilitaries are official or semi-official agents of the state, and subject to similar disciplines and constraints as the police or army. Some paramilitaries function as internal security forces and are used to secure regimes, including democratic ones, from internal threats such as military coups and separatist rebellions.

Paramilitaries may also perform other functions for the state, such as riot control, border security and even the elimination of political opponents. Many paramilitaries have developed deservedly sinister reputations, and some have been responsible for horrific acts of violence in Colombia, Indonesia, the Balkans, Rwanda and elsewhere.

Armies on the cheap

For governments, paramilitaries offer many advantages. They can be recruited rapidly, often from groups that are politically sympathetic to the regime. They are lightly equipped and do not need the complex weapons systems of conventional military forces.

The significance of paramilitaries lies in their institutional location outside of regular military and police commands and ministries. Indeed, there are often no formal lines of authority between state authorities and paramilitary leaders. This relative independence allows national governments to shrug off responsibility for human rights violations perpetrated by paramilitaries.

If paramilitaries grow and their influence expands, they can compete with formal state forces, often seeking to assert exclusive control over areas such as internal security. Where the decentralisation of security is unchecked, as has happened in Colombia with the growth of rightist paramilitaries, the state's monopoly of the use of force can be eroded, posing major problems for governments. In extreme cases paramilitaries may become renegades.

> Paramilitaries often survive long after the regimes that created them have been swept aside.

Their power and independence means that paramilitaries can—and often do—survive long after the regimes that created and sustained them have been swept aside. Unless they are reincorporated into the new regime, they can become a source of violent disruption and pose serious threats to the new political order.

Outsourcing war

One consequence of the end of the Cold War was a sharp downturn in defence spending around the world and equally sharp reductions in military aid to developing countries. Defence ministries—and rebel leaders—began seeking ways to increase efficiencies and reduce costs. The reliance on child soldiers and paramilitary organisations is in part a response to these pressures. So too is the growing drive to 'outsource' war.

Over the past decade more and more states have contracted out key military services to private corporations.

So-called privatised military firms, or PMFs, are the modern corporate variant of the mercenary armies of earlier eras. They sell war-related services rather than weapons (though some are arms traders as well). A small PMF may offer the advice of a few retired generals; a large transnational PMF may lease fighter jets complete with pilots.

Hundreds of PMFs have operated in more than 50 countries, and their global revenue has been estimated to exceed US$100 billion a year.[44]

This booming industry grew rapidly in response to the military downsizing that followed the end of the Cold

War in 1989. Around the world, 6 million military personnel were retired, and a huge market was created in surplus military equipment.[45]

The end of the Cold War also meant that US and Soviet military support to governments or insurgents fighting 'proxy wars' in the developing world largely dried up. This withdrawal of support created a demand for external military expertise that the private sector was quick to accommodate.

The drive toward privatisation

The growth of PMFs reflects a broader global trend toward the privatisation of public assets. Recent decades have been marked by greater outsourcing of government services, including those once perceived as defining the nature of the modern nation state: education, welfare, prisons and defence manufacturing. The privatised military industry has drawn its precedent, model and justification from the wider 'privatisation revolution'.[46]

The most obvious parallel to military outsourcing is found in domestic security services. In some countries, the number of personnel working in private security forces, and the size of their budgets, now greatly exceed those of public law-enforcement agencies.[47]

Privatised military firms are found in every continent except Antarctica,[48] and their growing influence is evident in both developed and developing countries. Saudi Arabia's military, for example, relies heavily on PMFs for operating its air defence system and for training and advising its land, sea and air forces.

The Democratic Republic of the Congo, though far poorer and less strategically important than Saudi Arabia, also depends on a private company, the Israeli corporation Levdan, to help train and support its military.

PMFs have influenced the process and outcome of numerous recent conflicts, including those in Angola, Croatia, Ethiopia-Eritrea and Sierra Leone.

Even the world's dominant military power has become increasingly reliant on this industry. From 1994 to 2002 the US Defense Department entered into more than 3000 contracts with US-based PMFs.[49] Halliburton (formerly guided by US Vice President Cheney) and its subsidiary KBR now provides logistics for every major US military deployment. Halliburton runs, or has run, US military bases in Georgia, Uzbekistan, Haiti, Rwanda, Somalia and the Balkans. Other firms have taken over much of the US military's training and recruiting—including the Reserve Officers Training Corps programs at more than 200 American universities.

PMFs have influenced the outcome of numerous recent conflicts, including those in Angola, Croatia, Ethiopia-Eritrea and Sierra Leone.

Many Americans might be surprised to learn that they carry PMF shares in their personal portfolios or pension funds, because of the purchase by L-3 (a Fortune 500 company) of Military Professional Resources Inc, a PMF that has trained the militaries of Croatia, Bosnia, Macedonia and Nigeria.

Iraq, Ethiopia, West Africa

PMFs played a significant role in the 2003 US invasion of Iraq, which the *Economist* magazine described as 'the first privatised war'.[50] Private military employees handled tasks from feeding and housing US coalition troops to maintaining complex weapons systems, such as the B-2 stealth bomber, F-117 stealth fighter and U-2 reconnaissance aircraft. The ratio of personnel employed by private contractors to US military personnel was roughly 1 to 10, compared to about 1 to 100 during the 1991 Gulf War.

Almost any military service or capability is now available on the global market. PMFs typically delay recruiting military specialists until after they have negotiated a contract with clients, which can range from governments and multinational corporations to humanitarian aid organisations and even suspected terrorist groups. The vast majority of recruited personnel are recently retired soldiers, already trained and ready to work. This means savings for the PMFs and their customers, since training costs have already been paid.

Once requiring huge investments in training, time and resources, the entire spectrum of conventional forces can be obtained today in a matter of weeks. Barriers to military strength have been dramatically lowered for those who can afford it. Clients with deep enough pockets can write out a cheque for military operations that previously would have been impossible to mount.

In Africa the armies of the Economic Community of West African States (ECOWAS) lack certain core military capacities, such as air support and logistics, that are critical to peacekeeping interventions. ECOWAS was able to intervene effectively in Liberia and Sierra Leone in the 1990s with help from International Charters Inc. of Oregon, which supplied assault and transport helicopters and former US Special Forces and Soviet Red Army veterans.

Andrew Testa / Panos Pictures

In Afghanistan, road travel between cities often requires armed convoys. Sustained insecurity creates a lucrative market for private military contractors.

Similarly, in 1998 Ethiopia leased from the Russian company Sukhoi an entire fighter wing of the latest Su-27s (roughly equivalent to the US F-15 fighter), along with pilots, technicians and mission planners. This private air force helped Ethiopia win its war with neighbouring Eritrea.

Types of private military firms

Different PMFs offer different services: each has its own capabilities and efficiencies.

- *Military provider firms* offer direct, tactical military assistance to clients, including servicing front-line combat operations. An example is Executive Outcomes, which in 1995 rescued the Sierra Leone regime from defeat in exchange for diamond concessions.
- *Military consulting firms* are not directly involved in combat. Instead, they employ retired senior officers and non-commissioned officers to provide strategic and training advice and expertise.
- *Military support firms* carry out multi-billion-dollar contracts to provide logistics, intelligence and maintenance services to armed forces, allowing soldiers to focus on combat duties.

There is even a US-based organisation, the International Peace Operations Association, that lobbies for PMFs to take over future UN peacekeeping operations, claiming that the private sector will provide more efficient and effective peacekeepers than often ill-trained and ill-equipped national forces.[51]

Paul Lowe / Panos Pictures

Targeting civilians

Many people believe that international terrorist attacks, genocides and other mass killings of civilians have increased in recent years. In fact genocides have declined remarkably since the end of the Cold War. Data on international terrorism are too unreliable to permit any confident statements about trends. However, the available evidence suggests that overall numbers of terrorist incidents have declined, while high-casualty attacks have increased.

Genocide

The year 2004 marked the 10th anniversary of the genocide in Rwanda, when government-backed militia drawn from the majority Hutu ethnic group systematically slaughtered an estimated 800,000 Rwandans, mainly from the minority Tutsi community.

In 2005 Europe marked the 10th anniversary of another genocide. In July 1995 Bosnian Serb forces rounded up and murdered more than 7000 Muslim men and boys from the small town of Srebrenica, a UN-designated 'safe haven'.

In neither case did the international community intervene until well after the slaughters had stopped.

Genocide has recently become an issue of profound political concern. But despite Rwanda, Srebrenica and a host of lesser massacres, the 1990s saw a steep worldwide *decline* in the number of mass killings of civilians.

As the debate about Darfur demonstrates, determining exactly what constitutes genocide is often problematic. The UN Genocide Convention defines genocide as 'acts committed with intent to destroy, in whole or part, a national, ethnical, racial or religious group'. But if strictly applied to Cambodia (1975–79), the UN's definition could mean that only those ethnic Chinese, Vietnamese and Chams who were killed could properly be considered victims of genocide—and not the 1 million ethnic Khmers (Cambodians) who were also slaughtered.[52]

What is politicide?

Some scholars have argued that the UN's definition of genocide is too limited, and have coined the term 'politicide' to describe policies that seek to destroy groups because of their *political* beliefs rather than their religion or ethnicity.[53] US Naval Academy political scientist Professor Barbara Harff defines genocides and politicides as acts perpetrated by governments (or in civil wars, by their opponents) that are 'intended to destroy in whole or in part a communal, political or politicized ethnic group'.

Genocides and politicides often take place during civil wars, as happened in Rwanda in 1994, or in their aftermath, as happened in Cambodia in 1975–79, where most of the mass killings were perpetrated by the Khmer Rouge *after* the fighting had stopped.

Figure 1.11 is drawn from Barbara Harff's genocide-politicide dataset. It plots the number of *events* that are classified as genocides or politicides, not the number of people killed. The trend is very similar to that of armed conflicts: an uneven rise until the end of the Cold War, followed by a sharp decline. But the drop in genocides and politicides in the 1990s is twice as steep as the decline in armed conflicts over the same period.

Figure 1.11 The rise and fall of genocide and politicide, 1956–2001

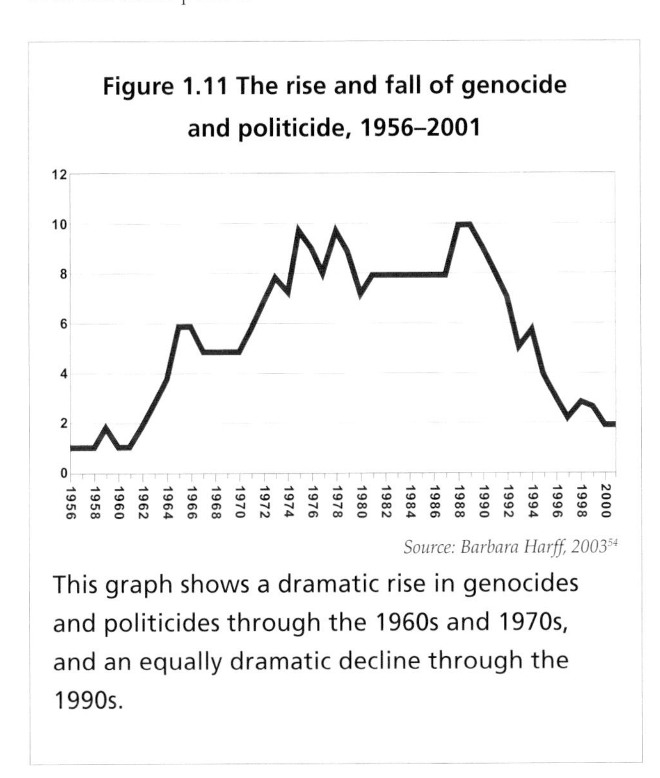

Source: Barbara Harff, 2003[54]

This graph shows a dramatic rise in genocides and politicides through the 1960s and 1970s, and an equally dramatic decline through the 1990s.

Distinguishing civil wars from genocides and politicides is not easy—except in the small number of cases where the latter take place in times of peace. But while parties in a civil war usually seek to *defeat* their politically defined enemy, politicide only occurs if they attempt to physically *eliminate* that enemy.

The considerable overlap between civil wars and politicides in the Harff dataset has led some researchers to argue that the distinction should be abandoned.

The numbers of genocides and politicides fell dramatically in the 1990s. But was there a similar fall in the number of people killed? No one knows with any certainty because until 2002 there was no systematic collection of data on deaths from genocides and politicides. (Part II of this report reviews the findings of the new Uppsala/Human Security Centre dataset that examines 'one-sided' political violence, a term that encompasses genocide and other slaughters of civilians, in 2002 and 2003.)

Excluding genocides and politicides can have a huge impact on war death tolls. In the case of Rwanda, for example, Uppsala estimates that fewer than 1000 people were killed in actual combat between government forces and rebels in 1994. By most estimates, 800,000 or more were slaughtered in the genocide.

Democide

Even genocide and politicide fail to encompass all the deaths from what the University of Hawaii's Rudolph Rummel calls 'death by government' or 'democide'.

'Democide' includes not only genocide, politicide and other massacres, but also deaths that arise from government actions (or deliberate failures to act) that kill people indirectly. Deaths from starvation in government-run forced labour camps would, for example, be an unambiguous example of democide.

The drop in genocides and politicides in the 1990s is twice as steep as the decline in armed conflicts over the same period.

Measuring democides is difficult because it requires knowledge of the *intentions* of political leaders.

The 1932-33 famine in Ukraine, which may have killed 7 million people, is a case in point. There is little doubt that the famine was a direct consequence of Stalin's agricultural policies, but it would only count as democide if those policies were intended to kill, or were knowingly pursued with a disregard for life.

Rummel estimates that between 1900 and 1987, 170 million people died as a consequence of intended government policies, or a 'knowing and reckless' disregard for life.[55] His democide database only extends to 1987, however, so we cannot determine whether the government-induced death tolls from indirect causes declined in tandem with deaths from combat in the 1990s.

But Rummel's research shows that autocratic regimes have by far the highest rates of 'death by government'. Given this, and given that there has been a steep decline in the number of autocracies since 1987, it would seem reasonable to assume that there has been a parallel decline in democide deaths as well.

Is international terrorism increasing?

So far, this report has shown that the numbers of armed conflicts, crises, battle-deaths and genocides have all declined in recent years. Can the same be said of international terrorism? In April 2004 a US State Department report argued that this was indeed the case.

This report—*Patterns of Global Terrorism 2003*—claimed that the 2003 total of 190 international terrorist attacks was the lowest since 1969, and that such attacks had declined by 45% between 2001 and 2003 (Figure 1.12).[56] US Deputy Secretary of State Richard Armitage asserted that the findings were 'clear evidence' that the US was prevailing in the war against international terrorism.[57]

Spinning the figures?

A month later, these claims were strongly contested when the *Washington Post* published a damning critique of *Patterns of Global Terrorism*. 'The only *verifiable* information in the annual reports', wrote Alan B. Krueger of Princeton University and David Laitin of Stanford University, 'indicates that the number of terrorist events has risen each year since 2001, and in 2003 reached its highest level in more than 20 years.'[58]

The Krueger-Laitin criticism placed a huge question mark not only against the claim that the US was 'winning the war on terror', but also against the whole system of data collection that the State Department had been using to map terrorism trends.

How could the State Department claim that there had been a 45% decrease in terrorist incidents between 2001 and 2003, while Krueger and Laitin—*using exactly the same data*—could assert that there had been a 36% increase?

Figure 1.12 Good news? International terrorist attacks, 1982–2003

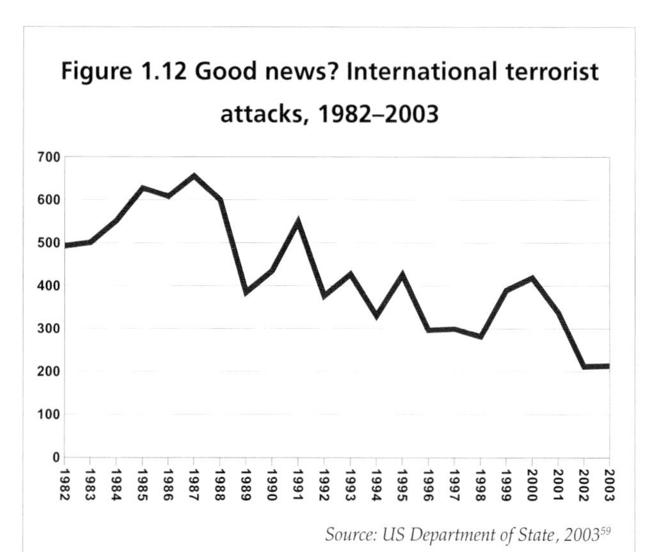

Source: US Department of State, 2003[59]

The total number of international terrorist incidents showed a clear decline from 1982 to 2003, according to the US State Department.

The State Department quickly conceded that there were numerous inaccuracies in the original 2003 report. For example, it had inexplicably failed to count terrorist acts that occurred after November 11, 2003—missing a number of major attacks. In June 2004 the State Department released revised statistics. The overall number of terrorist attacks was increased from 190 to 208.

But inclusion of the revised data made little difference to the previous trends and US officials did not respond to Krueger and Laitin's most telling criticism, which concerned the State Department's definition of international terrorism, and the way it subdivides terrorist acts.

The State Department defined international terrorism as premeditated acts of political violence perpetrated by clandestine sub-national groups against non-combatants and involving the citizens or territory of more than one country. Only attacks on 'civilians and military personnel who at the time of the incident were unarmed and/or not on duty', were judged as terrorist attacks.[60]

This definition excludes acts of terror perpetrated by states. And it also excludes the many car bomb and other attacks against *on-duty* US forces in Iraq since 2003, which President George W. Bush has routinely referred to as 'terrorism'.

The State Department also divided terrorist attacks into two categories:

- 'Significant' attacks which were those that involved loss of life, serious injury or major property damage (more than US$10,000). These incidents were listed individually in the annual terrorism reports.
- 'Non-significant' attacks which are neither defined nor listed.

Krueger and Laitin went back over the State Department's annual reports and extracted only those attacks that met the State Department's own criteria for 'significance'. Their findings are shown in Figure 1.13. 'The alleged decline in terrorism in 2003', they noted, 'was entirely a result of a decline in non-significant events.'[61]

The authors argued that when the State Department combined 'non-significant' together with 'significant' terror attacks it created a deeply misleading impression that allowed administration officials to claim that the 'war on terror' was being won. This was as true of the revised data published in June 2004 (which is presented in Figure 1.12) as it was of the flawed data released in April.

The State Department's revised interpretation of its data (Figure 1.12) shows an apparently encouraging trend: the total number of recorded terrorist incidents declined from around 665 in 1987 to 208 in 2003. But Krueger and Laitin's re-examination of the data (Figure 1.13) shows a steady if uneven increase: from 17 'significant' terror attacks in 1987, to more than 170 in 2003.

Figure 1.13 Bad news: Significant international terrorist attacks, 1982–2003

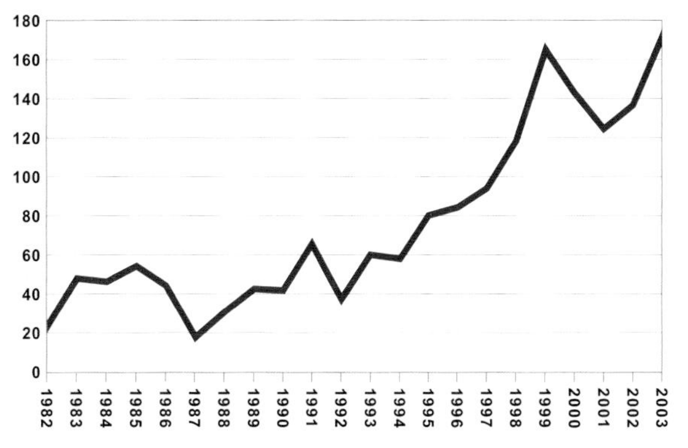

Source: Alan B. Krueger, 2004[63]

When only 'significant' terrorist attacks are counted, the State Department figures look very different. These attacks have increased more than eightfold over the last two decades.

Although there have clearly been problems with the way the State Department collected data in the past, what made *Patterns of Global Terrorism* so misleading was the manner in which the data were presented—in particular the failure to separate 'significant' from 'non-significant' attacks. But it is important to note that the trends presented in the State Department's reports are broadly consistent with another much-cited terrorism database, International Terrorism: Attributes of Terrorist Events (ITERATE).

Like *Patterns of Global Terrorism*, ITERATE's data map a downward trend in terrorist incidents of all types since the early 1980s.[62]

Casualties from international terrorism

Another way to determine the global impact of terrorism is to count not individual attacks but casualties—the numbers killed and wounded in international terrorist attacks each year. Figure 1.14 shows an uneven but clear upward trend from 1982 to 2003.

The peak for casualties in the mid-1980s was associated with a large number of terrorist attacks around the world. The 1995 peak, however, was due mostly to a single event, the Aum Shinrikyo cult's attack with sarin gas on the Tokyo subway. But the data on the Japanese attack are somwhat misleading. Although there were more than 5000 'casualties' from this attack, only 12 of them were deaths, and most of the others were people who attended hospital for relatively brief checkups.

The peak in 1998 was due primarily to the two terror bombings of US embassies in East Africa; the peak in 2001 was due to the September 11 World Trade Center attack, in which most of the casualties were deaths.

Figure 1.14 Casualties from international terrorism, 1982–2003

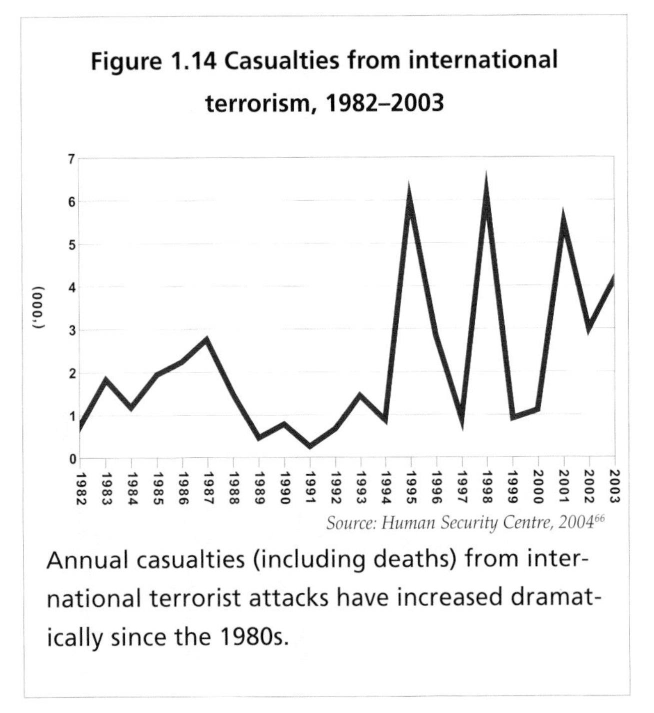

Source: Human Security Centre, 2004[66]

Annual casualties (including deaths) from international terrorist attacks have increased dramatically since the 1980s.

After the 2001 spike associated with September 11, the casualty total dipped in 2002, but even this relatively low point is higher than the highest point in the 1980s. In 2003 casualty numbers again increased.[64]

A new upsurge of international terrorism?

In April 2005 the State Department announced that *Patterns of Global Terrorism 2004*, due for release at the end of the month, would not include any quantitative data on terrorist incidents and that the task of compiling statistics would be taken over by the newly created National Counterterrorism Center (NCTC).[65]

At the end of April, responding to criticism that the Bush administration was hiding information that showed the US was losing the war on terrorism, the NCTC released the new data. It revealed a huge increase in 'significant' international terror attacks in 2004 compared with 2003—from 175 to 651. The casualty toll, at nearly 9000, was double that of 2003.[67]

South Asia experienced most of the attacks (327), followed by the Middle East (270), with just 54 attacks in the rest of the world. Most of the South Asian attacks were associated with the conflict over Kashmir, while most of the Middle East attacks took place in Iraq.[68]

Administration officials were quick to argue that no conclusions should be drawn from the greatly increased totals for 2004, since the NCTC had made much greater efforts to collect data than the State Department. Administration critics disagreed, arguing that the threefold increase in 'significant' attacks in 2004 compared with 2003 could not be explained simply by better reporting.

In October 2003, in a secret memo to senior administration officials, US Defense Secretary Donald Rumsfeld complained that, 'we lack metrics to know if we are winning or losing the global war on terror.'[69] Given the billions of dollars being spent by the US on the war against terrorism this was a remarkable admission. But there is now little doubt that the new data, taken with the earlier trend data on 'significant' terrorist attacks, indicate that the 'war on terror' is far from being won.

The indirect effects of terrorism

Far more people can die from the *indirect* consequences of major terror attacks than from the attacks themselves. According to the World Bank, the slowdown in the world economy that followed the September 11 terror attacks on the US in 2001 likely led to the deaths of 'tens of thousands' of children under the age of five.[70]

Anti-terrorist measures can also have unintended—and lethal—consequences. For example, in August 1998 the US launched a missile assault that destroyed the Shifa pharmaceutical factory in Sudan. The Clinton administration justified the attack on the grounds that the factory was producing precursors for chemical weapons. (No evidence has yet been published to demonstrate the truth of this charge.)

The strike was launched at night when no workers were on duty, so the number of direct casualties was minimal. But because the Shifa plant had been producing 50% of Sudan's drugs—medicines to treat malaria, tuberculosis and other endemic diseases in that desperately poor and conflict-ridden country—the attack caused a scarcity of vital medical supplies that likely caused thousands of Sudanese deaths.

Terrorists and weapons of mass destruction

Just how great a threat will international terrorism pose in the future? Worst-case scenarios see terrorists using nuclear or biological weapons to kill millions of people. William Perry, former US Secretary of Defense, has argued that there is an even chance of a nuclear terror strike within this decade. 'We're racing toward unprecedented catastrophe', he warned.[71]

> Fears that terrorists could acquire an 'off-the-shelf' nuclear weapon have yet to be realised.

While not impossible in the long term, such an event appears unlikely in the short and medium term, not because terrorists would be unwilling to use nuclear weapons, but because they lack the technological capacity to build them. Moreover fears that terrorists could acquire an 'off-the-shelf' nuclear weapon have yet to be realised.

In the late 1990s there were a number of claims, notably by General Alexander Lebed, former Secretary of the Russian Security Council, to the effect that Russia could not account for several of its 'suitcase bombs'.[72] In the hands of terrorists, these portable weapons would obviously pose a major threat. Without maintenance, however, small nuclear devices rapidly lose their effectiveness.[73]

More recently, David Albright, president of the Institute for Science and International Security in Washington DC, has estimated that there is a 10% to 40% chance that terrorists will build and detonate a 'dirty bomb' within the next 5 to 10 years.[74]

A dirty bomb is a conventional explosive device used to scatter radioactive material. But while such radiological weapons are relatively simple to make and use, and would generate considerable popular alarm, the damage they cause is minimal compared with a nuclear weapon.

Albright's estimates, like those of William Perry, are little more than educated guesses. But, at the very least, they suggest reasons for concern.

Biological weapons in terrorist hands may present the greatest potential threat to the greatest number of people in the short to medium term. Anthrax spores sprayed from an aircraft over a major city could kill hundreds of thousands, even millions, of people. But manufacturing and effectively dispersing weapons-grade biological agents is very difficult.

The Aum Shinrikyo cult in Japan launched at least nine attacks with biological agents, including anthrax, in the 1990s to absolutely no effect.[75] Despite ample resources, cult members failed to get access to agents of sufficient virulence, and lacked the technology or expertise to create the aerosols needed to disperse the agents effectively.

Terrorist assaults using even the most basic chemical and biological agents are, in fact, very rare. Worldwide there were just 27 such attacks reported in 1999, 49 in 2000, 25 in 2001, and 23 in 2002.[76] None of the agents deployed was capable of causing mass casualties, and the overwhelming majority were simple poisonous chemicals such as arsenic and chlorine. New developments in bio-technology may, however, lead to 'designer' biological weapons that would be easier for terrorists to acquire and use, and would have a far more devastating impact.

For many terrorist organisations, a car or truck bomb made out of fertiliser (usually ammonium nitrate) and diesel fuel remains the weapon of choice for mass-casualty attacks. The explosive ingredients are relatively easy to obtain and the bombs themselves are simple to make.

Fertiliser-diesel bombs were used in the 1995 Oklahoma City bombing (168 dead), the 1998 Real IRA attack in Omagh, Northern Ireland (29 dead), the 2002 Bali bombing (202 dead), and the November 2003 attacks in Turkey (53 dead).[77]

A small cargo ship loaded with fertiliser-diesel explosive and detonated in the port of a major city could kill hundreds, perhaps thousands.

What about domestic terrorism?

While most attention in the West focuses on *international* terrorism, *domestic* terrorism is far more deadly. There is widespread agreement that many more people die from domestic than international terrorism. But the highest numbers of domestic terrorist attacks take place in the context of civil wars where they are sometimes categorised as war crimes and not as terrorist attacks.

> A small cargo ship loaded with fertiliser-diesel explosive and detonated in the port of a major city could kill thousands.

The issue is further complicated because what insurgents describe as legitimate combat, governments typically see as terrorism. One man's terrorist—as a well-worn cliché puts it—is another man's freedom fighter. That the UN has consistently failed to agree on how terrorism should be defined underscores just how contested the term is. Without an agreed definition of terrorism, measurement is impossible.

Domestic terrorist groups are more likely to be found in large countries than small and—perhaps surprising to many—more often in democracies than in authoritarian states.[78] A 1999 FBI report revealed that 239 of the 327 terrorist attacks in the United States between 1980 and 1999 were perpetrated by domestic groups, most of them ideologically aligned with the extreme right.[79] Almost all these organisations were small—sometimes involving only a handful of individuals—and ineffectual.

It is sometimes claimed that democracy is to terrorism what oxygen is to life—that the very freedoms that characterise democratic states facilitate terrorist survival. This may be true, but surviving is very different from winning. No terrorist organisation has come close to overthrowing a democratic state.

Why international terrorism matters

In terms of numbers killed, international terrorism poses far less of a threat than do other forms of political violence or violent crime, but it remains a critically important human security issue for several reasons:

- The attacks of September 11, 2001, led to the most radical shift in Western security policy since the end of the Cold War.
- The 'war on terror' provided part of the rationale for two major conventional wars—in Afghanistan and Iraq.
- The anti-terror campaign has been associated with an extraordinarily high level of anti-Western sentiment in much of the Muslim world.[80]
- The number of 'significant' international terrorist attacks appears to have increased dramatically in 2004.
- The 'war on terror' has major implications for human security.

Finally, the global economic impact of a mass-casualty terror attack with weapons of mass destruction could push tens of millions of already poor people deeper into poverty, greatly increasing death rates from malnutrition and disease.

International terrorism is a human security issue for poor countries as well as rich.

Martin Adler / Panos Pictures

Fear of war, fear of crime

Most of this report describes and analyses objective data on the incidence and intensity of violence around the world. This section focuses on perceptions. How do people *feel* about political and criminal violence?

Human security is about perceptions as well as realities. Perceived threats can trigger interstate wars, violent civil conflict, political repression and genocide. And governments sometimes play on people's fears and exaggerate or fabricate threats to provide political justification for war or repression. Media coverage can have a strong, sometimes determining, influence on popular perceptions, and fear itself—of both criminal and political violence—can be a debilitating form of insecurity.

> Perceived threats can trigger interstate wars, violent civil conflict, political repression and genocide.

What is the extent of people's fears about their physical safety? How do these fears relate to objective risks? Is political violence perceived to be more threatening than violent crime?

These questions are addressed in this final section of Part I.

Why measure fear?

When assessing threats to security, policymakers and governments often ignore the views of those directly threatened. Although it might seem self-evident that human security policy should be informed by the concerns and priorities of individuals at risk, bottom-up perspectives are notably absent from human security research and policy agendas.

While objective data on battle-death tolls are available, when it comes to measuring fear there is a dearth of good research. This is hardly surprising. Usually the purview of a small elite, security policy has long been a top-down exercise that more often than not reflects the priorities of governments rather than those of their citizens.

Democratic accountability should be sufficient reason for taking people's security fears seriously. Individuals have the right to participate in decisions that fundamentally affect the safety of the communities they live in, particularly where scarce resources necessitate difficult trade-offs between different security goals. Should taxes be spent on strengthening military capacity, combatting terrorist threats, collecting small arms or training local police?

Determining the views of at-risk populations is also necessary to assess the scale and nature of the insecurities they face. The most commonly used measure of insecurity is the incidence of violence: the number of war deaths, murders, rapes and cases of torture. Yet such data ignore the impact that the *threat* of violence has on people's security. The most repressive regimes maintain control by creating a climate of fear; they seldom need to resort to actual violence.

In environments where people have adapted their behaviour to the level of threat, focusing exclusively on the incidence of violent acts can misrepresent the degree of risk. Declining crime rates, for example, may be the result of more people staying off the streets after nightfall rather than a real decrease in the risk of being attacked.

Some counter-intuitive findings

Understanding the public's perspectives on violence and fear can also help inform policy. A recent study of child soldiers, for example, found that girls who join armed groups are frequently fleeing abusive situations at home—a finding that challenges the conventional wisdom that child soldiers should be rapidly reintegrated with their families.[81]

> The most repressive regimes maintain control by creating a climate of fear; they seldom need to resort to actual violence.

While still patchy and ad hoc, the research that has focused on people's experiences of insecurity has produced interesting and sometimes surprising results. A focus group study in post-conflict Guatemala found that most violent acts are driven by economic rather than political motivations.[82] In Colombia, research that attempted to map fear geographically suggests that poor people living in crime-ridden urban neighbourhoods were most fearful when close to police stations.[83]

Major qualitative studies by development and humanitarian organisations have also produced important insights. The World Bank's *Voices of the Poor*—characterised as 'an unprecedented effort to gather the views, experiences and aspirations of more than 60,000 poor men and women from 60 countries'—reveals a consistent preoccupation with physical safety and suggests that poor people are particularly vulnerable to violence and intimidation. Rather than seeking protection from the police, poor people often fear them. Women in particular report feeling a pervasive threat of violence on the streets and sometimes in the home as well.[84]

> The views of citizens on security issues are frequently at odds with the policies of their governments.

The *People on War Report* prepared for the International Committee of the Red Cross employed a similar approach by soliciting the views of individuals caught up in humanitarian crises. Here the overwhelming concern for the physical safety of those polled was less striking than their policy preferences. Fully two-thirds of respondents in 12 war-torn countries called for greater international intervention on behalf of threatened populations.[85] It may not be surprising that people at risk favour international intervention, but it does contrast sharply with the views of many of their governments.

It is clear that the views of citizens on security issues are frequently at odds with both the prevailing wisdom of experts and the policies of their governments. Accurately assessing insecurity requires not only tabulating objective data on violence, but also measuring fear.

Measuring fear: The Gallup survey

In January 2004 Gallup International published one of the most ambitious global surveys ever to examine people's concerns about security. Carried out between November and December of 2003 for the World Economic Forum, it was based on interviews with 43,000 people in 51 countries.[86]

When Gallup asked respondents to rate the international security situation, only 20% worldwide rated it as 'good'. Just over twice as many, 41%, rated it as 'poor'.[87]

Although all respondents were asked to rate the security of the same international system, there were striking variations in the assessments of respondents from different regions (Figure 1.15).

Figure 1.15 Regional perceptions of international security

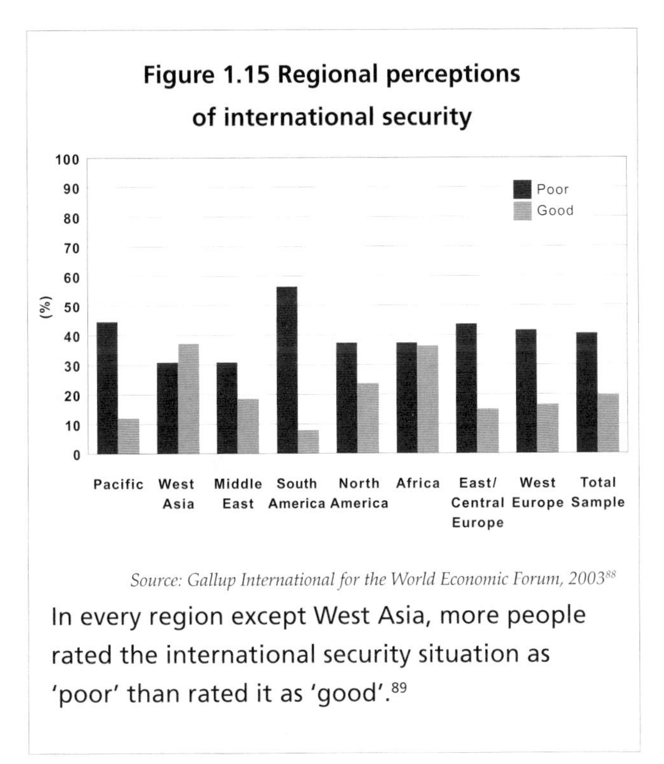

Source: Gallup International for the World Economic Forum, 2003[88]

In every region except West Asia, more people rated the international security situation as 'poor' than rated it as 'good'.[89]

- In war-torn Africa, 38% viewed international security as 'poor', but almost as many, 37%, rated it as 'good'.
- In the relatively peaceful Pacific region, for every respondent who rated global security positively, four rated it negatively.
- In South America the pessimism was even deeper: 57% rated global security 'poor' while a mere 8% rated it as 'good'.

Gallup not only found that perceptions of *global* security varied dramatically from region to region, it also revealed that people across the world had widely differing views on their own country's *national* security, with most being fairly pessimistic.

As Figure 1.16 shows, 35% of respondents in the global sample rated their country's national security as 'poor'. Just 27% characterised it as 'good'. Once again South America and the Pacific were the most pessimistic regions, even though their objective security situation was relatively benign.

In South America, for every respondent who rated his or her country's security as 'good' (6% of the total), more than 11 respondents (69%) rated it as 'poor'. Ironically, respondents in Africa, the region most afflicted by armed conflict, were considerably less pessimistic than those from the more secure South American and Pacific regions.

When participants around the world were asked what their country's national security would be like in 10 years' time, there was little difference between the optimists (30% of the global total) and the pessimists (29%). But regional differences were again striking. Respondents from regions affected by conflict, or recently emerging from it, such as Africa and West Asia, were considerably more optimistic

Figure 1.16 Regional perceptions of national security

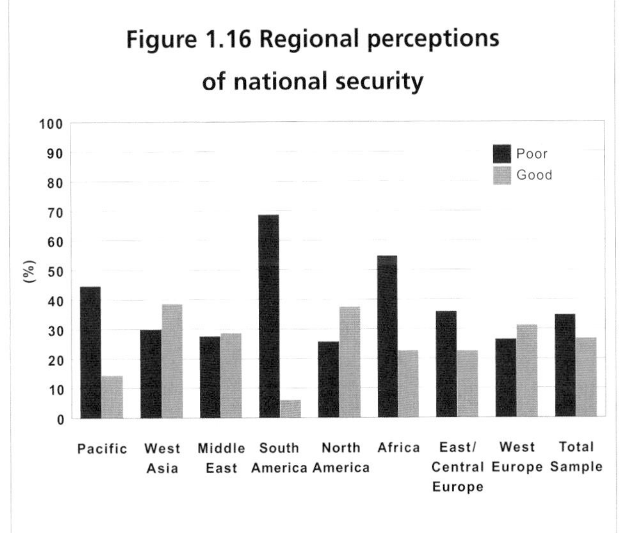

Source: Gallup International for the World Economic Forum, 2003

Individuals around the world were asked how they rated their national security situation. Respondents' perceptions were not always related to the objective risks.

about the future than those from the far more peaceful South American region.

The Gallup International poll suggests that people who are generally pessimistic about conditions at home are likely to perceive the international situation negatively as well—irrespective of the objective conditions. Pacific and South American respondents, for example, were not only pessimistic about international security, they were also deeply worried about the prevailing economic conditions in their own countries. However, Africans are pessimistic about both national security and economic conditions at home, while being among the most optimistic about the international security situation.

This survey suggest that people's fears about violence are important in their own right and have major social and political consequences, but they are not a reliable guide to the reality of global security.

What about violent crime?

For millions of people in the Democratic Republic of the Congo, Iraq and Nepal, armed conflict is an everyday reality. But in the world as a whole, only relatively small numbers of people, in a small number of countries, have any first-hand contact with political violence.

On first impression, violent crime might appear to be different. All countries are afflicted by it, and it is the cause of the death and injury of far more people than war and terrorism combined. Many more people have had direct or indirect experience of violent crime than of armed conflict.

Nevertheless, the overwhelming majority of people in most countries are not directly affected by criminal violence. And fear of violent crime tends to derive less from personal experience than from the media, peer-group opinion and a general sense of vulnerability.

Media reporting can create the impression that violent crime is more prevalent than it is in reality, and even that the incidence of violent crime is increasing when it is actually decreasing. One study found that television viewers who watch more than four hours of television a day believe violent crime to be more common than those who watch much less. And they tend to be more fearful of crime.[90]

As the findings of the Gallup International poll on people's views of national and international security demonstrated, there is no obvious relationship between fear and objective risk. People in relatively secure regions often fear political violence more than people in regions where the objective risks are far greater.

There is often a similar disconnect between fear of violent crime and the objective risk of becoming a violent-crime victim.

Many more people have had direct or indirect experience of violent crime than of armed conflict.

Women, for example, are most fearful of assault by strangers, yet are in fact much more likely to be victimised by someone they know. Women are also three times more fearful than men of becoming victims of violent crime—despite the fact that males are more likely to be assaulted.[91]

Even when fear of criminal violence is not warranted by the objective risks, it remains a major problem in its own right. Fear is detrimental not only to the individuals who experience it directly, but also to society. As people's fear of violent crime increases, their confidence erodes regarding the capacity of the state to fulfill one of its most basic obligations: to protect its citizens. And civility diminishes where people view their neighbours not as part of their community, but as threats to their security.

The geography of fear

To map popular concerns about violence around the world, the Human Security Centre commissioned Ipsos-Reid to conduct a global survey of people's fears and experiences of political and criminal violence in 11 countries around the world: Brazil, Canada, France, India, Japan, Russia, South Africa, Thailand, Turkey, the UK and the US.[92]

The survey, which polled more than 6000 people worldwide, revealed that neither war nor terrorism was the greatest source of fear for those polled. Criminal violence was a far greater concern. When people were asked what problems they thought their governments should address, however, economic and social issues took precedence, not only over war and terrorism, but over crime as well.

Figure 1.17 presents the responses to the survey question, 'There are many different potential threats and dangers to people's personal security in today's world. Thinking of all the threats that you might face in your life, which ONE is of the most concern to you now?'

Over a quarter of respondents (27%) around the world saw some form of 'criminal violence' as the greatest threat they faced. 'Criminal violence' here included not only 'being a victim of violence' (11% of total respondents) but also 'being a victim of theft or robbery' (10% of total respondents). Other specific risks mentioned in this category included kidnapping or abduction, identity theft, rape, sexual harassment or sexual assault, hate crime or mob violence, and domestic violence.

'Terrorism' (15%) followed criminal violence as the next most mentioned threat. War (8%) came in fifth, behind both 'health and economic threats'[93] (13%) and 'accidents/natural disasters' (12%).

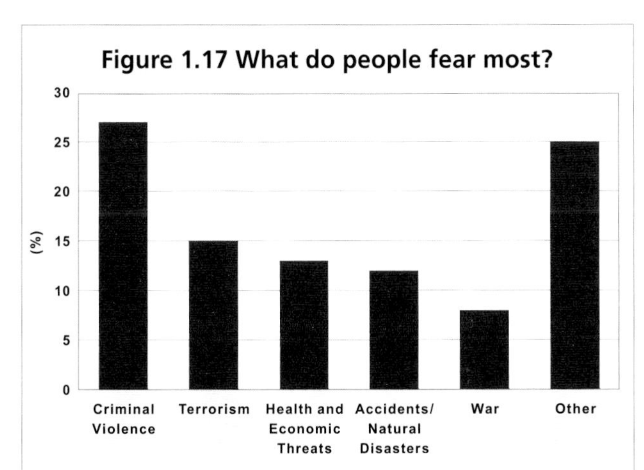

Figure 1.17 What do people fear most?

Source: Human Security Centre, 2005[94]

Asked what they saw as the greatest single threat to their personal security, half of those polled (50%) named criminal violence,[95] terrorism or war.

There were some interesting differences between countries in relation to 'terrorism'. No fewer than 51% of Indian respondents rated 'terrorism' as the issue of 'most concern', along with 22% of Russians, 17% of Americans and 13% of Canadians. Least concerned were the Thais (3%), Brazilians (2%) and South Africans (0%).

Francesco Zizola / Magnum Photos

A murder victim in Rio De Janiero, Brazil. Worldwide, more people say they fear violent crime than other forms of political violence.

'War'[96] was of relatively little concern to most respondents, but again, there were some notable differences among countries. Turkish respondents were most fearful (18% made it their top concern), followed by Japanese (15%) and Indian (13%) respondents. Very few South African (4%), British (3%) or Thai (2%) respondents ranked war as the greatest threat to their personal security.

Figure 1.18 illustrates people's specific experience of violence in the past five years. In the global sample, 11% of respondents reported that they had personally been attacked or threatened in the previous five years; 12% reported that someone in their household had been attacked or threatened.

Figure 1.19 shows the percentage of respondents in 10 countries who answered 'yes' to the question, 'In the past five years, have YOU personally been attacked or threatened by someone or by a group of people in a way that was violent?'

There were marked national differences. Only 1% of Japanese and Indians experienced violent attacks or threats,

Figure 1.18 How many people experience violence?

"In the past five years, have YOU personally been attacked or threatened in a way that was violent?"

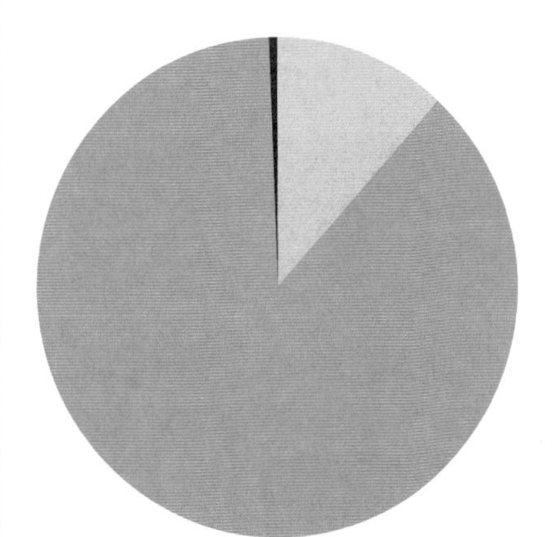

"In the past five years, has anyone in your household — NOT including yourself — been attacked or threatened in a way that was violent?"

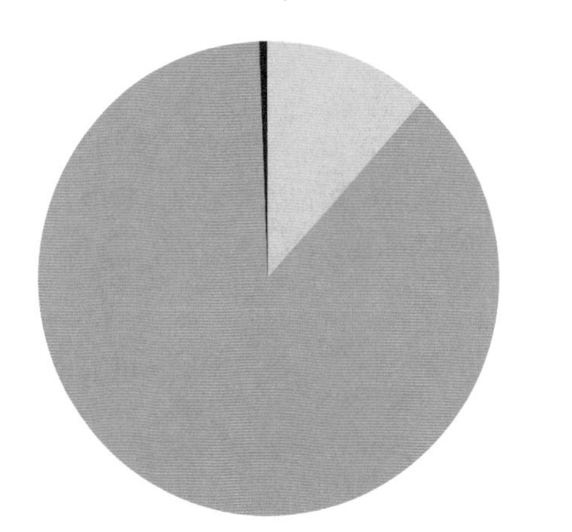

Source: Human Security Centre, 2005

Just 11% of respondents reported that they had been a victim of violence in the previous five years. 12% reported that someone in their household had been attacked or threatened.

compared with 15% of South Africans and Russians, and 20% of Brazilians. But as Figure 1.20 demonstrates, people's expectations of future violence are rarely in line with their past experience.

The survey showed marked divergences between perceived risks and actual experience. In nine of the countries surveyed the fear of future attack was greater than past personal experience of violent crime would suggest is justified.

Half the Thai respondents, for example, believed they would be victims of violence in the coming 12 months. Yet only 7% of Thais had been victims of any violent attack or threat during the previous five years. The difference was even greater for other countries. Just 1% of Indians and Japanese had personally experienced violence, but 10% and 14%, respectively, feared they would become crime victims in the next year. Only Russian respondents were more optimistic about the future than their experience over the past five years would seem to warrant.

Are people's income levels associated with their fears of violence? Yes, but not consistently. Figure 1.21 shows the percentages of individuals in three countries, broken down by income, who thought it was 'very likely' or 'somewhat likely' that they would be a victim of violence in the coming 12 months.

- In Brazil, there were more high-income respondents (85%) who thought themselves at risk of violence than low-income respondents (72%).

Figure 1.19 Which countries experience the most criminal violence?

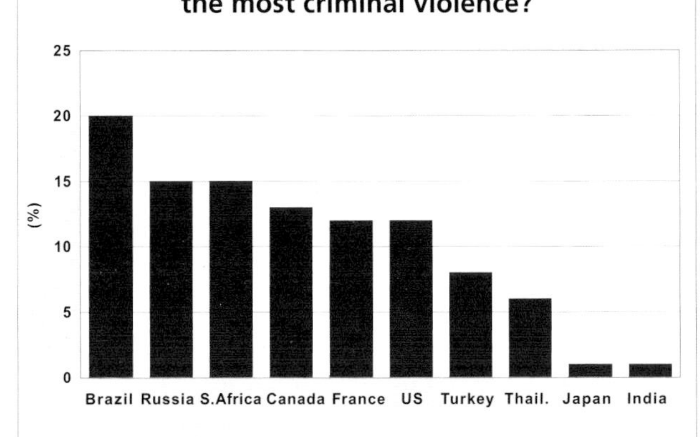

Source: Human Security Centre, 2005

The percentage of Brazilians attacked or threatened in the previous five years was 20 times greater than that of Indians or Japanese.

Figure 1.20 Expectations of violence: Experience versus reality

Country	Percentage of respondents who think it likely they will become victims of violence in the next year	Percentage of respondents who had actually been violently attacked or threatened in a violent way in the last five years	Percentage of respondents with a household member who had been violently attacked or threatened in the last five years
Brazil	75	20	27
Thailand	50	7	7
South Africa	48	15	24
France	33	12	16
Turkey	30	8	9
United States	17	12	12
Canada	16	13	14
Japan	14	1	4
Russia	13	15	16
India	10	1	1
All countries	22	11	12

Source: Human Security Centre, 2005

Pessimism about future violent crime threats is ubiquitous. In every country but Russia, substantially more people expected to fall victim to violence in the future than their past experience would warrant.

- But in Russia nearly three times as many low-income Russians (20%) as high-income Russians (7%) expected to become victims of violence.
- Around half of all South Africans questioned expected to experience violence in the coming year, more or less irrespective of income level.

What people want governments to address

In all 11 countries, respondents were asked, 'Of all the issues presently confronting your country, which ONE do you feel should receive the greatest attention from your country's leaders?'[97]

As Figure 1.22 indicates, over one-third of the respondents in the global sample believe that 'economic issues' (including jobs and taxes) should be the number one priority for governments, with another 20% naming 'social issues' (including poverty, health and education).

Across all 11 countries the number of people who wanted 'economic issues' or 'social issues' to be the top priority for governments was more than double that of those who named 'war' (a category that included other international issues), 'crime' (including violence, corruption and concerns about the justice system) or 'terrorism'.

Half of all South Africans expected to experience violence in the coming year, more or less irrespective of income level.

Figure 1.22 shows the global response, but there were many national differences. Respondents in Turkey, India and Japan, for example, wanted 'economic issues' to be the

Figure 1.21 The association between fear of violence and income

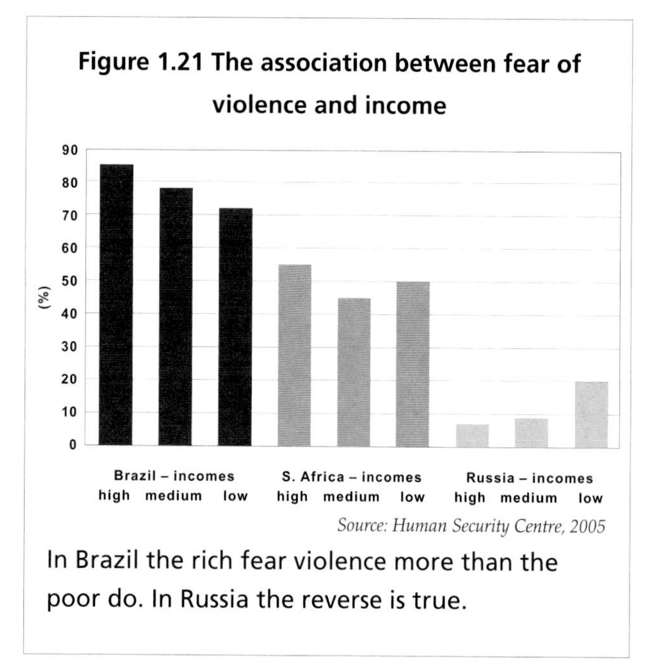

Source: Human Security Centre, 2005

In Brazil the rich fear violence more than the poor do. In Russia the reverse is true.

top priority (71%, 53% and 58%, respectively), while only 10% of British and 14% of Canadian respondents did.

> Human security is about freedom from the fear of violence as well as freedom from actual violence.

Not surprisingly, issues that citizens want their government to focus on tend to reflect their personal experiences. In Brazil and South Africa, both of which have very high crime rates, 21% and 37% of respondents, respectively, wanted their governments to focus on 'crime'. This compares with only 1% to 5% in Canada, Turkey and the United States, and 6% to 13% in France, India, Japan, Russia, Thailand and the UK.

More Americans than any other nationality wanted 'terrorism' to be the government's top priority, but even here the figure was only 10%. Surprisingly, only 9% of Indians polled wanted their government to make fighting terrorism the top priority, despite the fact that 51% of the Indians interviewed—far more than in any other country—had rated terrorism as the threat of most concern to them personally.

Only 2% of Thais and Canadians felt terrorism should be their government's number one concern, and less than 6% of respondents felt this way in the other countries polled.

Figure 1.22 Which issues should be the top priority for governments?

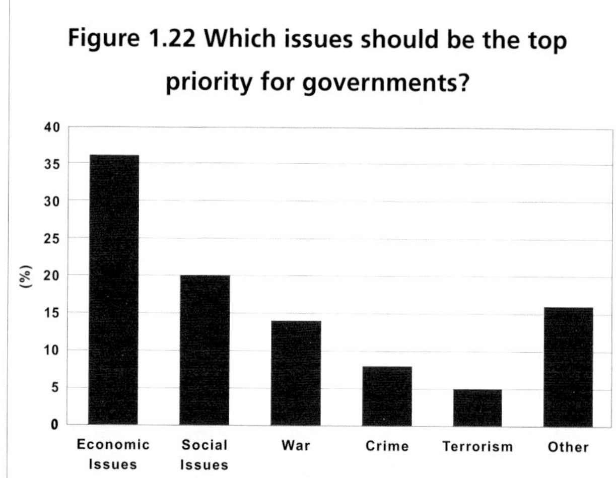

Source: Human Security Centre, 2005

Most people believe that addressing economic or social issues should be their government's number one priority—not war, terrorism or crime.

Conclusion

The Ipsos-Reid survey produces striking evidence that neither armed conflict nor terrorism is the greatest source of fear for many of the world's citizens. This should come as no surprise. Political violence, even civil war, tends to be localised. Criminal violence, unfortunately, remains ubiquitous. Human security is about freedom from the fear of violence as well as freedom from actual violence. What this poll shows is that people's fears of violence and the objective risk that they will become a victim of violence often differ radically. Fear is a function of many factors, not least of which is the media's fascination with war, terrorism and violent crime.

PART I

ENDNOTES

1. A recent study by two leading Swiss researchers, for example, claimed that 'with as many as five million casualties we have witnessed a higher death toll from violent conflict [in the 1990s] than in any other decade since World War II'. See Andreas Wenges and Daniel Möckli, *Conflict Prevention: The Untapped Potential of the Business Sector* (London: Lynne Rienner Publishers, 2002).
2. This finding comes from a new conflict termination dataset commissioned by the Human Security Centre. The complete findings will be reviewed in the *Human Security Report 2006*.
3. In the late 1990s, for example, analysis of aid, global economic growth data and government policies by the World Bank led to major shifts in official thinking about the effectiveness of development aid. See C. Burnside and D. Dollar, 'Aid, Policies and Growth', *American Economic Review* 90, 4 (September 2000): 847–868.
4. Development Data Group of the World Bank, Millennium Development Goals, The World Bank Group website, www.developmentgoals.org/ (accessed 1 June 2005).
5. The phrase 'development in reverse' comes from Paul Collier, *Breaking the Conflict Trap: Civil War and Development Policy* (Washington, DC: World Bank and Oxford University, 2003). The average costs of civil wars is calculated by Paul Collier and Anke Hoeffler, 'The Challenge of Reducing the Global Incidence of Civil War', Copenhagen Consensus Challenge Paper, Conflicts, 26 March 2004, http://www.copenhagenconsensus.com/Files/Filer/CC/Papers/Conflicts_230404.pdf (accessed 31 August 2005).
6. For more detail on definitions, see the Uppsala Conflict Database website at www.pcr.uu.se/database/definitions_all.htm #brd (accessed 4 August 2004).
7. In Figure 1.1, internationalised internal conflict is included in the intrastate conflict category.
8. John Lewis Gaddis, *The Long Peace: Inquiries into the History of the Cold War* (New York: Oxford University Press, 1989).
9. In this context, the term 'armed conflict' refers to conflicts in which one of the warring parties is a government.
10. Uppsala Conflict Data Program, Uppsala University; Center for the Study of Civil War, International Peace Research Institute, Oslo.
11. The definitions of region used by social scientists, geographers and cartographers often differ considerably. The *Human Security Report* relies on datasets that mostly define regions in conventional geographical terms. But the list of countries encompassed by a particular region may vary. For this reason care must be taken when comparing findings.
12. Figure 1.3 refers to interstate, colonial and internationalised intrastate conflicts. The latter are civil wars in which foreign countries intervene militarily. Figure 1.3 excludes all intrastate conflicts that have no foreign intervention.
13. Figure 1.4 refers to intrastate, interstate, colonial and internationalised intrastate conflicts. Conflict-years are only counted from the date of the country's independence or 1946, whichever is later.
14. Data provided by the Center for the Study of Civil War, International Peace Research Institute, Oslo, 2004.
15. Kyle Beardsley, David Quinn, Bidisha Biswas, et al., 'Mediation Style and Crisis Outcomes in the Twentieth Century', paper presented at the International Studies Association Conference, Montreal, March 2004.
16. See the background document commissioned by the Human Security Centre, Faten Ghosn and Glenn Palmer, 'A Short Investigation of Interstate Conflict since World War II: Has the Frequency or Severity Declined', at the *Human Security Report* website, www.humansecurityreport.info. Note that the authors are talking here about wars which, following the usual convention, they define as armed conflicts that have a battle-death toll of at least 1000 per year.
17. Ibid.
18. Bethany Lacina and Nils Petter Gleditsch, *Monitoring Trends in Global Combat: A New Dataset of Battle Deaths 2005* (Oslo: Centre for the Study of Civil War, 2004).
19. Note that the Lacina and Gleditsch data reported here only relate to conflicts in which a government was a party, whereas WHO claims to count deaths from state-based and non-state conflicts. But as the new Uppsala/Human Security Centre

dataset shows, non-state conflicts kill far fewer people on average than do state-based conflicts. The Uppsala/Human Security Centre dataset is discussed in detail in Part II of this report.

20. The Uppsala/Human Security Centre dataset's best estimate of battle-related deaths from state-based conflict in 2002 is 15,575 (as opposed to the 19,368 recorded by Lacina and Gleditsch). While the Lacina and Gleditsch dataset relies heavily on Uppsala's findings, the definition of 'battle-deaths' it employs is more inclusive than that of 'battle-related deaths'. See Bethany Lacina and Nils Petter Gleditsch, *Monitoring Trends in Global Combat: A New Dataset of Battle Deaths 2005.*
21. Colin D. Mathers, Christina Bernard, Kim Moesgaard Iburg, et al., 'Global Burden of Disease in 2002: Data Sources, Methods and Results', Global Programme on Evidence for Health Policy Discussion Paper No. 54, World Health Organization, December 2003 (revised February 2004).
22. Colin D. Mathers, Alan Lopez, Claudia Stein, et al., 'Deaths and Disease Burden by Cause: Global Burden of Disease Estimates for 2001 by World Bank Country Groups', Disease Control Priorities Project, Working Paper No. 18, April 2004, revised January 2005, http://www.fic.nih.gov/dcpp/wps/wp18.pdf (accessed 20 September 2005). Note that the discussion of the Uppsala/Human Security Centre dataset in Part II of this report marks the first publication of Uppsala's battle-related death data.
23. Bethany Lacina and Nils Petter Gleditsch, *Monitoring Trends in Global Combat: A New Dataset of Battle Deaths 2005.*
24. Ibid.
25. Drawn from data in Meredith Reid Sarkees, Frank Whelon Wayman and J. David Singer, 'Inter-State, Intra-State and Extra-State Wars: A Comprehensive Look At Their Distribution Over Time, 1816–1997', *International Studies Quarterly* 47 (March 2003): 49–70.
26. Ibid.
27. Coalition to Stop the Use of Child Soldiers, 'International Standards', Coalition to Stop the Use of Child Soldiers website, www.child-soldiers.org/resources/international-standards (accessed 26 March 2003).
28. Peter W. Singer, 'Caution: Children at War', *Parameters*, 1 December 2001, www.brookings.edu/views/articles/fellows/singer_20011203.htm (accessed 27 April 2005).
29. Peter W. Singer, 'Western Militaries Confront Child Soldiers Threat', *Jane's Intelligence Review*, 1 January 2005, www.brookings.edu/views/articles/fellows/singer20050115.htm (accessed 27 April 2005). As noted in Part III, the 300,000 figure may well be too high.
30. Ibid.
31. Ibid.
32. Peter W. Singer, 'Terrorists Must Be Denied Child Recruits', *Financial Times*, 20 January 2005.
33. Peter W. Singer, 'Western Militaries Confront Child Soldiers Threat'.
34. Stockholm International Peace Research Institute, *SIPRI Yearbook 2004* (Oxford: Oxford University Press, 2004).
35. Quoted by Edith Lederer, 'Global Arms Survey Finds US Most-Armed Nation,' *Common Dreams News Center*, http://www.commondreams.org/headlines03/0709-03.htm (accessed 4 August 2004).
36. Graduate Institute of International Studies, *Small Arms Survey 2003: Development Denied* (New York: Oxford University Press, 2003).
37. US Department of State, *World Military Expenditures and Arms Transfers 1999–2000* (Washington, DC: US Department of State, 2002).
38. Center for Arms Control and Non-Proliferation, 'Highlights of the FY'05 Budget Request', 02 February 2004, Center for Arms Control and Non-Proliferation website, http://armscontrolcenter.org/archives/000567.php (accessed 17 August 2005).
39. UN Department of Peacekeeping Operations, Background Note, 31 May 2005, http://www.un.org/Depts/dpko/dpko/archive/2005/bn0505e.pdf (accessed 12 August 2005).

40. Institute for Policy Studies and Foreign Policy In Focus, 'The Iraq Quagmire: The Mounting Costs of War and the Case for Bringing Home the Troops', Institute for Policy Studies website, http://www.ips-dc.org/iraq/quagmire/ (accessed 20 September 2005).
41. Arms Transfer Database, Stockholm International Peace Research Institute, 2004.
42. The International Institute for Strategic Studies, *The Military Balance 2002–2003* (Oxford: Oxford University Press, 2002).
43. Kit Collier, *The Armed Forces and Internal Security in Asia: Preventing the Abuse of Power* (Honolulu: East-West Center, 1999).
44. Peter W. Singer, *Corporate Warriors* (Ithaca, NY: Cornell University Press, 2003).
45. Peter Lock, 'Military Downsizing and Growth in the Security Industry in Sub-Saharan Africa', *Strategic Analysis* 22, 9 (December 1998): 1393–1426.
46. Peter W. Singer, *Corporate Warriors*, 66; Harvey Feigenbaum and Jeffrey Henig, 'Privatization and Political Theory', *Journal of International Affairs* 50 (Winter 1997): 338.
47. Martin Schonteich, 'Fighting Crime with Private Muscle: The Private Sector and Crime Prevention', *African Security Review* 8, 5 (1999): 17; Edward Blakely and Mary Snyder, *Fortress America: Gated Communities in the United States* (Washington, DC: Brookings Institution Press, 1997).
48. Peter W. Singer, *Corporate Warriors*, 10.
49. The Center for Public Integrity, 'Making a Killing: The Business of War', 28 October 2002, The Center for Public Integrity website, http://www.public-i.org/report.aspx?aid=177&sid=100 (accessed 7 September 2004).
50. 'Military Industrial Complexities', *Economist*, 29 March 2003, 56.
51. Doug Brooks, 'Help for Beleaguered Peacekeepers', *Washington Post*, 2 June 2003.
52. See the background document commissioned by the Human Security Centre, Barbara Harff, 'Genocide', at the *Human Security Report* website, www.humansecurityreport.info.
53. Barbara Harff, 'No Lessons Learned from the Holocaust? Assessing Risks of Genocide and Political Mass Murder Since 1955', *American Political Science Review* 93, 1 (February 2003): 65.
54. Barbara Harff, 'Genocide'.
55. R.J. Rummel, 'Power Kills: Genocide and Mass Murder', *Journal of Peace Research* 31, 1 (February 1994): 1–10.
56. US Department of State, *Patterns of Global Terrorism 2003* (Washington DC: Office of the Coordinator for Counterterrorism, 2004).
57. Note that the State Department was measuring only *international* terrorist attacks. Measuring *national* terrorism is far more problematic.
58. Alan B. Krueger and David Laitin, 'Faulty Terror Report Card', *Washington Post*, 17 May 2004. (Emphasis in the text added). The reference to 'verifiable' information is important because the State Department only provides written descriptions of the 'significant' terrorist attacks. Since there are no descriptions of 'non-significant' attacks their status cannot be verified.
59. US Department of State, *Patterns of Global Terrorism 2003*.
60. Ibid.
61. Alan B. Krueger and David Laitin, 'Faulty Terror Report Card'.
62. Todd Sandler and Walter Enders, 'An Economic Perspective on Transnational Terrorism', May 2003, http://www.cba.ua.edu/~wenders/EJPE_Sandler_Enders.pdf (accessed 17 August 2005).
63. Alan B. Krueger, Princeton University, 2004.

64. It is not prudent to rely on any single indicator when trying to gauge terrorism trends. On their own, counts of the number of attacks or casualties can give a false impression. In Latin America, for example, there are large numbers of terrorist attacks, but a very low level of casualties.
65. Sonni Efron and Paul Richter, 'New Office to Issue Terrorism Data', *Los Angeles Times*, 19 April 2005.
66. The Human Security Centre, University of British Columbia, 2004. Based on data in *Pattern of Global Terrorism 2003*, US Department of State, 2004 and 'An Economic Perspective on Transnational Terrorism', by Todd Sandler and Walter Enders.
67. National Memorial Institute for the Prevention of Terrorism, 'A Chronology of Significant International Terrorism for 2004', National Memorial Institute for the Prevention of Terrorism website, http://www.tkb.org/Home.jsp (accessed 20 September 2005).
68. Ibid.
69. 'Rumsfeld's War-on-Terror Memo', *USA Today*, 16 October 2003.
70. 'Poverty Warning After US Attacks', *BBC News*, 1 October 2001.
71. Cited in Nicholas D. Kristof, 'An American Hiroshima Is All Too Likely', *International Herald Tribune*, 12 August 2004.
72. Monterey Institute for International Studies, 'Suitcase Nukes: A Reassessment', Center for Nonproliferation Studies website, 23 September 2002, http://cns.miis.edu/pubs/week/020923.htm (accessed 7 September 2004).
73. Ibid.
74. Mike Nartker, 'Radiological Weapons: 'Dirty Bomb' Attack Is 40% Probability, Expert Says', *Global Security Newswire*, 18 November 2002, http://www.nti.org/d_newswire/issues/newswires/2002_11_18.html (accessed 7 September 2004).
75. Council on Foreign Relations, 'Terrorism: Questions and Answers', Council on Foreign Relations website, http://cfrterrorism.org/groups/aumshinrikyo.html (accessed 27 April 2005).
76. Wayne Turnbull and Praveen Abhayaratne, *2002 WMD Terrorism Chronology: Incidents Involving Sub-National Actors and Chemical, Biological, Radiological, and Nuclear Materials* (Monterey, CA: Monterey Institute of International Studies, 2003).
77. National Memorial Institute for the Prevention of Terrorism, 'MIPT Terrorism Knowledge Base, A Comprehensive Databank of Global Terrorism Incidents and Organizations', National Memorial Institute for the Prevention of Terrorism website, http://www.tkb.org/Home.jsp (accessed 20 September 2005).
78. William Eubank and Leonard Weinberg, 'Terrorism and Democracy: Perpetrators and Victims', *Terrorism and Political Violence*, 13, 1 (Spring 2001): 155–164.
79. Federal Bureau of Investigation, *Terrorism in the United States: 1999* (Washington, DC: US Department of Justice, Federal Bureau of Investigation, 1999).
80. Pew Research Center, 'A Year After Iraq: Mistrust of America in Europe Ever Higher, Muslim Anger Persists', Additional Findings and Analyses, Pew Research Center website, http://people-press.org/reports/display.php3?PageID=796 (accessed 15 August 2005).
81. Isobel McConnan and Sarah Uppard, *Children Not Soldiers: Guidelines for Working with Child Soldiers and Children Associated with Fighting Forces* (London: Save the Children Fund, 2001).
82. Caroline Moser and Cathy McIlwaine, *Violence in a Post-Conflict World: Urban Poor Perceptions from Guatemala* (Washington, DC: World Bank, 2000).
83. Ibid.
84. Deepa Narayan-Parker, *Voices of the Poor: Can Anyone Hear Us?* (New York: Oxford University Press for the World Bank, 2000).
85. Greenberg Research Inc., *The People on War Report* (Geneva: International Committee of the Red Cross, 1999).

86. Gallup International, 'Executive Summary: Voice of the People Survey 2003', 5 January 2004, Gallup International website, http://www.voice-of-the-people.net/ContentFiles/files/VoP2003/Executive%20Summary%20Report%20(January%209th %202004).pdf (accessed 6 February 2005).
87. Throughout this text, and in the related graphs, 'good' includes the ratings 'good' and 'very good', while 'poor' includes the ratings 'poor' and 'very poor'.
88. Gallup International, 'Executive Summary: Voice of the People Survey 2003'.
89. The definition of the regions in Figure 1.15 was determined by Gallup. For details see Gallup International, 'Executive Summary: Voice of the People Survey 2003'.
90. National Campaign Against Violence and Crime, 'Summary Volume: Fear of Crime, Commonwealth of Australia', May 1998, http://www.ag.gov.au/agd/www/rwpattach.nsf/viewasattachmentPersonal(E24C1D4325451B61DE7F4F2B1E1557 15)~no2_summary.pdf/$file/no2_summary.pdf (accessed 15 December 2004).
91. Hannah Scott, 'Stranger Danger: Explaining Women's Fear of Crime', *Western Criminology Review* 4, 3 (2003): 203.
92. The survey questioned 6043 people in 11 countries. In each country, Ipsos-Reid representatives used comparable interview techniques. UK respondents weren't asked the full range of questions, so some of the results cover 10 countries, and some cover 11. Some surveys were limited to a few cities; others were national in scope. All interviews were carried out between August 30 and October 5, 2003. All respondents were older than 18, but upper age limits differed. In the US, 1005 people were interviewed; elsewhere, the target was 500 per country. The questions were asked in local languages. But this language was not necessarily the mother tongue of all respondents. Moreover, abstract concepts such as 'security' do not translate in precisely the same way from language to language and from culture to culture. Some caution should therefore be used in interpreting these results.
93. In Figure 1.17, 'health and economic threats' include epidemics, environmental crises, famine, economic collapse and terminal illness.
94. Source data commissioned from Ipsos-Reid by the Human Security Centre; see Ipsos-Reid website, http://www.ipsos.ca/ (accessed 10 May 2005).
95. In Figures 1.17 and 1.22, 'criminal violence' and 'crime' refer to violence, hate crime/mob violence, rape, sexual harassment/ sexual assault, domestic violence, kidnapping/abduction, theft/robbery and identity theft.
96. In Figures 1.17 and 1.22, 'war' refers to interstate war, nuclear war, political violence, revolution and civil war.
97. No list of options to choose from was given to the interviewees.

Andrew Testa / Panos Pictures

PART II

THE HUMAN SECURITY AUDIT

Part II reviews a new global dataset that provides a comprehensive portrait of global political violence for the years 2002 and 2003. It also surveys trends in human rights abuse, criminal violence and human trafficking. It concludes with a discussion of the methodological challenges facing researchers measuring human insecurity.

PART II

THE HUMAN SECURITY AUDIT

Leo Erken / Panos Pictures

Introduction

Research findings published here for the first time help illuminate both the scope and the depth of human insecurity around the world. But obtaining accurate data remains a major challenge.

Mapping trends in political violence is important both for researchers seeking to understand their causes, and for governments and international organisations attempting to evaluate the impact of security policies.

Part II begins with a detailed review of the new dataset on global political violence that the Human Security Centre commissioned from Uppsala's Conflict Data Program specifically for this report.

The Uppsala/PRIO dataset that was featured in Part I only provides data on the number of 'state-based' conflicts—that is, those waged between a state and another state, or a state and an armed rebel group.

The Uppsala/PRIO dataset does *not* count:

- 'Non-state' conflicts—intercommunal and other armed conflicts in which a government is not one of the warring parties.
- 'One-sided' violence—cases of unopposed deadly assaults on civilians, like that in Rwanda in 1994.
- Death tolls from state-based and non-state conflict, or from one-sided violence.

The new Uppsala/Human Security Centre dataset provides data on all of the above.

Because the new dataset thus far covers just two years—2002 and 2003—it does not yet provide trend data. Even so, it has produced some arresting findings. It reveals, for example, that there have been far more conflicts taking place around the world than are counted by the Uppsala/PRIO dataset. Indeed, in both 2002 and 2003 there were *more* non-state than state-based armed conflicts.

This raises an obvious question. How can we be sure that *all* armed conflicts have declined since the end of the Cold War when we have no record of non-state conflicts before 2002? This question is examined—and answered—in the section that follows.

In the absence of official statistics, Uppsala and the compilers of other conflict datasets rely on reports from the media, NGOs, academics and governments to count battle-related death tolls. The fact that many battle-related deaths are simply not reported, plus Uppsala's strict

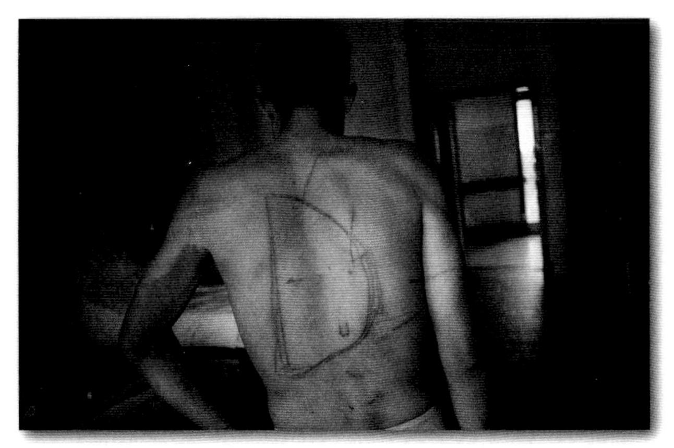

Andrew Testa / Panos Pictures

Torture and other gross human rights abuses are often perpetrated in secret, making the collection of reliable trend data very difficult.

data coding rules, mean that a degree of under-counting is inevitable.

Other methods of estimating war deaths, including epidemiological surveys, are in principle more accurate. But they cannot be used to create global datasets.

Another issue that complicates our understanding of trends in political violence is the attachment that the media, and some policymakers, have to many of the myths of contemporary global security, some of which were briefly discussed in the Overview. As one UN report on the difficulties of data collection noted:

> When it comes to statistics ... numbers take on a life of their own, gaining acceptance through repetition, often with little inquiry into their derivations. Journalists, bowing to the pressures of editors, demand numbers, any number. Organizations feel compelled to supply them, lending false precision and spurious authority to many reports.[1]

A classic case of 'numbers taking on a life of their own' is the endlessly reiterated claim that 90% of those killed in today's wars are civilians. In fact, the 90% figure is completely without foundation. (See 'The myth of civilian war deaths' by Kristine Eck of Uppsala University's Conflict Data Program.)

Political violence is a term that embraces more than simply war, genocide and terrorism. It also encompasses state repression: torture; extrajudicial, arbitrary and summary executions; the 'disappearance' of dissidents; the use of death squads; and incarceration without trial. All of these are as much part of the human security agenda as they are of the human rights agenda.

But mapping global and regional trends in human right abuse is extremely difficult. The UN's Human Rights Commission is far too politicised a body to even contemplate such an exercise, while the major human rights organisations resist as a matter of principle any attempt to quantify human rights abuse.

Researchers running one little-publicised project—the Political Terror Scale (PTS) now located at the University of North Carolina, Asheville—have been collating and coding data on human rights violations around the world for more than 20 years. PTS data are coded in such a way that making comparisons between countries is relatively simple.

PTS researchers Linda Cornett and Mark Gibney used PTS data to track regional trends in human rights violations from 1980 to 2003 for the *Human Security Report.* Taken as a whole the data reveal little significant variation—certainly nothing like the dramatic post–Cold War decline in armed conflicts.

However, the regional trend data indicate that the human rights situation worsened somewhat in four out of six regions around the world from 1980 to 2003, but that after 1994 it improved modestly in five of the six regions.

In most states, most of the time, far more people are killed or injured by criminal violence than by warfare. But attempts to map the incidence of violent crime around the world confront major data problems. The fact that only a small percentage of countries report violent crime statistics in a regular and timely manner, plus pervasive problems of under-reporting and under-recording, mean that efforts to produce reliable global or regional trend data on violent crime confront nearly insurmountable difficulties.

The discussion of global homicide and rape trends in the section on criminal violence draws on a paper commissioned for this report by Graeme Newman of the State University of New York in Albany. This section also includes a discussion by Luke Dowdney of Viva Rio on children and violent crime in Rio de Janeiro.

Human trafficking is another crime that often involves violence, and has been described by UNICEF as the 'largest slave trade in history.'[2] There are no reliable data on the numbers trafficked each year, but there is widespread agreement that trafficking has become a significant cause of human insecurity.

The final section in Part II asks whether or not it is possible to create a human security index modelled on the UN's Human Development Index. It draws on data from the Uppsala Conflict Data Program, the Political Terror Scale and a relatively new World Bank dataset on political violence and stability, to present a comparison of the world's least secure states. The fact that so many of the same countries appear in all three 'least secure' lists speaks to the interrelated nature of war, human rights violations and political instability.

Sven Torfinn / Panos Pictures

A new global dataset

Commissioned by the Human Security Centre, and published here for the first time, this dataset provides the most comprehensive picture yet of the incidence, scope and intensity of political violence around the world.

Counting wars is a complex and often contested business. Most datasets that measure the incidence of armed conflict, including the 1946 to 2003 Uppsala/PRIO dataset that provided much of the data for Part I of this report, only count the number of 'state-based' conflicts—those in which a government is one of the warring parties.

> One-sided violence is distinguished from armed conflict because it involves the slaughter of defenceless civilians rather than combat.

But relying solely on counts of state-based conflicts means ignoring the very large number of conflicts in which a government is *not* involved—intercommunal conflicts between ethnic and religious groups, or fights between rival warlords, for example. The Uppsala Conflict Data Program describes these as 'non-state' conflicts.

Similarly, most armed conflict datasets don't count cases of what Uppsala calls 'one-sided' violence—the unopposed killing of 25 or more civilians during a calendar year. This category is distinguished from armed conflict because it involves the slaughter of defenceless civilians rather than combat.

To gain a more comprehensive picture of the incidence and intensity of political violence around the world, the Human Security Centre commissioned the Uppsala Conflict Data Program to collect data on the two previously uncounted categories, *as well as* on the number of deaths associated with the three types of political violence.

Although the new dataset thus far only covers two years, it has already produced some surprising findings. Some examples:

- *All* categories of political violence declined between 2002 and 2003.
- There were more non-state conflicts than state-based conflicts in both 2002 and 2003.
- Non-state conflicts killed two to five times fewer people on average than did state-based conflicts. The reported deaths from one-sided violence were lower still.

- In 2003 less than 5% of all armed conflicts were fought between states.
- In 2003 sub-Saharan Africa experienced more cases of political violence of all types than any other region.

Figure 2.1 records a modest worldwide decline (10%) in cases of political violence of all types (armed conflicts and one-sided violence) between 2002 and 2003.

Regionally, Africa and then Asia experienced the greatest number of cases of political violence. But while Asia showed a small increase (4%) from 2002 to 2003, there was a significant decrease (21%) in Africa.

In 2002 only one of the 66 armed conflicts (that between India and Pakistan) was coded as an interstate conflict.[3] In 2003 two of the 59 ongoing armed conflicts were coded as interstate conflicts (the fighting between India and Pakistan and the US-led invasion of Iraq).

Figure 2.2 tells us about the number of *countries* in each region that suffered from political violence in 2002 and 2003. Since some countries experience several conflicts

WHAT'S NEW ABOUT THE UPPSALA/HUMAN SECURITY CENTRE DATASET?

The Uppsala/Human Security Centre dataset covers the three main categories of political violence. This report publishes the new data for 2002 and 2003.[4] The *Human Security Report 2006* will publish the data for 2004 and 2005.

Category of political violence[5]

State-based armed conflicts

Conflicts between states or between a state and a non-state actor, with at least 25 battle-related deaths per year. Includes all interstate wars and those civil wars where the state is a warring party. Updated data on the number of state-based armed conflicts compiled by the Uppsala Data Program are published each year in the *Journal of Peace Research* and the *SIPRI Yearbook*.

What's new? Data on the number of reported battle-related deaths for each conflict and the death rate (fatalities per 100,000 population) for each country experiencing conflict.

Non-state armed conflicts

Conflicts in which none of the warring parties is a government and which incur at least 25 battle-related deaths per year.

What's new? Data on the number and location of non-state conflicts and the numbers killed have never before been systematically collected and published annually.

One-sided violence

The deliberate unopposed slaughter of at least 25 civilians in one year by a government or political group. Includes genocides, politicides and other violent assaults on civilians.

What's new? Barbara Harff's dataset (see Part I) counts genocides and politicides and the death tolls associated with them. However, the one-sided violence considered in the new dataset is a broader category that goes beyond genocide and politicide.

What's counted?

- The number of cases of political violence (armed conflicts plus cases of one-sided violence).
- The number of countries experiencing political violence.
- The number of reported deaths from political violence.
- The number of reported deaths per 100,000 population.

Figure 2.1 Cases of armed conflict and one-sided violence, 2002–2003

	State-based			Non-state			One-sided			Total: All types		
	2002	2003	Change	2002	2003	Change	2002	2003	Change	2002	2003	Change
Africa	15	10	-5	26	25	-1	17	11	-6	58	46	-12
Americas	2	1	-1	2	2	0	2	1	-1	6	4	-2
Asia	12	14	+2	5	2	-3	11	13	+2	28	29	+1
Europe	1	1	0	0	0	0	1	1	0	2	2	0
Middle East	2	3	+1	1	1	0	2	4	+2	5	8	+3
Total	32	29	-3	34	30	-4	33	30	-3	99	89	-10

Source: Uppsala/Human Security Centre dataset, 2005[6]

Between 2002 and 2003 there was a small decline in cases of political violence around the world.

Figure 2.2 Number of countries experiencing political violence, 2002–2003

	State-based			Non-state			One-sided			Total: All types		
	2002	2003	Change	2002	2003	Change	2002	2003	Change	2002	2003	Change
Africa	13	9	-4	8	7	-1	11	9	-2	18	13	-5
Americas	2	1	-1	2	2	0	1	1	0	3	2	-1
Asia	6	8	+2	3	1	-2	5	5	0	7	9	+2
Europe	1	1	0	0	0	0	1	1	0	1	1	0
Middle East	2	3	+1	1	1	0	1	4	+3	3	4	+1
Total	24	22	-2	14	11	-3	19	20	+1	32	29	-3

Source: Uppsala/Human Security Centre dataset, 2005

Worldwide there was a small decline in the number of countries experiencing political violence in 2003.

in a single year, the figures are significantly lower than in Figure 2.1.

Africa was the only region to show a marked year-on-year change. Between 2002 and 2003 Africa became significantly more secure, with 28% fewer countries being affected by political violence.

As Figure 2.3 indicates, the seven countries that had the highest number of conflicts and cases of one-sided violence in 2002 were India (10), the Democratic Republic of the Congo (9), Somalia (8), Nigeria (7), Ethiopia (6) and Sudan and Burma (Myanmar) (with 5 each).

In 2003 India again suffered the highest number of armed conflicts and cases of one-sided violence (15), followed by Uganda (7), the Democratic Republic of the Congo and Ethiopia (with 6 each), and Nigeria, Somalia and Sudan (with 5 each).

Has the number of conflicts really declined?

The armed conflict statistics that Uppsala/PRIO update each year, and that are published in the Stockholm International Peace Research Institute's *SIPRI Yearbook* and the *Journal of Peace Research*, have become a valued and trusted source of information on the trends in armed conflict around

Figure 2.3 Cases of armed conflict and one-sided violence by country, 2002–2003[7]

	State-based		Non-state		One-sided		Total	
	2002	2003	2002	2003	2002	2003	2002	2003
Africa								
Algeria	1	1	0	0	1	1	2	2
Angola	2	0	0	0	1	0	3	0
Burundi	1	1	0	1	3	2	4	4
CAR	1	0	0	0	0	0	1	0
Chad	1	0	0	0	0	0	1	0
Congo-Brazzaville	1	0	0	0	1	0	2	0
DRC	0	0	5	4	4	2	9	6
Eritrea	0	1	0	0	0	0	0	1
Ethiopia	2	1	3	4	1	1	6	6
Ghana	0	0	1	0	0	0	1	0
Côte d'Ivoire	1	1	1	0	0	0	2	1
Liberia	1	1	0	0	1	1	2	2
Madagascar	0	0	1	0	0	0	1	0
Morocco	0	0	0	0	0	1	0	1
Nigeria	0	0	6	4	1	1	7	5
Rwanda	1	0	0	0	0	0	1	0
Senegal	0	1	0	0	1	0	1	1
Somalia	1	0	7	5	0	0	8	5
Sudan	1	2	2	2	2	1	5	5
Uganda	1	1	0	5	1	1	2	7
Americas								
Colombia	1	1	1	1	2	1	4	3
Ecuador	0	0	0	1	0	0	0	1
Mexico	0	0	1	0	0	0	1	0
Asia								
Afghanistan	1	1	2	2	0	0	3	3
India	6	7	1	0	3	8	10	15
Indonesia	1	1	0	0	3	2	4	3
Myanmar (Burma)	2	1	2	0	1	0	5	1
Nepal	1	1	0	0	2	0	3	1
Pakistan	1	1	0	0	0	1	1	2
Philippines	2	2	0	0	2	1	4	3
Sri Lanka	0	1	0	0	0	0	0	1
Thailand	0	0	0	0	0	1	0	1
Europe								
Russia	1	1	0	0	1	1	2	2
Middle East								
Iraq	0	1	1	1	0	0	1	2
Israel and the Palestinian Territories	1	1	0	0	2	2	3	3
Saudi Arabia	0	0	0	0	0	1	0	1
Turkey	1	1	0	0	0	1	1	2

Source: Uppsala/Human Security Centre dataset, 2005

Individual country counts of state-based conflicts, non-state conflicts and cases of one-sided violence provide a detailed picture of the location of political violence around the world.

the world. Yet few, if any, non-specialists will have been aware that a whole category of conflict was excluded from these publications.

The single most important finding from the new Uppsala/Human Security Centre dataset is that in 2002 and 2003 there were more non-state conflicts than there were state-based conflicts.

- Of the 66 armed conflicts in 2002, 34 (52%) were non-state conflicts, and 32 (49%) were state-based.
- Of the 59 armed conflicts in 2003, 30 (51%) were non-state conflicts, and 29 (49%) were state-based.

This raises an important question about one of the central claims made in Part I of this report—namely, that the number of armed conflicts has declined quite dramatically in the past dozen years. That claim was based on trends revealed in the Uppsala/PRIO dataset on state-based conflicts.

How can we be sure that there has been a major decline in *all* armed conflicts since the end of the Cold War if the Uppsala/PRIO dataset counts only state-based conflicts?

> In 2002 and 2003 there were more non-state conflicts than there were state-based conflicts.

It is at least theoretically possible that non-state conflicts increased more than state-based conflicts decreased during this period. If this were true, there would have been a net *increase,* not decrease, in armed conflicts of all types over the past decade, and the central thesis of this report could not be supported.

But we *can* be confident that non-state conflicts declined in the post–Cold War era. Indeed, the decline may well be steeper than the drop in state-based conflicts. Why?

First, there are the findings of the Minorities at Risk Project at the University of Maryland on violence between communal groups from 1990 to 1998. Project director Ted Robert Gurr concluded that during this period 'serious intercommunal conflict [i.e., non-state conflict] followed the same rise-and-fall path of violent ethnic challenges to states [i.e., state-based conflict]'. The intercommunal conflicts examined in Gurr's study declined by more than 50% between 1993 and 1998.[8]

Second, Monty G. Marshall of the Center for International Development and Conflict Management has created a dataset that counts the number of countries experiencing all forms of warfare—including non-state conflict—each year from 1946 to 2004.[9] Marshall's data reveal an even steeper decline since the end of the Cold War than the Uppsala/PRIO state-based conflict dataset.[10]

Together, the studies by Gurr and Marshall indicate that non-state conflicts have followed the same downward trend in the post–Cold War years as state-based conflicts—and that the decline in non-state conflict has likely been greater than the decline in state-based conflict. It follows that the number of armed conflicts of all types has declined.

Can we trust the death toll data?

In addition to tracking the number of armed conflicts and cases of one-sided violence around the world, the Uppsala/Human Security Centre dataset provides a count of reported, verifiable and codable deaths from political violence in every country each year.

The dataset also records whether the deaths were caused by governments or non-state armed groups, and whether the conflict was about the struggle for control of the government or over territory.[11]

Estimating the number of armed conflicts or cases of one-sided violence is relatively easy. Determining the numbers killed by political violence is both more difficult and requires more resources.

Once it was possible to count bodies on the battlefield when an engagement was over. Not any more. The typical conflict today is spread over huge areas and many months—sometimes years. Fighting, particularly between non-state actors, often takes place in remote areas.

Many of the estimates of war deaths that get publicised in the media and used by governments, NGOs and even UN agencies are simply guesses—and are often greatly exaggerated.

In 1995, for example, there were widely publicised claims that some 200,000 people had been killed in the fighting in Bosnia and Herzegovina. This figure was not based on any serious assessment of the evidence and was subsequently found to be hugely inflated.[12]

> Many of the estimates of war deaths that get publicised in the media and used by governments, NGOs and even UN agencies are simply guesses.

Uppsala's approach to data collection is cautious, conservative and subject to stringent coding rules that inevitably lead to a degree of under-counting. However, Uppsala's methodology is currently the only one that can produce annual national, regional and global trend data for all three categories of political violence and publish them in a timely manner.

Three approaches to estimating war deaths

A number of different methodologies are currently used to measure war deaths in a systematic manner. Each of the following approaches has advantages and disadvantages—and each serves different analytic and policy purposes.

Report-based methodologies

The Uppsala/Human Security Centre and Correlates of War datasets and the International Institute of Strategic Studies' Armed Conflict Database[13] all rely on *reports* of deaths from political violence.

In Uppsala's case, the relevant information is culled electronically from the huge Factiva news database using purpose-built automated software.[14] The selected data are then reviewed and coded. This approach, as noted above, has a systematic bias toward under-counting. There are two main reasons for this.

First, some deaths simply never get reported. This is particularly true of conflicts where the media are excluded, such as in Chechnya. Deaths that are not reported cannot be recorded.

Second, Uppsala's stringent coding rules require:

- That there be a minimum of 25 deaths per year.
- That the cause of death be identified as political rather than criminal violence.
- That the group responsible for the deaths be reliably identified.

The case of Iraq clearly shows the effect this last requirement can have on battle-related death counts.

Most of the killings that have taken place during the post-war insurgency in Iraq have been carried out by unidentified perpetrators and cannot, therefore, be coded. This means that thousands of instances of what are very likely acts of political violence have gone unrecorded.

The coding difficulties in the Iraq case are unusual, but they highlight the need to record a new category of deaths—those that are likely due to political violence but are not codable for lack of sufficient information. This category will be included in future *Human Security Reports.*

Epidemiological surveys

Epidemiological surveys in wartorn countries are mostly undertaken to provide information for humanitarian agencies whose primary interest is the health *consequences* of war, not its causes. But such surveys are increasingly used to estimate death tolls from combat-related violence, as well as deaths from war-exacerbated disease and malnutrition.

Standard population health survey methodologies based on a randomly chosen sample of the population are used to establish death rates from various causes. Death rates during or after the conflict are then compared with pre-conflict death rates to determine the war-induced 'excess' death rate. ('Excess' deaths are those that would not have occurred had there been no conflict.)

When the sample size is large enough and appropriately selected, researchers can have considerable confidence in the accuracy of the extrapolated death toll estimates.

In-depth historical investigations

Another approach to counting war deaths, one developed by Patrick Ball and colleagues at the Human Rights Data Analysis Group,[15] relies on exhaustive historical investigations of particular conflicts using painstakingly cross-checked reports from human rights organisations, data from exhumations, extensive interviews and other relevant sources. In-depth historical investigations have been carried out in Guatemala, Peru, Kosovo, East Timor and Haiti, and their findings are typically used to provide information on gross human rights abuses for truth and reconciliation commissions[16] or as evidence for war crimes tribunals.

These studies tend to uncover large numbers of deaths that have not been previously reported.

The strengths of report-based methodologies

In June 2005 the *Small Arms Survey 2005* (SAS)[17] published a comparison of estimates of death totals compiled by various report-based datasets (including Uppsala's) with those of epidemiological surveys and in-depth historical investigations. It found that the death estimates of the report-based methodologies were two to four times lower than death estimates produced by the other methodologies.

> Neither epidemiological surveys nor in-depth historical studies can be used to produce timely global and regional death toll data.

While the SAS analysis of Uppsala's data was problematic for a number of reasons,[18] its claim that report-based methodologies under-count battle-related deaths was clearly correct.

So if epidemiological surveys and in-depth historical analyses like those undertaken by the Human Rights Data Analysis Group produce a more complete picture of the numbers of people killed by political violence, why doesn't the *Human Security Report* rely on them to provide death toll data?

The short answer is that neither epidemiological surveys nor in-depth historical studies can be used to produce timely global and regional death toll data. There are a number of reasons for this:

- **Global coverage.** Only methodologies like Uppsala's record deaths for all conflicts in all countries each year.
- **National coverage.** Many epidemiological surveys carried out in post-conflict societies, or those still at war, focus only on the areas that are of greatest concern to humanitarian agencies. But the findings of surveys of a particular region of a country cannot be extrapolated to generate national death toll estimates.
- **Comparability.** Different epidemiological surveys have different coding rules, which makes comparisons problematic. For example, some surveys lump murders and combat-related deaths together under a single descriptive category of 'violent deaths'. Others distinguish between deaths caused by political violence and those caused by criminal violence.
- **Timeliness.** In order to establish comparable annual death toll estimates, data for each country in conflict must be collected and published in a timely manner. Only report-based methodologies currently do this.
- **Cost.** Nationwide epidemiological surveys and in-depth historical studies are expensive (relative to report-based methodologies). Currently, there is simply no funding available to conduct them annually for every country experiencing political violence.
- **Feasibility.** Even when funding is available, epidemiological surveys and in-depth historical analyses normally require the permission, if not the cooperation, of governments. Sometimes that permission will not be granted. Report-based approaches are not similarly constrained.

Each of the three approaches to measuring death tolls reviewed here serves a different purpose and each adds to our understanding of political violence around the world.

But while in-depth historical studies and epidemiological surveys provide the most detailed picture of the human costs of political violence in individual conflicts, they cannot be used to create annually updated datasets that track national, regional and global trends in deaths from political violence. And it is the data on *trends* that are of greatest importance to policymakers and to researchers investigating the causes of war and peace. A systematic bias in the recorded death toll data toward under-counting does not compromise their value in tracking trends.

Trend data are important not only because they help policymakers determine whether or not their policies are working, but because they also reveal long-term changes that might otherwise be overlooked. For example, the rapid rise in the number of armed conflicts around the world during the 'Long Peace' of the Cold War passed largely unnoticed by a scholarly community that were focused on relations between the major powers and the East-West confrontation. This dramatic shift only became obvious when reliable trend data were published. The same trend data revealed the subsequent substantial drop in armed conflicts in the post–Cold War era.

The 1946 to 2002 Lacina and Gleditsch battle-death dataset reviewed in Part I provides another example of the utility of trend data. While the accuracy of many of the individual death tolls, for particular countries in particular years, can certainly be challenged, the finding that there has been a dramatic decrease in the deadliness of conflict over the past 50-plus years is not in question. This surprising finding helps us understand how changes in the modes of combat during this period have made warfare much less deadly.

Trend data are important because they help policymakers determine whether or not their policies are working.

Deaths from political violence: The new dataset

Globally, state-based conflicts killed more people (57% of the total in 2002, and 75% in 2003) than either non-state conflicts (26% in 2002, 14% in 2003) or one-sided violence (18% and 10%). But as Figure 2.4 shows, there was considerable regional variation.[21]

Remarkably, in spite of the Iraq war in 2003, the reported global death count from all forms of political violence held virtually steady from 2002 to 2003.

Figure 2.4 Numbers of reported deaths from political violence, 2002–2003*

	State-based			Non-state			One-sided			Total: All types		
	2002	2003	Change	2002	2003	Change	2002	2003	Change	2002	2003	Change
Africa	6659	5935	-724	4556	3464	-1092	3217	1584	-1633	14432	10983	-3449
Americas	1157	487	-670	595	129	-466	188	115	-73	1940	731	-1209
Asia	5979	4854	-1125	1778	149	-1629	1138	812	-326	8895	5815	-3080
Europe	753	480	-273	0	0	0	34	59	+25	787	539	-248
Middle East[19]	1027	8817	+7790	200	181	-19	306	248	-58	1533	9246	+7713
Total	15575	20573	+4998	7129	3923	-3206	4883	2818	-2065	27587	27314	-273

Source: Uppsala/Human Security Centre dataset, 2005

*Fatality figures are 'best estimates'[20]

From 2002 to 2003 total reported deaths from all categories of political violence decreased in all regions except the Middle East, where the Iraq war drove deaths from state-based conflict dramatically upward.

Figure 2.5 Numbers of reported deaths from political violence by country, 2002–2003*

	State-based		Non-state		One-sided		Total		Death rate**	
	2002	2003	2002	2003	2002	2003	2002	2003	2002	2003
Africa										
Algeria	150	198	0	0	156	25	306	223	1.0	0.7
Angola	729	0	0	0	57	0	786	0	5.7	0.0
Burundi	460	955	0	43	385	144	845	1142	12.0	16.2
CAR	159	0	0	0	0	0	159	0	4.2	0.0
Chad	418	0	0	0	0	0	418	0	5.1	0.0
Congo-Brazzaville	116	0	0	0	55	0	171	0	5.4	0.0
DRC	0	0	3184	2063	877	91	4061	2154	7.6	4.2
Eritrea	0	57	0	0	0	0	0	57	0.0	1.3
Ethiopia	50	25	138	143	226	56	414	224	0.6	0.3
Ghana	0	0	36	0	0	0	36	0	0.2	0.0
Côte d'Ivoire	600	121	26	0	0	0	626	121	3.7	0.7
Liberia	500	1589	0	0	200	369	700	1958	21.2	59.4
Madagascar	0	0	79	0	0	0	79	0	0.5	0.0
Morocco	0	0	0	0	0	45	0	45	0.0	0.2
Nigeria	0	0	490	206	45	50	535	256	0.4	0.2
Rwanda	59	0	0	0	0	0	59	0	0.7	0.0
Senegal	0	40	0	0	33	0	33	40	0.3	0.4
Somalia	132	0	512	368	0	0	644	368	6.9	3.9
Sudan	2254	2321	91	309	74	173	2419	2803	7.5	8.5
Uganda	1032	629	0	332	1109	631	2141	1592	9.2	6.5
Americas										
Colombia	1157	487	569	99	188	115	1914	701	4.4	1.6
Ecuador	0	0	0	30	0	0	0	30	0.0	0.2
Mexico	0	0	26	0	0	0	26	0	0.0	0.0
Asia										
Afghanistan	400	168	187	149	0	0	587	317	2.1	1.1
India	2008	1899	1500	0	538	531	4046	2430	0.4	0.2
Indonesia	112	429	0	0	252	88	364	517	0.2	0.2
Myanmar (Burma)	230	40	91	0	37	0	358	40	0.7	0.1
Nepal	2425	1064	0	0	233	0	2658	1064	11.0	4.4
Pakistan	265	144	0	0	0	54	265	198	0.2	0.1
Philippines	539	1085	0	0	78	65	617	1150	0.8	1.4
Sri Lanka	0	25	0	0	0	0	0	25	0.0	0.1
Thailand	0	0	0	0	0	74	0	74	0.0	0.1
Europe										
Russia	753	480	0	0	34	59	787	539	0.6	0.4
Middle East										
Iraq[22]	0	8313	200	181	0	0	200	8494	0.8	35.1
Israel and the Palestinian Territories	971	425	0	0	306	148	1277	573	13.2	5.8
Saudi Arabia	0	0	0	0	0	43	0	43	0.0	0.2
Turkey	56	79	0	0	0	57	56	136	0.1	0.2

Source: Uppsala/Human Security Centre dataset, 2005

*Fatality figures are 'best estimates'.

**Number of fatalities per 100,000 of population, rounded to the nearest decimal. Population data come from the World Bank's *World Development Indicators* database and are for 2002.

Reported death counts and death rate data for individual countries reveal a more detailed picture of the costs of political violence.

As it was, the Iraq war meant that the body count for the Middle East increased at least sixfold, and likely much more. Elsewhere, deaths from political violence fell substantially from 2002 to 2003: in the Americas by a massive 62%, in Europe by 32%, in Asia by 35% and even in wartorn Africa by 24%.

Most of the increase in the battle-related death toll in the Middle East is attributable to state-based conflict in Iraq. In all other regions, deaths from state-based conflict dropped significantly—down 11% in Africa and 58% in the Americas.

Non-state conflict death tolls were down everywhere, from a 10% fall in the Middle East to a massive 92% drop in Asia.

And from one-sided violence, reported deaths fell in all regions except Europe. The decrease ranged from 19% in the Middle East to 51% in Africa.

Figure 2.5 shows that in 2002 the five countries with the highest number of reported deaths from all three forms of political violence were the DRC, India, Nepal, Sudan and Uganda.

In 2003 the picture had changed significantly. The five countries with the highest number of reported deaths from political violence were Iraq,[28] Sudan, India, the DRC and Liberia.

However, these reported death-count figures overstate the significance of high absolute numbers of deaths in more populous countries. A different picture emerges

THE MYTH OF CIVILIAN WAR DEATHS

In World War I, 5% of fatalities were civilian; in World War II, fatalities rose to 50%; and in the 1990s, 90% of war deaths were civilian.

Similar claims are regularly made by UN agencies (including UNDP[23] and UNICEF[24]) and are quoted in the European Union's security strategy.[25] Many journalists, NGOs, academics and policymakers accept the 90% figure as an uncontested truth.

And yet it has no basis in fact.

The claim can be traced back to two sources. In 1991 Uppsala University published *Casualties of Conflict*,[26] which contained the claim that 'nine out of ten victims (dead and uprooted) are civilians'. On the back cover of the book, however, the parenthetical words were dropped, leaving only the statement that 'nine out of ten victims of war and armed conflict today are civilians'.

For Uppsala, the category of 'victim' included refugees as well as war dead. But some readers wrongly equated 'victim' with 'fatality'. What the Uppsala data suggested was far less dramatic: approximately 67% of those killed in conflicts during 1989 were civilians. Today the figure is likely much lower.

The other contemporary source of the myth—also from 1991—is Ruth Leger Sivard's *World Military and Social Expenditures*.[27] Sivard wrote that 'in 1990 [the proportion of civilian to combatant deaths] appears to have been close to 90%'. But Sivard's estimate included fatalities from war-related famines, which is not what most people have in mind when they talk about civilians being *killed* in war. Moreover, there are no global data on deaths caused by war-related famine and (more importantly) disease—so it is not clear what sources Sivard used to arrive at her conclusion.

What then can be said about civilian fatalities in war? Prior to 1989 information was so poor that it was virtually impossible to make even crude estimates of the global civilian death toll. Even today, our estimates of civilian deaths are based on information that is never complete and is rarely accurate. Data collected by the Uppsala Conflict Data Program suggest that between 30% and 60% of fatalities in 2002 were civilians.

It is precisely because it is so difficult to distinguish between combatant deaths and civilian deaths that Uppsala embraces both in its 'battle-related deaths' category.

Indeed, the only claim we can make with any confidence is that the oft-cited 90% civilian death rate for the 1990s is a myth.

when countries are ranked by their death *rates*. In 2002 the countries with the highest death *rates* were Liberia (21.2 deaths per 100,000 of the population), Israel and the Palestinian Territories (13.2), Burundi (12.0), Nepal (11.0) and Uganda (9.2).

And in 2003 the countries with the highest death rates were Liberia (59.4), Iraq (35.1), Burundi (16.2), Sudan (8.5) and Uganda (6.5).

For state-based conflict, the five countries with the most reported battle-related deaths in 2002 were (in order) Nepal, Sudan, India, Colombia and Uganda; in 2003 they were Iraq, Sudan, India, Liberia and the Philippines.

For non-state conflict, the five countries with the most reported battle-related deaths in 2002 were the DRC, India, Colombia, Somalia and Nigeria; and in 2003 they were the DRC, Somalia, Uganda, Sudan and Nigeria.

And for one-sided violence, the five countries showing most reported deaths in 2002 were Uganda, the DRC, India, Burundi, and Israel and the Palestinian Territories; in 2003 they were Uganda, India, Liberia, Sudan, and Israel and the Palestinian Territories.

The findings of the new dataset suggest that governments kill far fewer civilians than do rebel groups. In 2002, 23% of those who died in one-sided political violence were killed by governments, while 77% were killed by non-state groups. In 2003, 32% were killed by governments and 68% by non-state groups. These figures should be viewed with some caution, however, as they may reflect government control over local media as much as real differences in death rates.

Conclusion

The new Uppsala/Human Security Centre dataset has already generated a number of important and surprising findings, but its full potential will not be realised until annual data have been collected for some years and clear trends can be ascertained.[29] The *Human Security Report 2006* will publish the 2004 and 2005 data, enabling the presentation of four-year trends in all categories for the first time.

As the previous discussions have shown, we can be confident about the accuracy of data on the number of armed conflicts and cases of one-sided violence, but obtaining good data on the number of battle-related deaths and deaths from one-sided violence will always pose a much greater challenge.

Data collection on the human costs of war remains a complex and contested business.

Martin Adler / Panos Pictures

Measuring human rights abuse

Despite growing attention to human rights, no government, international organisation or NGO collects quantified global or regional data on human rights abuse. Determining whether such abuse is increasing or decreasing is extremely difficult.

There is more to security than counting conflict numbers, war deaths or terrorist attacks. Core human rights violations—such as torture; extrajudicial, arbitrary and summary executions; the 'disappearance' of dissidents; and the use of government-backed death squads—are also an integral part of the human security agenda. But mapping trends is problematic.

The UN's Commission on Human Rights is mandated to monitor and report on the human rights situation in member states, but it has signally failed to do so in any consistent and impartial manner.

Major human rights organisations provide detailed accounts of human rights abuses in individual countries, but they have long resisted any attempt to provide quantified measures of violations. They point to the inherent unreliability of much of the data and argue that brutalising 10 citizens is as unacceptable as brutalising a thousand. Any system of ranking that might imply that the former is more tolerable than the latter should be rejected, they argue.

But without quantitative annual audits, neither governments, international agencies, nor the human rights community can determine global or regional trends in core human rights abuse. And knowing whether abuse is increasing or decreasing is a necessary condition for evaluating the impact of human rights policies.

The Political Terror Scale

A little-known dataset developed at Purdue University some 20 years ago, and now maintained at the University of North Carolina, Asheville, by researchers Linda Cornett and Mark Gibney, goes a significant way toward addressing the measurement challenge.[30]

The Political Terror Scale (PTS) uses annual reports from Amnesty International and the US State Department to measure the human rights situation in individual countries.[31] The higher a country ranks on the five-level scale, the worse its human rights record.

- **Level 1.** Countries operate under a secure rule of law. People are not imprisoned for their views, and torture is rare or exceptional. Politically motivated murders are extremely rare.

- **Level 2.** There is a limited amount of imprisonment for non-violent political activity. Few persons are affected, and torture and beatings are exceptional. Politically motivated murder is rare.
- **Level 3.** Imprisonment for political activity is more extensive. Politically motivated executions or other political murders and brutality are common. Unlimited detention for political views, with or without a trial, is also commonplace.

In five regions the human rights situation has improved since 1984.

- **Level 4.** The practices of Level 3 affect a larger portion of the population. Murders, disappearances and torture are a common part of life. But in spite of the pervasiveness of terror, it directly affects only those who interest themselves in politics.
- **Level 5.** The terrors characteristic of Level 4 affect the whole population. The leaders of these societies place no limits on the means they use, or the thoroughness with which they pursue, personal or ideological goals.

This scale assumes a constant interval between each level—so a Level 4 score is taken as equivalent to two Level 2 scores. This assumption allows researchers to sum the scores for all the counties in a region. The total score is then divided by the number of countries to arrive at an average score for the region.

What do the PTS trend data reveal?

The PTS indicates that the level of human rights abuse in the developing world appears to have remained relatively constant for the 24 years that the researchers have been collating data. (There are not enough data on human rights abuses in the developed world to chart trend lines.) There is certainly nothing comparable to the dramatic rise and fall in armed conflicts for the same period, or to the long-term downward trend in battle-deaths.

In five out of the six regions in the developing world for which data have been collected the human rights situation has improved modestly since 1994.

There is good reason to believe that human rights abuses have been under-reported in the past and that this under-reporting is reflected in the PTS data. If this is indeed the case then the human rights situation in the developing world has likely improved over the last 20-plus years.

The data for the four regions in Figure 2.6 show a small net increase in human rights abuse over the whole 24-year period.[32] But in the Middle East and North Africa, sub-Saharan Africa, and South Asia, the data reveal a modest decline in abuse from the early to mid-1990s to 2003. In East/Southeast Asia and the South Pacific the human rights situation worsened from the mid-1990s.

In Eastern Europe and Central Asia, and in Latin America and the Caribbean, the trend data indicate a net improvement in the human rights situation over two decades (Figure 2.7).

How reliable are the PTS trend data?

The measurement methodology used in the Political Terror Scale confronts a number of challenges. First, the method

Figure 2.6 Political repression 1980–2003: A net increase in four regions

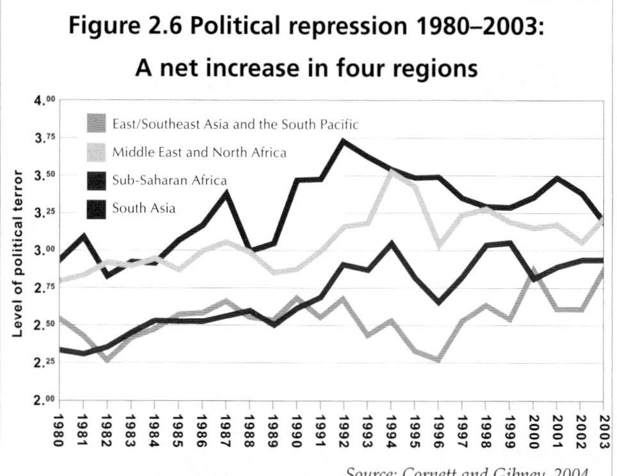

Source: Cornett and Gibney, 2004

In four developing country regions the data indicate that human rights abuse rose slightly over the 24-year period. But in three of the four regions, there has been a modest improvement in the past decade.

Figure 2.7 Political repression 1980–2003: A decrease in two regions

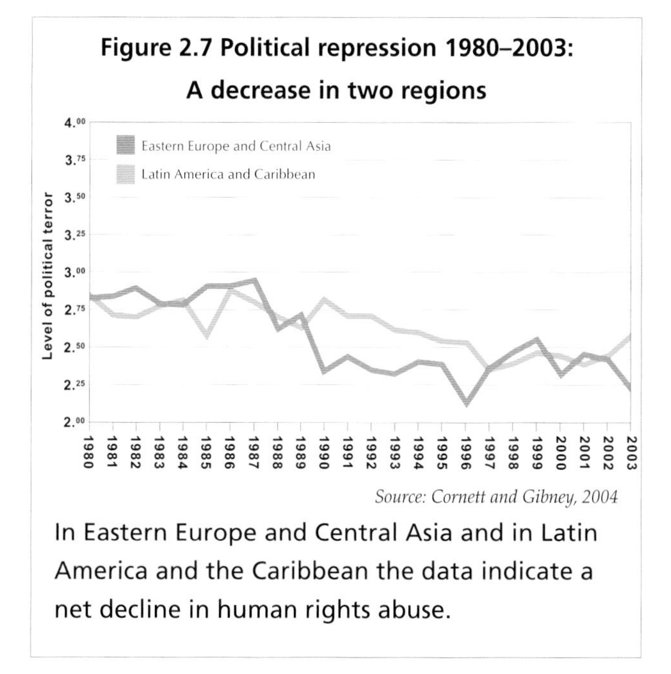

Source: Cornett and Gibney, 2004

In Eastern Europe and Central Asia and in Latin America and the Caribbean the data indicate a net decline in human rights abuse.

used to determine a country's annual PTS ranking on the five-point scale is inherently subjective, relying heavily on coders' judgments of the scope and intensity of human rights abuses.

Second, the Amnesty International and State Department reports are far more comprehensive today than they were two decades ago. Both organisations rely on media reports. One recent study found that the percentage of articles mentioning 'human rights' in the *Economist* and *Newsweek* more than doubled between 1980 and 2000.[33] This suggests that abuse levels were likely under-reported in the past.

Better reporting today means that fewer human rights abuses go unrecorded than in the past.[34] This in turn means that the human rights situation today is almost certainly better than the trend data suggest.

Third, the Political Terror Scale coding practices have likely undergone subtle changes over the years, according to Cornett and Gibney. For example, levels of abuse in Latin America that would be scored as Level 3 today may well have been counted as Level 2 in the early 1980s when gross human rights abuses were more common, and countries were generally held to lower standards. If such an unconscious coding shift has indeed occurred, this again suggests that abuse levels in the past were likely higher than the trend data indicate.

Fourth, the PTS fails to 'capture the all-pervasive *threat* of violence in a totalitarian state'.[35] When governments rule by fear, they may not need to resort to physical coercion.

Fifth, the dataset is not population-weighted: data from Nepal are given the same significance as data from China, which has over 50 times more people.

There may well have been more human rights abuse in the past than the trend data suggest.

Sixth, data for developing countries are not reproduced here because the Amnesty and State Department reports have not always covered them consistently or in depth.

Taken together, these data challenges suggest we should approach the PTS findings with some caution. But notwithstanding the qualifications, in the absence of any other data, the Political Terror Scale sheds much-needed light on a murky corner of human insecurity.

Martin Adler / Panos Pictures

Tracking criminal violence

Why include criminal violence in a global human security audit? Because violent crime kills far more people than war and terrorism combined. And while less than one-sixth of states are currently afflicted by armed conflict, all suffer from criminal violence.

Political violence and murder share obvious similarities: both involve intentional killing. They are also very different. While war is a quintessentially political activity, homicide is not. Armed conflicts engage large numbers of fighters and require considerable organisation. Most criminal violence, by contrast, involves individuals or small groups, and requires little complex organisation.

Some scholars argue that the traditional distinction between war and violent crime breaks down in many of today's civil wars. Ohio State University's John Mueller, for example, contends that many armed conflicts are now little more than collective criminal violence waged by gangs of thugs for private gain. Similarly, Paul Collier, former director of the World Bank's research department, has described rebellion as a 'quasi-criminal activity'.[36]

The traditional distinction between crime and war breaks down in other ways. In some cases, rebels resort to violent crime to generate funds for military ends. In others, governments label armed resistance directed against them as 'criminal violence' in order to delegitimise it.

A nexus of criminal and political violence

There is another reason to include criminal violence in a human security audit. Political violence and violent crime can be causally related.

One recent study found that homicide rates increase by an average of 25% for some five years following the end of civil wars.[37] This is not surprising. War erodes the legal and normative restraints on violence that prevail in times of peace. And wartime habits of violence can carry over into peacetime.

Civil wars are often followed by revenge killings, while demobilised soldiers frequently wind up unemployed, turning to violent crime in order to support themselves and their families.

Despite the obvious connections between criminal and political violence, both governments and researchers have traditionally dealt separately with violent crime and armed conflict.

In government, violent crime is the responsibility of justice departments, while war remains the province of foreign ministries and defence departments. Among researchers, criminologists deal with violent crime, while political scientists focus on war. These divisions of labour make sense much of the time, but not where political and criminal violence overlap so much that they become virtually indistinguishable.

The international community is now beginning to pay more attention to the links between political and criminal violence. This is particularly true in post-conflict reconstruction programs, and is evident in the strong emphasis being placed on reintegrating former fighters into society and on reforming the police, judiciary and security forces.

In addition, rising international concern about terrorism following September 11, 2001, has led to much greater cooperation between crime fighters and security services in counterterrorist operations around the world.[38]

The data challenge

It is far from easy to determine global trends in criminal violence.

First, definitions of violent crime vary. For example, deaths from terrorism, war and genocide are not usually defined as homicides. But in some countries, some of the time, they are. Definitions of sexual assault also vary considerably.

> The international community is now beginning to pay more attention to the links between political and criminal violence.

Second, bureaucracies in developing countries have fewer resources and less experience in collecting and collating data. They may be more susceptible to political interference. Sometimes there is no clear distinction between the military and the police, which increases the likelihood that deaths from terrorism or armed conflict will be recorded as criminal acts.

Third, international agencies use varying data collection methods, which can lead to widely divergent estimates. The World Health Organization, for example, estimated the homicide rate for Africa in 2000 at 22 per 100,000 people.[39] Interpol's estimate for the same year was less than one-third of WHO's: 6 per 100,000.[40]

Fourth, major problems arise from under-reporting and under-recording. Rape is universally under-reported and in some countries under-recorded.

Fifth, statistics are often simply unavailable—in most years fewer than 50% of governments provide homicide and rape data to Interpol.

Finally, the countries that fail to provide data are disproportionately poor, which means they are much more likely to have been involved in civil wars. Both poverty and a recent history of warfare are associated with higher than average homicide rates.[41] It is likely, therefore, that global and regional violent crime rates significantly understate the real level of violence.

All of these factors, taken together, hinder the effective collection and analysis of regional crime data.[42] And this in turn makes attempts to track trends in violent crime inherently problematic.

The global homicide rate

The following discussion draws on an analysis of global crime trends produced for the Human Security Centre by Graeme Newman, editor of the UN publication *Global Report on Crime and Justice*.[43] It focuses on two major threats to human security—homicide and rape.

Figure 2.8 shows the reported global homicide rates from 1959 to 2001. The trend line is relatively stable, but with two significant peaks. It is likely, however, that the two peaks reflect either misreporting, or political violence in certain countries being counted as homicides.

The 1975 to 1976 peak appears to be the result of a huge and inexplicable increase in the number of reported homicides in Nigeria (from about 1500 in 1974 to more than 42,000 in 1975) and in Peru (from just over 400 to nearly 6000 between 1975 and 1976). In neither of these countries were there then reports of major

Figure 2.8 World homicide rates, 1959–2001

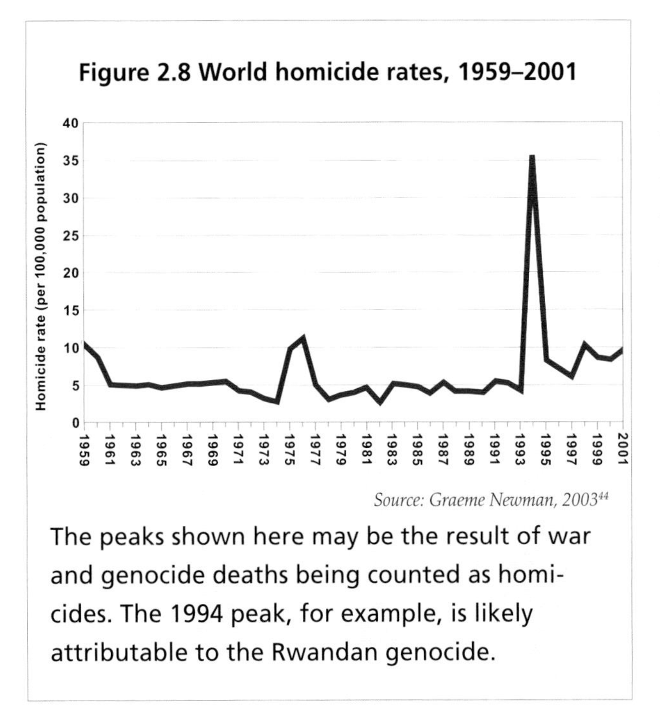

Source: Graeme Newman, 2003[44]

The peaks shown here may be the result of war and genocide deaths being counted as homicides. The 1994 peak, for example, is likely attributable to the Rwandan genocide.

armed conflict or genocide. Since real homicide rates would not increase so steeply in such a short period of time, this increase has no obvious explanation—other than misreporting.

And the 1994 peak likely reflects the decision by the Rwandan government to categorise as homicides the estimated 800,000 deaths from the genocide.

If these anomalous spikes are ignored, then the global homicide rate appears to have been relatively stable for some 40 years. Certainly, there have been no changes remotely comparable to the dramatic increases and decreases in battle-deaths during the same period.

Homicide, North and South

Comparing the reported homicide rates for developing and industrialised countries further illustrates the difficulty of analysing the data (Figure 2.9).

The volatility shown in the trend line for developing countries reflects the fact that some of these countries experienced civil war and genocide, and that deaths from these causes were being reported as homicides. In Figure 2.9, the peaks caused by the Rwandan genocide and the increased 'homicide' counts in Nigeria and Peru become even more obvious.

The sharp upsurge in 2001 is mostly due to a sevenfold increase in the Africa-wide homicide rate from 2000 to 2001. Since 'normal' homicide rates never increase so steeply in so short a period, this spike can almost certainly be attributed to recording war deaths as homicides—or to misreporting.

Figure 2.9 Homicide rates in industrialised and developing countries, 1959–2001

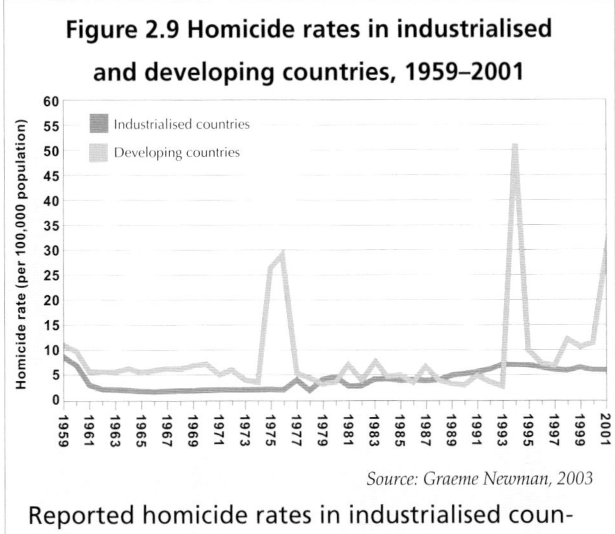

Source: Graeme Newman, 2003

Reported homicide rates in industrialised countries are stable compared with those in the developing world.

A world view of rape

Tracking global rape trends (Figure 2.10) became possible only after 1976, when Interpol began analysing the statistics for rape and other sexual offences separately. Although more common than homicide, rape remains chronically under-reported. In 1996 the United Nation's Office on Drugs and Crime (UNODC) conducted a crime victim survey in 10 industrialised countries and found that, on average, only one in five cases of sexual violence was ever reported to authorities.[45]

The reasons for under-reporting vary considerably. Chief among them is the desire of many rape victims to avoid the social stigma associated with sexual assault, and the personal trauma of recounting the ordeal and participating in the police investigation and in any subsequent trial. Many victims also fear, often with good reason, that their accusations will not be taken seriously.

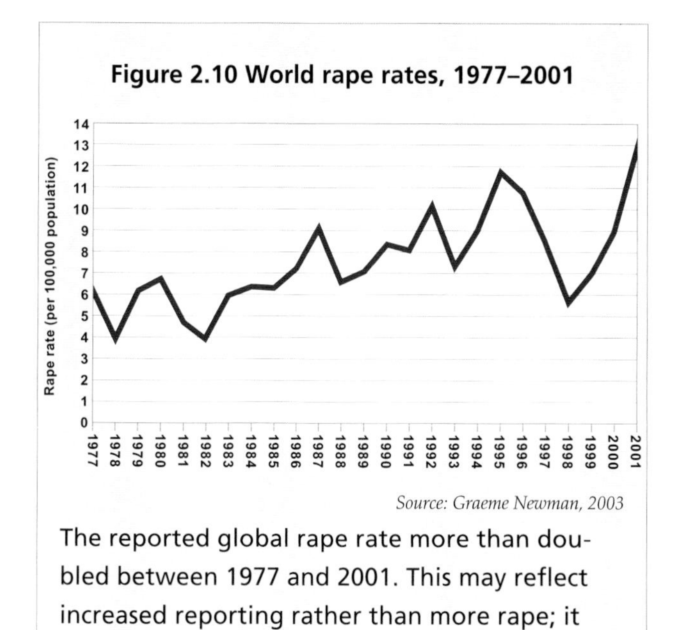

Figure 2.10 World rape rates, 1977–2001

Source: Graeme Newman, 2003

The reported global rape rate more than doubled between 1977 and 2001. This may reflect increased reporting rather than more rape; it could reflect both.

As with homicide statistics, fewer than 50% of countries around the world publish rape statistics in any given year. However, as the UN's *Global Report on Crime and Justice* has pointed out, the number of countries (not individuals) reporting sexual violence increased in the 1990s, reflecting the growing seriousness with which rape is being viewed internationally.[46]

Establishing statistical trend data on sexual offences is further complicated by different definitions of rape. Marital rape, for example, is counted as a crime in some countries but not in others.

Part of the reason for the volatility in the reported world rape rate is that the incidence of rape—like that of homicide—can increase dramatically during civil strife or genocide. For example, the spikes in the global rape rate between 1992 and 1997 correspond to periods of political violence in Rwanda and the former Yugoslavia, where extremely high levels of rape were reported.

But this explanation does not account for other peaks and troughs: the doubling between 1998 and 2001, for example. Much of this volatility may be due to inaccurate reporting and recording.

The regional rape statistics offer some insight into the problems of getting accurate data. For example, the so-called New World countries of the United States, Canada, Australia and New Zealand had the highest reported incidence of rape in the world for most of the period under review (1977 to 2001)—well over 10 times that of Asia.

Is this because rape really is more prevalent in these countries? Or do the relatively low reported rape rates in Africa (prior to 1993), Central and Eastern Europe, and Asia reflect serious under-reporting of sexual violence?

The latter is certainly part of the answer. In many countries in these regions, victims of sexual violence have little legal recourse and may become the victims of reprisals if they report the rape to authorities.

Under-reporting and under-recording are also greater where the police and the judiciary fail to take sexual violence seriously, or fail to act on, or even to record, complaints from victims. In many industrialised countries, public information campaigns have increased the sensitivity of policing bureaucracies to the problem of rape, and have led to an increase in reporting.

Much of the volatility in the reported rape rate may be due to inaccurate reporting and recording.

But none of this can explain why reported rape rates are *several times* higher in the New World states than in Western Europe. We do know from UNODC's 1996 crime victim survey that the difference between Western Europe and North America is not a result of differences in *reporting* rates—these are not great enough to explain the large differences in the *recorded* rape rates between Europe and North America.[47] If the disparities between Europe and the New World countries are not a function of differences in the rate of reporting, how can they be explained?

Part of the answer may be that some states in Australia and some provinces in Canada still subsume the crime of rape into the broader category of 'sexual assault', which also includes lesser offences that occur more frequently.

CHILDREN, DRUGS AND VIOLENCE IN RIO

Violence and illegal narcotics often go hand in hand. Nowhere is this more so than in Rio de Janeiro, where criminal drug gangs use armed children to help run the trade. Thousands of children have been killed in violent shoot-outs with the police or rival cartels.

An estimated 5000 to 6000 youths and adolescents were involved in Rio de Janeiro's drug trade in 2003.[48] Employed and armed by the main drug factions, they take part in violent confrontations with rival groups and with security forces, in much the same way that child soldiers fight in rebel armies.

The drug gangs seek to control the Rio slums through territorial and paramilitary domination.[49] There are frequent armed disputes over territory, often leading to violent showdowns with police.

Rio's annual criminal death toll is so high that it sometimes exceeds the death toll in Colombia, where a violent civil war has been waged for decades. There were an estimated 60,000 conflict-related deaths in Colombia from the 1980s to 2003.[50] During the same period, Rio de Janeiro reported 49,913 firearms fatalities, 70% of them attributed to drug-related violence.[51]

From December 1987 to November 2001, 467 Israeli and Palestinian youth were killed in Israel and the occupied territories.[52] During the same period, 3937 under-18-year-olds were killed by gunfire in the municipality of Rio de Janeiro alone.[53]

The similarities between children recruited into the drug trade and into rebel armies are striking. Although joining a drug ring in Rio is by and large voluntary, many poor children have few other options and may get involved when they are as young as eight years old. The majority are 15 to 17 years old, as is true in many documented cases of child soldiers.[54]

Like child soldiers, youth working for Rio's drug cartels also function within a hierarchical structure maintained through orders and punishment, including summary executions. Drug lords provide the youth with arms, including assault rifles, machine guns and grenades, and the youth openly display these in the communities they patrol.

Children involved in the drug trade are sometimes targeted by police for summary execution. In 2001 officers killed a total of 52 under-18-year-olds during police operations.[55]

Military solutions to Rio de Janeiro's drug trafficking disputes are unlikely to work. Wars end but the drug trade doesn't—and this is where the parallel to the plight of child soldiers breaks down. Criminal gangs will continue to compete for control of the drug trade as long as the drugs remain illegal and people continue to buy them. While demobilisation programs make sense for child soldiers once peace agreements are signed, peace agreements have no counterpart in the constant violent struggle to control the drug trade. And to categorise children working in drug gangs as soldiers may serve only to legitimise the already high levels of lethal state force used against them.

Efforts to ease the plight of children affected by, and involved in, organised armed violence is not, of course, restricted to Rio. Viva Rio, a Brazilian NGO working to reduce violence against children, is collaborating with the International Action Network on Small Arms to coordinate research in other countries where children are involved in gang violence.

Additionally, the Children and Youth in Organized Armed Violence (COAV) program is working with local partners in Colombia, Ecuador, El Salvador, Haiti, Honduras, Jamaica, Nigeria, Northern Ireland, the Philippines, South Africa and the United States. Its focus is on children and youth employed or otherwise participating in organised armed criminal violence where there are elements of a command structure and power over territory, local population or resources. This definition helps distinguish COAV's work from that of researchers dealing with child soldiers or violent youth crime perpetrated by individuals. Violent youth groups encompassed by this mandate range from 'institutionalised' street gangs in El Salvador, Honduras and the United States, to politically motivated armed groups known as 'popular organisations' in Haiti, to vigilante groups and ethnic militia in Nigeria. Through comparative analysis, COAV is seeking to understand the causes of youth-organised armed violence and to identify creative solutions and best-practice policy responses.[56]

Andrew Testa / Panos Pictures

We can reliably document trends in political violence but not for violent crime—global statistics on murder and rape are simply too problematic.

This explanation cannot, however, account for the extraordinary volatility in reported rape rates in the New World nations, where the average reported rape rate for the four countries more than halved, and then more than doubled, *twice,* between 1977 and 1983. Indeed, there is no obvious explanation for these changes—it is impossible to believe that *real* rape rates could change so dramatically and quickly.

No firm conclusions

Global *political* violence data for the post–World War II era show unmistakable and highly significant trends. There are no comparably clear trends in global *criminal* violence, at least not for homicide and rape.

The most serious problem with the homicide statistics is the lack of data for many countries and the erratic reporting in many others. With respect to sexual violence, determining whether the apparent increase in the world rape rate is due to better reporting and recording, or is due to a real increase in the incidence of rape, or to both, is simply impossible.

As long as these problems continue to compromise the collection and collation of violent crime statistics, it will be impossible to track trends in global or regional homicide and rape rates with any real degree of confidence.

Mikkel Ostergaard / Panos Pictures

Human trafficking

The trafficking of human beings has burgeoned into a multi-billion-dollar industry that is so widespread and damaging to its victims that it has become a cause of human insecurity.

Associated with the worldwide liberalisation of transport, markets and labour, the breakup of the Soviet Union, and a doubling in world migration over the past 40 years, human trafficking has become a major source of revenue for organised crime.

According to the US State Department, 'Human trafficking is the third largest criminal enterprise worldwide, generating an estimated $9.5 billion in annual revenue.'[57]

The State Department's estimate is just for the revenue generated by trafficking itself. The illicit profits for the traffickers generated by the victims *after* they arrive in the country of destination are many times higher. A recent report by the International Labour Organization (ILO) estimated these to be some US$32 billion a year.[58]

The US State Department claims that 'at least' 600,000 to 800,000 individuals are trafficked across national frontiers each year. Of these, it is believed that approximately 80% are women and girls and up to 50% are minors.[59] If those who are trafficked *within* borders are included, the total number of victims could be as high as 4 million.

But the illegal nature of the trade, the low priority given to data collection and research, and the frequent reluctance of victims to report crimes, or to testify for fear of reprisals, combine to make gauging the numbers trafficked each year extremely difficult.

According to an analyst from the UN's Global Programme against Trafficking in Human Beings, 'Even though some high-quality research exists most of the data are based on "guesstimates", which, in many cases, are used for advocacy or fund-raising purposes'.[60]

According to the US State Department, 'human trafficking is the third largest criminal enterprise worldwide'.

Recent research by the International Organization for Migration's (IOM) Counter-Trafficking Service shows that between 2001 and 2003 the number of victims of international trafficking referred to the IOM decreased in Kosovo by 67%, in Macedonia by 46% and in Moldova by 35%. In Albania the decline was 90% between 2000 and 2003. Numbers of victims receiving 'assistance' from the IOM in Bosnia and Herzegovina declined by 75% between 2001 and 2003.[61]

These findings do not necessarily mean that trafficking has declined—there are other possible explanations—but at the very least they raise questions about the conventional wisdom that it is steadily increasing.

What is human trafficking?

These findings do not necessarily mean that trafficking has declined—there are other possible explanations. But at the very least these data raise questions about the claim that the trade in human beings is steadily increasing.

In November 2000, the UN General Assembly adopted a new protocol that defines trafficking (including trafficking within countries) as:

> The recruitment, transportation, transfer, harbouring or receipt of persons, by means of the threat or use of force or other forms of coercion, of abduction, of fraud, of deception, of the abuse of power or of a position of vulnerability or of the giving or receiving of payments or benefits to achieve the consent of a person having control over another person, for the purpose of exploitation. Exploitation shall include, at a minimum, the exploitation of the prostitution of others or other forms of sexual exploitation, forced labour or services, slavery or practices similar to slavery, servitude or the removal of organs.[62]

Cross-border trafficking should not be confused with people-smuggling. Traffickers seek to exploit their victims for long-term profit. People-smuggling ends once human cargoes are delivered across borders.[63]

However, as the ILO has noted, in practice 'it is often difficult to distinguish ... between workers who have entered forced labour as a result of trafficking and those who have been smuggled.'[64]

Trafficking takes place in three stages: recruitment, transportation and exploitation.

Recruitment

Cross-border traffickers frequently use false promises of well-paid overseas employment to recruit their victims. Positions are advertised in legitimate employment agencies, in mainstream magazines, in newspapers or on the Internet.

Women are the major victims of trafficking, and most are trafficked into some form of prostitution. Some are aware that they will be employed as sex workers, but few understand the degree to which they may be indebted, intimidated, exploited and controlled.[65]

> These findings raise questions about the conventional wisdom that trafficking is steadily increasing.

An IOM study reported that among trafficked females who had been interviewed by researchers, 10% had been kidnapped.[66] Another study estimated that 35% of minors trafficked from Albania were abductees.[67] Abductors are often acquaintances, relatives or friends of the family. In some cases, children are simply sold by their parents or guardians.[68]

Transportation

The second stage in cross-border trafficking is transportation to the target country—which is usually, but not always, the promised destination. Here, traffickers often use people-smuggling networks, relying on corrupt police and bribed border guards and customs officials to help move their human cargoes expeditiously across frontiers.

But increasingly, trafficked persons travel openly, on legal or forged travel documents, which are often obtained with help from their traffickers.[69]

Exploitation

The final stage in the trafficking chain is 'employment' in a wide variety of businesses that seek cheap, compliant workers, and whose operators ask few questions about the origin of their employees.

A study by the United Nation's Office on Drugs and Crime (UNODC) found that 85% of women, 70% of children and 16% of trafficked men are used for sexual exploitation.[70] The ILO, on the other hand, estimates that only 43% of victims are trafficked into commercial sexual exploitation.[71] The fact that two separate UN organisations come out with such different figures serves again to remind how uncertain all estimates in this area are.

Male victims tend to be exploited as forced labour, drug vendors and beggars—even as combatants in armed conflicts.

Controlling victims

To realise their profits, traffickers must ensure that their 'investments' are safeguarded, making the control of victims a top priority.

Debt bondage is one of the commonest methods. Victims are often grossly overcharged for transportation, and when the costs of accommodation, food and clothing are added to this debt and exorbitant interest rates are charged, escape from indebtedness can become virtually impossible.

> Wartorn countries may be used as transit routes. Mass displacement and loss of livelihoods create a huge potential supply of victims.

Violent coercion—rape, beatings and threats to family and loved ones—is also often used to intimidate the victims. One study of trafficked women assisted by the IOM found that some 55% had been beaten and sexually abused.[72]

To discourage escape, traffickers may withhold their victims' identification and travel documents, reducing the prospect of successful escape and return home. Victims without legal residency rights in their destination country are reluctant to appeal to the authorities for help, in case doing so puts them at risk of prosecution, deportation, or both.

Human trafficking and conflict

Armed conflicts create new opportunities for traffickers. Wartorn countries may be used as transit routes, while mass displacement and loss of livelihoods create a huge potential supply of victims.[73] Women and girls are frequently trafficked within and across borders to provide sexual services to combatants and to work as cooks, cleaners and porters. The longer a war persists, the more extensive the displacement, and the more prolonged and widespread the suffering and poverty, the greater the opportunities for traffickers.

A 2002 report from the US State Department described abuse by government-backed militias in the long-running civil war in impoverished southern Sudan. This included 'capture through abduction (generally accompanied by violence); the forced transfer of victims to another community; subjection to forced labor for no pay [and] denial of victims' freedom of movement and choice'.[74]

The aftermath of war also provides opportunities for traffickers. In Bosnia and Herzegovina, Sierra Leone and other societies struggling with post-war reconstruction, peacekeepers and humanitarian and aid workers generate a strong demand for sex workers, one that traffickers have been quick to meet. Involvement of UN peacekeepers in trafficking has become a major source of concern for the UN's Department of Peacekeeping Operations.

Human trafficking and poverty

The victims of trafficking mostly originate in countries plagued by weak or corrupt governments, economic decline, poverty, social upheaval, organised crime and violent conflict. In failing states and some former communist countries, weak law enforcement has permitted the organised crime networks involved in trafficking to flourish largely unchallenged.

Poverty appears to be the single most significant driver of human trafficking. In a 2001 report on nine coun-

Teun Voeten / Panos Pictures

Kosovo: women forced into prostitutions have often been trafficked from the former Soviet Union.

tries in West and Central Africa, the ILO's International Programme on the Elimination of Child Labour found that 'countries that have widespread poverty, low education levels and high fertility rates tend to be those from which children are trafficked.'[75]

In Eastern Europe and the former Soviet Union, high unemployment, low wages and the disappearance of social safety nets following the collapse of communism have made the blandishments of traffickers more attractive to potential victims, while governments have done little to try to control the trade. Trafficking of women and girls is also driven in part by sexual and ethnic discrimination.

Responsibility for trafficking does not rest solely with the traffickers. Without the strong demand for trafficked labour from brothel owners, sweatshop operators and others, there would be no trade in human beings. And without demand from consumers for cheap sex and the goods made by ultra-cheap labour, there would be no brothels or sweatshops.

Responsibility is also shared by governments in recipient countries, which have done little to combat the trade.

Combatting trafficking

Over the last few years, in part as a result of increased media attention, there have been signs that the problem is being taken more seriously. In Europe, for example, there has been a concerted effort to create and harmonise legislation aimed at bringing down the criminal organisations that run the big trafficking networks.

Recognition of the need to combat trafficking is growing in the rest of the world as well. By August 2005, 117 countries had signed, and 87 countries had become parties to, the new UN trafficking protocol, which entered into force in December 2003.[76]

This new protocol makes a strong call for the protection of victims. But Europol, in its 2003 report, *Crime Assessment: Trafficking of Human Beings into the European Union,* notes that, notwithstanding this commitment, it is still the victims of trafficking that too often bear the brunt of legal censure, while their exploiters walk free. 'Women soliciting in public are criminalised, initially for offences related to the selling of sexual services and subsequently for offences arising from their illegal entry to and residence in the country and lack of valid documentation.'[77]

The case for a more victim-sensitive approach to combatting trafficking is pragmatic as well as moral. Prosecuting traffickers—and dismantling the networks that support them—is far more likely to succeed with the cooperation of victims. No one is better positioned than the victims to identify—and testify against—the exploiters.

Ahikam Seri / Panos Pictures

Creating a human security index?

It is not possible at present—and may not even be desirable—to produce a reliable human security index. But it is possible to determine which countries are most threatened by political violence, human rights abuse and instability.

Every year the much-cited *Human Development Report* produced by the United Nations Development Programme (UNDP) ranks countries around the world according to their citizens' quality of life. It draws on data about life expectancy, educational achievement and income to create a single composite measure that it calls the Human Development Index (HDI).

UNDP's annual ranking exercise generates intense interest, a great deal of media coverage—and considerable controversy. In 2004 Norway, Sweden and Australia ranked on top of the index, while Sierra Leone, Niger and Burkina Faso took the bottom places.

Composite indices like the HDI can serve a number of purposes. They can:

- Encapsulate in a single measure a range of complex data.
- Facilitate comparisons between countries over time.
- Stimulate public discussion.
- Be used to bring pressure to bear on governments.[78]

In recent years there has been considerable debate about creating a human security index, and two such indices have already been developed. Both focus primarily on development issues; neither includes any measure of violence; neither is regularly updated.[79]

There are a number of possible measures of human insecurity that might be combined to make a composite index, including battle-related death rates, 'indirect' death rates, and homicide and rape rates.

In recent years there has been considerable debate about creating a human security index.

Is it possible to combine indicators of this kind into a single composite human security index?

The short answer is that it is certainly not currently possible, and that it is probably not desirable.

There are a number of practical challenges. The most serious is that the existing datasets used to measure human insecurity are not comprehensive enough—

and many are not updated annually. Data on homicide and rape are missing for most of the least secure countries in the world and there are no global data on indirect deaths—those deaths caused by disease and the lack of food, clean water and health care that result from war.

Moreover, even if it were possible to create a single composite human security index, it is not clear that doing so would be desirable. While composite indices have distinct advantages, simplicity also has a downside. Composite indices can conceal more information than they convey. Presenting the data from individual human security datasets separately, rather than aggregating them into a single index, conveys more information—and conveys it more clearly.

Aggregating very different measures—death rates and rankings of human rights violations, for example—also raises difficult questions about how to weight the different measures when combining them.

And while providing useful insights into the least secure countries, such measures are not very useful for determining the most secure countries, the majority of which are found in the developed world.

Here the difficulty is that there is not much insecurity to measure. By definition, highly secure countries rarely experience warfare, so very few suffer battle-related deaths. And human rights measures for some of the most secure countries are also missing from the Political Terror Scale dataset. The World Bank instability indicator does include the more secure industrialised countries, but it is too narrow to serve as a useful measure on its own. Differentiating among countries that are not afflicted by war, are highly stable politically and have very low levels of political repression is extraordinarily difficult.

Nevertheless these two datasets, along with the Uppsala/Human Security Centre dataset, measure important dimensions of human insecurity. The statistics they provide form the basis of Figure 2.11, and give three parallel measures of the world's least secure countries:

- *The Uppsala/Human Security Centre dataset.* The figures shown are the 'best estimates' of death rates from political violence in 2003. They include both battle-related deaths and deaths from one-sided violence.
- *The Political Terror Scale* from the University of North Carolina, Asheville, which measures core human rights abuse. Countries are scored on a scale from 5 (worst) to 1 (best), based on human rights violations in 2003.[80]
- The World Bank's composite *Political Instability and Absence of Violence Index*,[81] a measure that gauges the probability that a government 'will be destabilised or overthrown by possibly unconstitutional and/or violent means, including domestic violence and terrorism.'[82] Countries are ranked on a scale from 0 (worst) to 100 (best).

Are these the world's least secure countries?

Figure 2.11 reveals a remarkable overlap between these three measures of human insecurity. Countries plagued by high levels of political violence and human rights abuse tend also to be politically unstable, and vice versa.

But the absence of any measure of criminal violence is a major concern. A number of countries that experience neither wars nor political instability nevertheless have very high levels of criminal violence.

The Ipsos-Reid survey finding that many people fear criminal violence more than they fear political violence (see Part I) gives further weight to the argument that criminal violence data should be included in any composite index of human security.

An even bigger omission is the absence of any data on indirect deaths. As we show in Part IV of this report, war-related disease and malnutrition kill far more people than combat does.

Figure 2.11 The world's least secure countries?

Fatalities from political violence		Core human rights abuses				Political instability/violence	
	Rate per 100,000 (2003)		Amnesty International (2003)	State Dept. (2003)	Average ranking (2003)		World Bank (2002)
Liberia	59.4	Colombia	5	5	5	DRC	0.0
Iraq	35.1	DRC	5	5	5	Liberia	0.5
Burundi	16.2	Iraq	5	5	5	Afghanistan	1.1
Sudan	8.5	Sudan	5	5	5	Burundi	1.6
Uganda	6.5	Algeria	5	4	4.5	Côte d'Ivoire	2.2
Israel/Palestinian Terr.	5.8	Indonesia	5	4	4.5	Sudan	2.7
Nepal	4.4	Israel	5	4	4.5	Somalia	3.2
DRC	4.2	Liberia	5	4	4.5	Colombia	3.8
Somalia	3.9	Afghanistan	4	4	4	Palestinian Terr.	4.3
Colombia	1.6	Angola	4	4	4	Iraq	4.9
Philippines	1.4	Brazil	4	4	4	CAR	5.4
Eritrea	1.3	Myanmar (Burma)	4	4	4	Georgia	5.9
Afghanistan	1.1	Burundi	4	4	4	Nepal	6.5
Côte d'Ivoire	0.7	Cameroon	4	4	4	Congo-Brazzaville	7.0
Algeria	0.7	CAR	4	4	4	Algeria	7.6
Senegal	0.4	China	4	4	4	Zimbabwe	7.6
Russia	0.4	Congo-Brazzaville	4	4	4	Nigeria	8.6
Ethiopia	0.3	Côte d'Ivoire	4	4	4	Angola	9.2
Indonesia	0.2	Ethiopia	4	4	4	Chad	9.2
Ecuador	0.2	India	4	4	4	Uganda	10.3
India	0.2	Nepal	4	4	4	Israel	10.8
Saudi Arabia	0.2	North Korea	4	4	4	Indonesia	11.4
Turkey	0.2	Pakistan	4	4	4	Rwanda	11.9
Nigeria	0.2	Palestinian Terr.	4	4	4	Guinea	12.4
Morocco	0.2	Philippines	4	4	4	Pakistan	13.0
Pakistan	0.1	Russia	4	4	4	Yemen	13.0
Sri Lanka	0.1	Somalia	4	4	4	Sierra Leone	14.1
Thailand	0.1	Uganda	4	4	4	Haiti	14.6
Myanmar (Burma)	0.1	Zimbabwe	4	4	4	Myanmar (Burma)	15.1

Source: Human Security Centre, 2005

Three different measures of human insecurity give three separate 'least secure' rankings. There is a high degree of overlap between the rankings.[83]

PART II

ENDNOTES

1. UNESCO Bangkok, 'Trafficking Statistics Project', UNESCO Bangkok website, www.unescobkk.org/index.php?id=1022 (accessed 1 August 2005).
2. 'UNICEF Official Cites "Largest Slave Trade In History"', *UN Wire* 20 February 2003, http://www.unwire.org/UNWire /20030220/32139_story.asp (accessed 1 August 2005).
3. In 2002 the US and its allies were fighting al-Qaeda, which is not a state.
4. For Uppsala's analysis of the 2002 and 2003 political violence data, see the *Human Security Report* website at www.human securityreport.info.
5. For more detailed information on definitions, see the *Human Security Report* website at www.humansecurityreport.info. See also the Uppsala Conflict Data Program's database at www.pcr.uu.se/database/.
6. These data are current as of September 2005 but may be subject to slight revision as new information becomes available. Note that coding decisions mean that there are sometimes slight differences in the information contained in Figures 2.1–2.5. For example, Uppsala argues that since the ultimate goal of al-Qaeda is the overthrow of the US, the conflict should be coded as a conflict over control of the government of the US. The conflict is consequently counted in the Americas conflict total in Figures 2.1 and 2.2. In Figure 2.3, which lists the numbers of cases of armed conflict and one-sided violence by location, the USA vs. al-Qaeda conflict is counted in Afghanistan's conflict total because that is where the fighting occurred. In Figures 2.4 and 2.5, battle-related deaths and deaths from one-sided violence are counted in the country where they occur.
7. Due to coding rules, the total number of conflicts in each region in Figure 2.3 may not exactly match the total number of conflicts in each region in Figure 2.1. The interstate conflict between India and Pakistan in 2002 and 2003 is counted once in the Asia total in Figure 2.1. However, it is counted twice in Figure 2.3 (which lists the number of cases of armed conflict and one-sided violence by country): once in India's total and once in Pakistan's total (fighting occurred in both countries). Similarly, the US vs. al-Qaeda conflict is included in Afghanistan's total (and Asia's) in Figure 2.3, whereas in Figure 2.1 it is included in the Americas regional total.
8. Ted Robert Gurr, 'Containing Internal War in the Twenty-First Century', in Fen Osler Hampson and David M. Malone, eds., *From Reaction to Conflict Prevention: Opportunities for the UN System* (Boulder: Lynne Rienner, 2002).The author notes that the sample was not comprehensive since it only examined intercommunal conflicts among groups that were also involved with conflicts with a government.
9. Professor Marshall was previously at the Center for International Development and Conflict Management at the University of Maryland.
10. Monty G. Marshall, 'Global Conflict Trends', Figure 3, Center of Systemic Peace website, 1 February 2005, http://mem bers.aol.com/CSPmgm/conflict.htm (accessed 19 June 2005). For a comparison with trend data on the number of states with armed conflicts that is derived from Uppsala's state-based data, see Monty G. Marshall, 'Measuring the Societal Impact of War', in Fen Osler Hampson and David M. Malone, eds., *From Reaction to Conflict Prevention: Opportunities for the UN System.*
11. Although this information is not published in this report, it is available on the *Human Security Report* website at www .humansecurityreport.info.
12. Small Arms Survey, *Small Arms Survey 2005,* (London: Oxford University Press, 2005).
13. For information on the Correlates of War dataset, see www.correlatesofwar.org/. For information on the International Institute of Strategic Studies' Armed Conflict Database, see http://acd.iiss.org/armedconflict/MainPages/dsp_WorldMap.asp.
14. For information on the Factiva database operated by Dow Jones and Reuters, see www.factiva.com. The database draws on some 9000 media sources around the world, including local, national and international newspapers, leading business magazines, trade publications and newswires. Uppsala also draws on other sources of data, including primary source material.

15. For an account of the methodology used in these studies, see the American Association for the Advancement of Science website at http://shr.aaas.org/hrdag/.
16. Note that some commissions are truth commissions while others are truth *and* reconciliation commissions.
17. Small Arms Survey, *Small Arms Survey 2005.*
18. The treatment of Uppsala's data by the *Small Arms Survey* (SAS) is problematic for a number of reasons. Before 2002 Uppsala did not collect death toll data on non-state conflicts or on one-sided violence, so large numbers of deaths from political violence were not being counted. But deaths in these categories *were* being measured in the epidemiological surveys and the in-depth historical investigations referenced in the SAS. By the time of the Iraq war, Uppsala *was* collecting data on death tolls from non-state conflicts and one-sided violence, but here the SAS's comparison is problematic for a different reason. The SAS's analysis compares Uppsala's 'best estimate' of reported and codable battle-related deaths in Iraq in 2003 with those of a much-cited epidemiological survey published in the British medical journal the *Lancet* (L. Roberts, R. Lafta, R. Garfield et al., 'Mortality Before and After the 2003 Invasion of Iraq: Cluster Sample Survey', *Lancet* 364 (20 October 2004): 1857–1864). Uppsala's estimate of deaths is 8494, while the *Lancet* estimate for the year is 22,980—a figure more than twice as large. The *Lancet* survey estimate is for all deaths from political violence from the date the war started to the end of 2003. But Uppsala's dataset compilers were unable to code any of the killings during the post-war insurgency, primarily because the perpetrators could not be identified, so the only battle-related deaths Uppsala codes for 2003 are for the short period in March and April when the conventional war was being waged. In the Iraq case, when 'like' really is being compared with 'like'—when war-related deaths from violence are compared over the same period of time—there is no appreciable difference between Uppsala's death count and that of the *Lancet* survey. This single example doesn't refute the claim that in general the Uppsala's data collection approach under-counts battle-related deaths—as noted previously the very nature of Uppsala's methodology makes this inevitable. The SAS's evaluation of the Uppsala data suggests that more case studies—and more detailed analysis—are necessary to get a better estimate of the degree to which under-counting is taking place in the report-based methodologies.
19. Note that the Middle East figures should be considerably higher, since Uppsala was unable to code the fatalities in Iraq during the post-war insurgency.
20. The Uppsala/Human Security Centre dataset records 'best', 'low' and 'high' estimates for each category of political violence each year. The 'best estimate' is the figure that Uppsala regards as being most credible, based on the most authoritative available information. In Figures 2.4 and 2.5 only the 'best estimates' are published, but the 'high' and 'low' figures are available on the *Human Security Report* website at www.humansecurityreport.info.
21. Note that the numbers recorded in this figure and the following figure do not represent the total number of deaths from political violence but rather the number of *reported* and *codable* deaths. These totals are almost certainly lower than the true death toll.
22. Note that the death toll for Iraq is only for the period of the conventional war (20 March 2003 to 9 April 2003), not the subsequent insurgency.
23. United Nations Development Programme, *Human Development Report 1998: Consumption for Human Development* (New York: United Nations Development Programme, 1998).
24. Graça Machel, *Impact of Armed Conflict on Children* (New York: United Nations and United Nations Children's Fund, 1996), http://www.unicef.org/graca/graright.htm (accessed 10 August 2005).
25. European Union Institute for Security Studies, *A Secure Europe in a Better World* (Paris: European Union Institute for Security Studies, 2003), http://www.iss-eu.org/solana/solanae.pdf (accessed 10 August 2005).
26. Christa Ahlström and Kjell-Åke Nordquist, *Casualties of Conflict—Report for the World Campaign for the Protection of Victims of War* (Uppsala: Uppsala University, Department of Peace and Conflict Research, 1991).
27. Ruth Leger Sivard, *World Military and Social Expenditures,* 14th ed. (Washington, DC: World Priorities, 1991).

28. See endnote 22.
29. Uppsala has collected data on one-sided violence back to the mid-1990s, which will be used to graph trends in the 2006 *Human Security Report*. Subject to funding, the same backdating exercise will be undertaken for non-state conflicts.
30. See the background document commissioned by the Human Security Centre, Linda Cornett and Mark Gibney, 'Tracking Terror: The Political Terror Scale 1980–2001', at the *Human Security Report* website, www.humansecurityreport.info.
31. The Political Terror Scale counts human rights abuses by any group—government or non-government. Most abuse, however, is by governments.
32. The definitions of regions correspond approximately with the categories used by the US Department of State. The exact definitions are spelled out in Linda Cornett and Mark Gibney, 'Tracking Terror: The Political Terror Scale 1980–2001'. See the *Human Security Report* website, www.humansecurityreport.info.
33. For a discussion of this issue, see James Ron, Howard Ramos and Kathleen Rodgers, 'Transnational Information Politics: Amnesty International's Country Reporting, 1986–2000', Department of Sociology, McGill University, 11 August 2004, http://www.gwu.edu/~psc/news/ISQ%20submission2.pdf (accessed 1 August 2005).
34. Ibid.
35. Linda Cornett and Mark Gibney, 'Tracking Terror: The Political Terror Scale 1980–2001'.
36. John Mueller, *The Remnants of War* (Ithaca: Cornell University Press, 2004); Paul Collier, 'Rebellion as a Quasi-Criminal Activity', *Journal of Conflict Resolution* 44 (2000): 839–853.
37. Paul Collier and Anke Hoeffler, 'Murder by Numbers: Socio-Economic Determinants of Homicide and Civil War', Centre for the Study of African Economies Working Paper Series, no. 2004–10, http://www.csae.ox.ac.uk/workingpapers/pdfs/2004-10text.pdf (accessed 10 August 2005). The authors found no evidence that the causal relationship went the other way: that high rates of homicide increased the risk of civil war.
38. In July 2004, for example, the *9/11 Commission Report* argued for 'integrated all-source analysis' of international terrorism. National Commission Report, 22 July 2004, http://www.9-11commission.gov/report/911Report.pdf (accessed 20 June 2005).
39. World Heath Organization, *The World Health Report: 2004: Changing History* (Geneva: World Heath Organization, 2004), www.who.int/whr/2004/en/ (accessed 20 June 2005).
40. See Interpol data in the background document commissioned by the Human Security Centre, Graeme Newman, 'Human Security: A World View of Homicide and Rape', at the *Human Security Report* website www.humansecurityreport.info.
41. Paul Collier and Anke Hoeffler, 'Murder by Numbers: Socio-Economic Determinants of Homicide and Civil War'.
42. There are several methodological difficulties in compiling and presenting this data over time. During the past 40 years there has been a dramatic increase in the number of countries in the international system, and many borders have changed. Not all countries keep accurate records. Some of the countries that do keep records compile and report them annually; others do so less frequently.
43. UN Office for Drug Control and Crime Prevention, *Global Report on Crime and Justice* (New York: Oxford University Press, 1999).
44. Graeme Newman, 'Human Security: A World View of Homicide and Rape'.
45. Cited in Bree Cook, Fiona David and Anna Grant, *Sexual Violence in Australia*, Research and Public Policy Series no. 36 (Canberra: Australian Institute of Criminology, 2001), http://www.aic.gov.au/publications/rpp/36/ (accessed 24 June 2005).
46. UN Office for Drug Control and Crime Prevention, *Global Report on Crime and Justice*.
47. Bree Cook, Fiona David and Anna Grant, *Sexual Violence in Australia*.
48. Louise Rimmer, 'Cool Hand Luke', *The Scotsman*, 16 August 2003, http://news.scotsman.com/index.cfm?id=887492003 (accessed 7 June 2004).

49. Josinaldo Aleixo de Souza, *Socibilidades emergentes—Implicações da dominação de matadores na periferie e traficantes nas favelas* (PhD diss., Universidade Federal do Rio de Janeiro, 25 September 2001).
50. Stockholm International Peace Research Institute, SIPRI Year Book, 2004: *Armament Disarmament and International Security* (Oxford: Oxford University Press, 2004).
51. DATASUS, 'Sistema de informações sobre mortalidade', Ministério de Saúde, Secretaria da Saúde do Governo do Estado do Rio de Janeiro, http://tabnet.datasus.gov.br/cgi/deftohtm.exe?sim/cnv/obtrj.def (accessed 7 June 2004).
52. Israeli Information Center for Human Rights in the Occupied Territories, 'Minors Killed Since 9 December 1987', http://www.btselem.org/English/Statistics/Minors_Killed.asp (accessed 7 June 2003; site discontinued).
53. DATASUS, 'Sistema de informações sobre mortalidade'.
54. Rachel Brett and Margaret McCallin, *Children: The Invisible Soldiers*, 2nd ed. (Stockholm: Rädda Barnen, 1998).
55. Secretaria de Segurança Pública do Estado do Rio de Janeiro (SSP-RJ), SSP-RJ website, http://www.ssp.rj.gov.br/ (accessed 10 August 2005).
56. Details of COAV's research and a regularly updated news service focusing on children and armed violence can be found at www.coav.org.br.
57. The US Department of State, 'Trafficking in Persons Report', 14 June 2004, http://www.state.gov/g/tip/rls/tiprpt/2004/34021.htm (accessed 7 February 2005).
58. International Labour Office, *A Global Alliance Against Forced Labour* (Geneva: International Labour Office, 2005), http://www.ilo.org/dyn/declaris/DECLARATIONWEB.DOWNLOAD_BLOB?Var_DocumentID=5059 (accessed 3 June 2005).
59. The US Department of State, 'Trafficking in Persons Report', 3 June 2005, http://www.state.gov/g/tip/rls/tiprpt/2005/46606.htm (accessed 3 June 2005).
60. Kristiina Kangaspunta, 'Mapping the Inhuman Trade: Preliminary Findings of the Database on Trafficking in Human Beings', *Forum on Crime and Society* 3 (December 2003): 81–103, www.unodc.org/pdf/crime/forum/forum3_note1.pdf (accessed 3 June 2005).
61. International Organization for Migration, *Changing Patterns and Trends of Trafficking in Persons in the Balkan Region* (Geneva: International Organization for Migration, 2004), www.iom.int/iomwebsite/Publication/ServletSearchPublication?event=detail&id=3831 (accessed 5 June 2005).
62. Article 3(a) of the protocol to Prevent, Suppress and Punish Trafficking in Persons, Especially Women and Children, supplementing the United Nations Convention against Transnational Organized Crime, http://www.unodc.org/pdf/crime/a_res_55/res5525e.pdf (accessed 20 January 2005).
63. The UK-based NGO Anti-Slavery International describes the difference between the two as follows: 'Human trafficking involves deceiving or coercing someone to move—either within a country or abroad through legal or illegal channels—for the purpose of exploiting him or her. Smuggling is assisting someone for a fee to cross a border illegally.' *See Human Trafficking Q&A*, Anti-Slavery International, http://www.antislavery.org/homepage/antislavery/trafficking.htm#qanda (accessed 20 January 2005).
64. International Labour Office, *A Global Alliance Against Forced Labour*.
65. L. Kelly and L. Regan, 'Stopping Traffic: Exploring the Extent of, and Responses to, Trafficking of Women for Sexual Exploitation in the UK', *Police Research Series* 125 (London: Home Office Policing and Reducing Crime Unit, 2000).
66. Elizabeth Kelly, *Journeys of Jeopardy: A Review of Research on Trafficking in Women and Children in Europe* (Geneva: International Organization for Migration, 2002).
67. Cited in Elizabeth Kelly, *Journeys of Jeopardy: A Review of Research on Trafficking in Women and Children in Europe.*
68. Ibid.
69. International Organization for Migration, *Changing Patterns and Trends of Trafficking in Persons in the Balkan Region.*

70. Kristiina Kangaspunta, 'Mapping the Inhuman Trade: Preliminary Findings of the Database on Trafficking in Human Beings'.
71. International Labour Office, *A Global Alliance Against Forced Labour*. The difference may be due to the fact that UNDOC's data come mostly from European countries, while the ILO data are drawn from all regions of the world.
72. Elizabeth Kelly, *Journeys of Jeopardy: A Review of Research on Trafficking in Women and Children in Europe*.
73. Elisabeth Rehn and Ellen Johnson Sirleaf, *Women, War and Peace* (New York: United Nations Development Fund for Women, 2002), http://www.unifem.org/resources/item_detail.php?ProductID=17 (accessed 19 January 2005).
74. US Department of State, *Slavery, Abduction and Forced Servitude in Sudan* (Washington: US Department of State, Bureau of African Affairs, 2002), http://www.state.gov/p/af/rls/rpt/10445.htm (accessed 21 February 2005).
75. International Labour Organization, *Combating Trafficking in Children for Labour Exploitation in West and Central Africa* (Geneva: Intenational Labour Orgainization, 2001), http://www.ilo.org/public/english/standards/ipec/publ/field/africa/central.pdf (accessed 19 January 2005).
76. Protocol to Prevent, Suppress and Punish Trafficking in Persons, United Nations Office on Drugs and Crime website, http://www.unodc.org/unodc/en/crime_cicp_signatures_trafficking.html (accessed 30 August 2005).
77. European Law Enforcement Organisation, '*Crime Assessment: Trafficking of Human Beings into the European Union*', The European Police Office website, http://www.europol.eu.int/index.asp?page=publ_crimeassessmentTHB (accessed June 4 2005; document no longer available).
78. Philip Alston, 'Toward a Human Rights Accountability Index', *Journal of Human Development* 1 (2000): 250.
79. AVISO, 'The Index of Human Security', Aviso, January 2000, http://www.gechs.org/aviso/avisoenglish/six_lg.shtml (accessed 15 June 2005); Gary King and Christopher J.L. Murray, 'Rethinking Human Security', *Political Science Quarterly* 116 (2002–2002).
80. The 2003 Political Terror Scale data are used here. The full data table is available in the Political Science Department of the University of North Carolina at http://www.unca.edu/politicalscience/faculty-staff/gibney.html (accessed 10 September 2004).
81. World Bank, 'Governance Indicators: 1996–2002', World Bank Institute website, http://www.worldbank.org/wbi/governance/govdata2002/index.html (accessed 10 September 2004); Daniel Kaufmann, Aart Kraay and Massimo Mastruzzi, 'Governance Matters III: Governance Indicators for 1996–2002', World Bank Institute website, http://www.worldbank.org/wbi/governance/pubs/govmatters3.html (accessed 10 September 2004). Note that the data for the 'political stability and absence of violence' measure are for 2002. Since this measure does not change greatly from year to year, we feel comfortable using the 2002 data. Iraq would be an obvious exception since 2003 saw a war and subsequent violent occupation.
82. World Bank, 'Questions and Answers: Governance Indicators', World Bank Institute website, http://info.worldbank.org/governance/kkz2004/q&a.htm (accessed 3 June 2005).
83. All countries that experienced deaths from political violence in 2003 are listed. The 29 countries with the highest levels of human rights abuses are listed, as are the 29 countries with the worst political instability and violence scores.

Sven Torfinn / Panos Pictures

PART III

ASSAULT ON THE VULNERABLE

Part III examines the impact of war on those generally considered to be the most vulnerable—refugees, women and children. As is often the case in this field, analysis is complicated by the lack of reliable data.

PART III

ASSAULT ON THE VULNERABLE

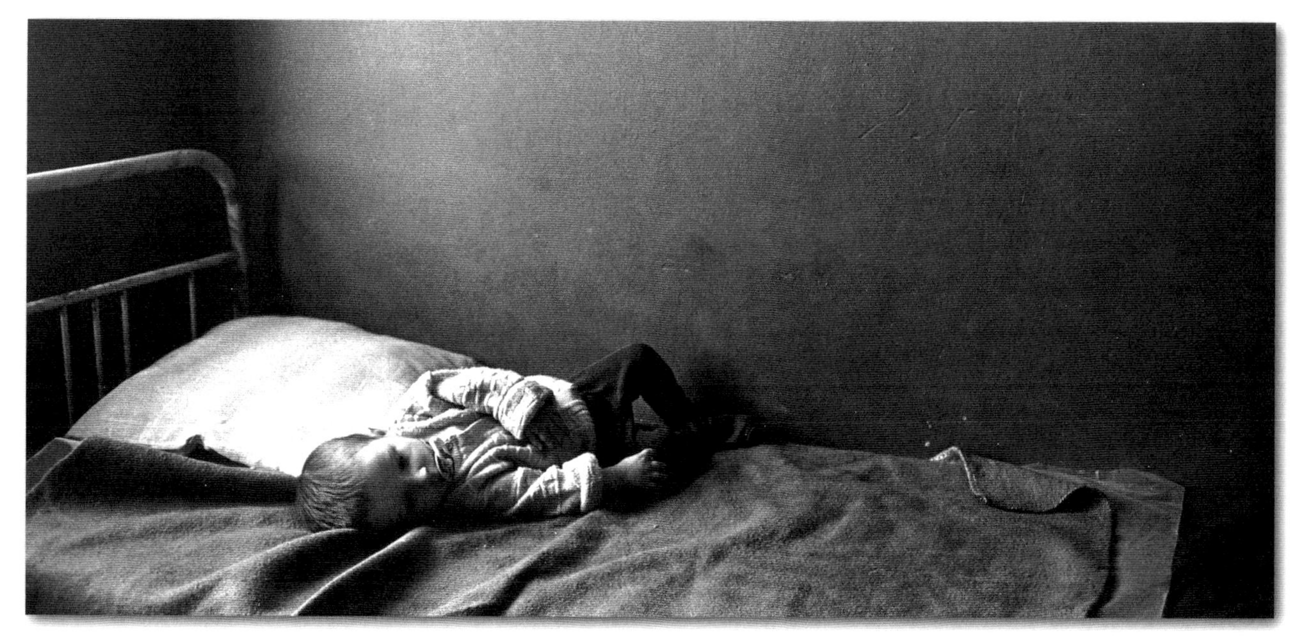

Leo Erken / Panos Pictures

Introduction

When conflict causes people to flee their homes, their vulnerability to predation, disease and malnutrition increases—often dramatically. Gender is also an important determinant of wartime vulnerability—often in surprising ways.

Although war-induced displacement is one of the few human security issues for which there are official data, determining trends is hampered by the fact that more than half the displaced persons around the world are not counted by the UN.

The United Nations High Commissioner for Refugees (UNHCR) collects data only on what it calls 'persons of concern' to the organisation. This includes all refugees, but less than half of the estimated 24 million internally displaced persons (IDPs).

The plight of IDPs is generally worse than that of refugees. As a new survey by the Global IDP Project of the Norwegian Refugee Council points out:

> IDPs did not receive sufficient humanitarian assistance from their governments. In fact, three in four IDPs, more than 18 million people, could not count on their national authorities for the provision of adequate assistance.[1]

But refugees and IDPs are not simply victims. As Fred Tanner and Stephen Stedman point out, 'Throughout the 1990s, refugee camps were used as staging grounds and resource bases for combatants in areas experiencing some of the world's most protracted wars.' (See: 'Militarising refugee camps'.) In fact, according to the UNHCR some 15% of refugee camps are militarised.

The question of people's vulnerability to the various impacts of war is more complex than often assumed. For example, one of the most frequently cited claims about today's displaced persons is that 80% of them are women and children—an assertion that conveys the impression of unique vulnerability to displacement.[2] In fact, a recent UNHCR analysis of refugee and IDP trends indicates that women and children make up 70.5%[3] —not 80%—of displaced persons.[4] Since women and children (i.e., boys and girls under 18 years of age) make up at least 70% of the population in many war-affected countries, this figure does not constitute evidence that they are uniquely vulnerable.

In armed conflict women and girls are *far* more vulnerable to sexual assault and predation than men. Here again the absence of reliable data makes tracking trends extraordinarily difficult. It is not even possible to determine whether wartime sexual violence is increasing or decreasing. Such information is critical for governments seeking to understand if policies designed to reduce the incidence of wartime sexual violence are working or not.

Despite the absence of global data, case study evidence suggests that displaced women may be twice as vulnerable to sexual assault as those who do not flee their homes. Insofar as this finding is generally true, the more than five-fold increase in the numbers of displaced people between 1970 and the early 1990s was likely associated with a major increase in war-related sexual assaults.

Similarly, the decline in both the number of displaced persons and the number and deadliness of armed conflicts since the end of the Cold War may well have led to a net decrease in wartime sexual violence—notwithstanding the recent wave of assaults in Darfur, the Democratic Republic of the Congo and elsewhere.

> Amoung children, those under five years of age are by far the most vulnerable to death from war-induced malnutrition and disease.

With the critically important exception of sexual violence, there is considerable evidence to suggest that *men*, not women, are more vulnerable to the major impacts of armed conflict. Of course, it is not surprising that far more men get killed on the battlefield than women, since they make up the overwhelming majority of combatants. But case study evidence also suggests that women are less likely to be victims of 'collateral damage', and non-combatant males are more likely to be subject to mass killing than non-combatant females. Further, some recent epidemiological survey evidence finds that males are more likely to die from war-induced malnutrition and disease than females.[5]

What these findings suggest is that women are more resilient and less vulnerable to the impacts of armed conflict than much of the literature that focuses on women as victims suggests. The increased participation of women in government military forces, rebel groups and even terrorist organisations also serves to remind us that depicting women simply as passive victims of political violence can be profoundly misleading.

Of course, children are the most vulnerable of all. The discussion on child soldiers draws on recent research by the Coalition to Stop the Use of Child Soldiers and Brookings Institution analyst Peter W. Singer. Here the focus is not so much on the economic and strategic imperatives that impel the recruitment of children and that were briefly reviewed in Part I, but on how children under arms are used and abused.

Most analysts believe that there has been a dramatic increase in the use of child soldiers over the past three decades, driven in part by economic imperatives. Physically vulnerable and easily intimidated, children make cheap, expendable soldiers. Armed with modern light weapons, they can be swiftly transformed into efficient, low-cost killers.

But lack of reliable data again confounds attempts to determine whether numbers of child soldiers have recently been increasing or decreasing. Both governments and rebel forces routinely lie about their use of child soldiers and few if any records are kept, making the task of estimating numbers extremely difficult.

The estimate of 300,000 child soldiers worldwide dates back almost a decade, yet it is repeatedly cited as if it were current. However, given the dramatic decline in the number of wars since then—and the consequent demobilisation of fighters, including children—it would be surprising if child soldier numbers had not fallen along with those of regular forces during this period.

Whatever the numbers, there is no doubt that children generally—and not just child soldiers—suffer most from the impact of armed conflict and displacement. Among children, those under five years of age are by far the most vulnerable to death from war-induced malnutrition and disease. In some conflicts more than 50% of the 'indirect deaths' from armed conflicts are children in this category.

This 'indirect death' phenomenon is examined in more depth in Part IV, and will be a major focus of the *Human Security Report 2006*.

Sven Torfinn / Panos Pictures

The plight of the displaced

While the number of refugees around the world has steadily declined in recent years, the number of internally displaced persons has grown considerably. Many are sick and hungry, most lack protection and few have adequate shelter.

For four decades the number of refugees around the world has tracked the number of armed conflicts—growing inexorably, though unevenly, from the 1960s to the early 1990s, then falling commensurately as the numbers of wars declined in the 1990s, from a record high of 17.8 million in 1992 to 9.7 million in 2003. The recent upsurge of peace agreements in Africa, the world's most violent continent, suggests that this trend will continue, at least in the short term.

Most displaced persons are not refugees, however. Of the estimated 33 million displaced people around the world in 2003, about 24 million were internally displaced persons (IDPs), and although the data are unreliable, it appears that their numbers have increased significantly since 1995 (see Figure 3.1).[6] Unlike refugees, IDPs do not cross national borders in search of safety—they remain within their home country.[7]

Figure 3.1 Refugees and internally displaced persons, 1964–2003

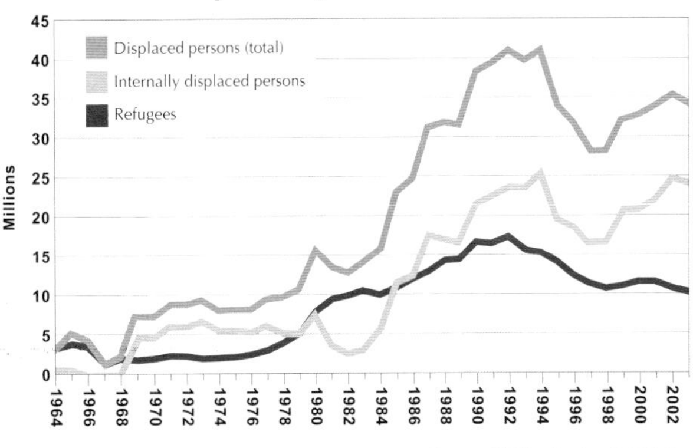

Source: Philip Orchard, 2004[8]

From the mid-sixties to the early 1990s, numbers of all displaced persons, both refugees and IDPs, rose dramatically, from about 5 million to 42 million. But while the number of refugees declined between 1992 and 2003, the number of IDPs increased.

Note: Refugee figures from 1964–1975 are estimates by UNHCR based on the arrival of refugees and/or recognition of asylum seekers.

World War II and its aftermath

More than 30 million people were displaced as a result of World War II, confronting the new UN Relief and Rehabilitation Administration (now the United Nations High Commissioner for Refugees, or UNHCR) with a huge task of repatriation and local integration.[9] By 1946, however, the looming Cold War made the repatriation of refugees to the Soviet Union and Soviet-controlled areas politically unpalatable to Western governments. Resettlement became the preferred option. As James Hathaway put it, accepting refugees from Communist regimes, 'reinforced the ideological and strategic objectives of the capitalist world'.[10] Cold War politics rather than humanitarian need tended to determine who was granted asylum. In the 1980s, for example, the United States accepted only 3% of Salvadorean and Guatemalan applications for asylum, but 75% of those from the Soviet Union.[11]

For much of the Cold War the UNHCR and host and donor states assumed that most refugees would remain in their country of asylum for extended periods.[12] But over the years the rising numbers of asylum seekers and the increasing reluctance of host countries to absorb them, plus opportunities for some refugees to return home, led to a major shift in policy. Once again, repatriation became the name of the game. Between 1991 and 1996 the UNHCR repatriated more than 9 million refugees.[13]

In the West the end of the Cold War swept away any remaining ideological motive for accepting refugees, most of whom now came from the poorest countries of the developing world.[14] Opportunistic European politicians began blaming unemployment and rising crime rates on refugees, asylum seekers and illegal migrants. Governments argued that many who claimed to be asylum seekers were really economic migrants with no real need of international protection. The claim was doubtless true in some cases.

And governments had reason to be concerned about costs. In 2002–03 the cost of housing and support for the 41,000 asylum seekers in the UK was nearly US$2 billion—'roughly twice the amount the UNHCR spends each year to support and care for 21 million refugees in its camps around the world'.[15]

IDPs: Greater numbers, greater problems

In 2003 there were an estimated 23.6 million IDPs worldwide, up from an estimated 3 million in 1982. The protection provided for these displaced people varies from non-existent to barely adequate. According to the Norwegian Refugee Council, in 13 of the 52 countries that have IDPs, governments provide no protection at all, while 9 million IDPs in 22 other countries receive occasional protection. UN humanitarian agencies operate in only 21 countries—less than half the number of countries with IDPs.[16]

It isn't obvious why IDP numbers apparently rose between 1995 and 2002 while both the numbers of armed conflicts and refugees fell. Several possibilities present themselves.

In the West the end of the Cold War swept away any remaining ideological motive for accepting refugees.

First, the scope of the problem is better understood now than it was a decade ago—despite attempts by governments to invoke sovereignty and non-interference to quash criticism. This is thanks in part to the work of the Representative of the Secretary-General on Internal Displacement, but also to the increased numbers of NGOs and UN agency staff on the ground. So part of the increase in IDP numbers may be due simply to an increase in reporting.

Second, in many countries embroiled in conflict, 'ethnic cleansing' campaigns mean that returning refugees have no secure homes to go to. When refugees return to their own countries, the global refugee total goes down, but the global IDP total may go up.

Third, in many contemporary wars, civilians are not only victims of 'collateral damage', they are deliberately targeted by rebel groups and even government forces. Mass killing of civilians in guerrilla wars is most likely to occur when guerrillas pose a major threat to the regime and are strongly supported by the civilian population.[17]

MILITARISING REFUGEE CAMPS

The flight of Rwandans following the genocide in 1994 may have been the largest and most rapid mass exodus in African history and is deeply misunderstood.

Between July 14 and 18, 1994, some 850,000 people fled from Rwanda into eastern Zaire (now the Democratic Republic of the Congo), joining several hundred thousand who had travelled there in the previous month. By August, between 1.7 and 2 million Rwandans were living in makeshift camps in Zaire and Tanzania.

Many of the displaced were not fleeing the genocide; they were its perpetrators. The slaughter of more than 800,000 Rwandan Tutsi and moderate Hutu had ended in the middle of July 1994, not because the international community had finally been galvanised into action, but because the Rwandan Patriotic Front (RPF), a largely Tutsi force that had been fighting the Rwandan government for three years, had prevailed.

The genocide had been organised and directed by elements of the Rwandan government and army that had opposed a power-sharing deal with the RPF to end the civil war. When all seemed lost militarily, the *genocideurs* forcibly marched hundreds of thousands of Rwandan Hutus out of the country—an exodus fueled by Hutu fears that the RPF would seek violent retribution. But the genocide's organisers and killers blended into the refugee camps in Zaire—where they, like other refugees, received assistance—and quickly gained control. As Médicins Sans Frontières has pointed out, 'those responsible for the genocide ... remained living with impunity in camps run by the United Nations, and the very system established to protect the refugees became the source of their peril.'[18]

According to the UNHCR, militarised camps such as those in Zaire now pose the single largest threat to refugee security. Although the great majority of refugee crises do not foment refugee militarisation, a small but significant number (15%) do have this effect. Throughout the 1990s refugee camps were used as staging grounds and resource bases for combatants in areas experiencing some of the world's most protracted wars: Afghanistan, Bosnia, Burundi, East Timor, Liberia, Rwanda, Sudan and the Palestinian Territories.

The fact that some of the most powerful member states of the United Nations used refugees as pawns in larger geopolitical conflicts ensured the UNHCR was denied resources necessary to stop the use of camps as de facto military bases. In its commitment to long-term relief assistance, the UNHCR was inadvertently supporting warring groups intent on exploiting refugee populations and humanitarian assistance as a means of continuing their violent struggles.

Recognising the dilemma, some refugee workers argue that host governments should provide better camp security. But in today's world, many host governments are either complicit in the political and military manipulation of refugees (as in Pakistan, Thailand and the Democratic Republic of the Congo) or simply lack the capacity to protect refugee populations (as in Lebanon).

The UNHCR has proposed measures to deal with the problem—ranging from modest preventive initiatives, to the creation of an international military force tasked with policing the camps and separating combatants from refugees.

While admirable in principle, these proposals will have little impact in practice as long as the international community continues to ignore the manipulation of refugees by host governments, neighbours, regional powers and, not least, the major powers.

In such cases, flight is often the only option. But seeking sanctuary across borders may not be possible for a variety of reasons—including the refusal of governments to allow displaced persons to leave the country and the reluctance of governments in potential host countries to accept them.

Finally, while the number of armed conflicts declined between 1995 and 2002, the number of people killed in sub-Saharan Africa increased dramatically, but temporarily, at the end of the century. Some of the increase in IDPs was almost certainly a response to this increase in violence.

Failures to protect the displaced

When civilians become strategic targets, those who seek to help them—including humanitarian agencies—may themselves be targeted. This is one reason for the upsurge of attacks on humanitarian workers during the 1990s.[19] The greater the danger to humanitarian workers, the more likely those workers are to be withdrawn from the field and the less protection and assistance will be available to the displaced and vulnerable.

In 2002 a four-year survey by the Norwegian Refugee Council's Global IDP Project reported that:

> The global IDP crisis is one of the great humanitarian challenges of our time. In most of the 48 countries covered, IDPs struggle to survive with inadequate shelter, few resources and no protection. Warring parties often block humanitarian aid, unnecessarily worsening malnutrition and disease. Moreover IDPs—mainly women and children—have no one to protect them from multiple human rights violations: including attacks, torture, forced labour and sexual exploitation.[20]

IDPs are entitled to the same legal protection under human rights and humanitarian law as other civilians, and they are supposed to be protected by their governments. But some governments lack the capacity to protect displaced citizens; others simply don't care. Sometimes governments themselves cause displacement. When this happens IDPs have no one to turn to for protection—except on those rare occasions when the international community can be persuaded to mount a 'humanitarian intervention'. And even when governments—often grudgingly—permit aid agencies access to internally displaced populations, the situation on the ground is often too dangerous to allow unprotected agency personnel to operate effectively.

The ability of the international community to assist the displaced is further complicated by inadequate response capacity. In February 2004 Refugees International reported that field assessments by its staff revealed that UNHCR was failing to meet its core responsibility in protecting refugees—let alone IDPs—in every country assessed. Even official agency reports on the response to IDP needs are negative. A recent assessment by the UN's new Internally Displaced Persons Unit concluded that the international community's response to IDP needs was ad hoc and plagued by egregious failures.[21]

> When civilians are stategic targets, those who seek to help them—including humanitarian agencies—may themselves be targeted.

Agency turf battles are a further impediment, but the fundamental problem is that humanitarian agencies simply lack the capacity to address protection needs in the field effectively. Among official agencies and NGOs, there is general agreement that the most effective way to address this is through better collaboration. But while the 'collaborative approach' is widely agreed to be sensible, it requires a degree of cooperation that has yet to be achieved.

In the meantime—unable to depend on either their own governments or the international community—most displaced persons have no choice but to rely on their own coping mechanisms.

Nick Danziger / Press Images Europe

War and sexual violence

Sexual violence has been an intimate partner of armed conflict throughout human history, but because of chronic under-reporting by both victims and authorities, determining its extent in war is extraordinarily difficult.

Men and women die—and suffer—in wars quite differently. Far more men are killed in battle than women. Indeed, according to the World Health Organization (WHO) nearly 90% of all direct war deaths in 2002 were men.[22] But women are far more vulnerable to sexual violence and predation.[23] In the world's war zones, women and girls are overwhelmingly non-combatants—and rarely have the means to protect themselves.

The history of sexual violence in 20th century wars illustrates the scope of the problem:

- During Japan's infamous assault on the Chinese city of Nanking in December 1937, more than 20,000 and possibly as many as 80,000 women were raped and killed. In 1934–1945 the Japanese forced between 100,000 and 200,000 mostly Asian women, most of them Korean, into prostitution as 'comfort women'.[24]
- In the final phases of World War II, Russian soldiers raped and gang-raped hundreds of thousands of women in the assault on, and subsequent occupation of, Germany.[25]
- In 1971 hundreds of thousands of Bengali women were sexually assaulted by West Pakistani forces in the uprising and subsequent savage repression that killed more than a million people and eventually led to the creation of Bangladesh from what had been East Pakistan.[26]
- In the 1994 Rwandan genocide, as many as 500,000 women and girls may have been victims of sexual violence.[27] According to Gerald Chamina, Rwanda's prosecutor general, 'Rape was the worst experience of victims of the genocide. Some people paid to die, to be shot rather than tortured. Their prayers were for a quick and decent death. Victims of rape did not have that privilege.'[28]
- In the war in Bosnia, an estimated 20,000 to 50,000 women were sexually assaulted.[29]

In the new century the assaults have continued:

- In Burma, Refugees International reported in 2003 that a government-backed reign of terror had resulted in the sexual violation of thousands of women from the Karen, Karenni, Mon and Tavoyan ethnic minorities.[30]
- In Sudan in early 2005, government forces and militias were responsible for rape and other acts of sexual violence throughout the region of Darfur. These and other

acts were conducted on a 'widespread and systematic basis, and therefore may amount to crimes against humanity'.[31]

- In the Democratic Republic of the Congo, government troops and rebel fighters have raped tens of thousands of women and girls, 'but fewer than a dozen perpetrators have been prosecuted by a judicial system in dire need of reform'.[32]

Displacement and sexual violence

A major survey in post-war Sierra Leone found that the rate of sexual assault against women and girls who had been displaced was 17%, almost double that of those who had not fled their homes.[33] Nationwide that rate translates into 94,000 to 122,000 victims among the displaced females alone.[34] Nearly a third of the assault victims among the displaced had been gang-raped.

Unarmed and rarely able to exercise their rights, displaced women and girls become easy targets for sexual violence and exploitation. And while refugee camps provide food and shelter for women fleeing the chaos of war, they often fail to protect them from predation.

> No one knows whether the incidence of sexual violence in war is increasing or decreasing.

There have been a number of well-documented recent cases of aid workers and peacekeepers coercing women and girls into providing sexual services in exchange for protection, assistance and support for children and other family members:

- One 2002 report on camp conditions in Guinea, Liberia and Sierra Leone cited numerous stories of sexual violence and exploitation by peacekeepers and humanitarian workers.[35]
- In January 2005 a UN inquiry substantiated allegations of sexual abuse by peacekeepers and civilian UN workers in the Democratic Republic of the Congo.[36]

Is the violence increasing or decreasing?

No one knows whether the incidence of sexual violence in war is increasing or decreasing. Statistics on rape and other forms of sexual assault in conflict zones remain virtually non-existent and many post-conflict epidemiological surveys do not ask questions about sexual violence because they are too sensitive.

Victims are often reluctant to report that they have been sexually assaulted because they fear being stigmatised or further victimised. Many hold a well-founded belief that authorities will do little to provide redress.[37]

This chronic under-reporting has allowed authorities to downplay the problem, with the result that rape and related crimes have tended to be treated as an unfortunate form of 'collateral damage'. As Human Rights Watch has argued:

> Rape has long been mischaracterised and dismissed by military and political leaders as a private crime, the ignoble act of the occasional soldier. Worse still, it has been accepted precisely because it is so commonplace. Longstanding discriminatory attitudes have viewed crimes against women as incidental or less serious violations.[38]

Despite the lack of reliable statistics, wartime sexual violence has received far more attention in recent years—and few doubt that it is widespread. But it is unclear whether the incidence of attacks is increasing, or simply that more are being reported. Both could be true. However, some inferences can be drawn from the association between sexual violence and population displacement.

As noted earlier, in the civil war in Sierra Leone the sexual assault rate among displaced women was close to twice that of those who had not fled their homes. If a similar relationship exists in other conflict zones around the world, then war-related sexual violence would have risen as the numbers of displaced people increased.

From the beginning of the 1970s to the early 1990s, the number of people displaced, many as a result of armed conflict, increased from 8 million to more than 40 million. So *if* the Sierra Leone pattern applies universally, then the incidence of conflict-related sexual violence would also have risen massively over the same period.

After 1992 the numbers of displaced persons around the world declined, so the same logic would suggest that—all other things being equal—the number of victims of sexual violence would have declined as well.

Another possibility is that the *rate* of sexual assaults per hundred thousand of the population increased in some conflicts, while the *total* number of victims of such assaults decreased worldwide as the number of conflicts declined.

Clearly more research is needed before any definitive conclusions can be reached on this issue. And researchers need to bear in mind that rates of sexual violence can differ dramatically from conflict to conflict. One recent study found, for example, that wartime sexual violence rates in the conflicts in Bosnia and Sierra Leone were many times higher than those in Israel-Palestine, Sri Lanka and El Salvador.[39]

Rape as a weapon of war

There is some case study evidence to suggest that 'strategic rape'—sexual assault that is encouraged by military leaders as a means of furthering war aims—has been rising. One recent study reported that rape had been used as a 'weapon of war' in at least 13 countries between 2001 and 2004.[40]

Rape can be used to humiliate and demoralise enemies, while the mere threat of sexual violence can induce people to flee their homes—a central goal of 'ethnic cleansing'. For example, in July 2004 Amnesty International reported that the Arab militias ('Janjawid') in the Darfur region of Sudan had raped women in public as part of a deliberate effort to humiliate, punish, control, engender fear and displace whole communities.[41] During the Rwandan genocide a decade earlier, rapes were 'often staged as public performances to multiply the terror and degradation.'[42]

So-called strategic rape is particularly effective against traditional 'honour and shame' societies, where the perceived integrity of the family and the community is bound up with the virtue of women. When used this way rape becomes a cultural weapon as well as a physical outrage, one that brings shame and humiliation to the victim's entire family. This happened in Kosovo, where Muslim women were specifically targeted, in part because the perpetrators believed that once women had been raped, traditional cultural norms would ensure that they would be ostracised and could then neither marry nor have children.[43]

Sexual violence is most prevalent when, as is the case with strategic rape, it is encouraged and legitimised by political authorities. But even without official encouragement most wars involve a dramatic erosion in the norms that restrain anti-social behaviour in times of peace. And the general lawlessness and impunity that war brings in its train means that once the fighting starts there is often little to deter individuals from acting out their violent desires. Where pre-war social norms against sexual violence are weak, the risk of rape in war is correspondingly greater.

The fate of the victims

Many wartime victims of sexual violence confront a tragic dilemma. If they do not reveal that they have been violated they cannot seek treatment, which puts their health, and sometimes their lives, at risk. Disclosing that they have been raped, on the other hand, may mean being stigmatised and rejected by the very people they would normally turn to for support.

> Sexual violence is most prevalent when it is encouraged and legitimised by political authorities.

Victims of sexual violence are at high risk of contracting diseases from their attackers—the most deadly being HIV/AIDS. Other diseases, such as chlamydia, gonorrhea, syphilis and venereal warts, often produce no symptoms in women, so infections go untreated. This can result in more serious conditions—the most common being pelvic inflammatory disease and infertility. In poor countries, non-existent or inadequate health services compound the problem.

MEN AS VICTIMS, WOMEN AS WARRIORS

Many analyses of gender and conflict ignore or underestimate the gender-based violence directed against males, and pay little attention to the active roles women play in warfare.

In December 2004 Amnesty International released a major report on the vulnerabilities of women in armed conflicts. The press release stated, 'Women and girls bear the brunt of armed conflicts fought today both as direct targets and as unrecognised "collateral damage".'[44]

The Amnesty report is part of a growing body of policy-oriented research that uses gender as a lens to study the impact of armed conflict. This research has helped sensitise policymakers to the special vulnerabilities of women in war and in post-war environments. But the 'gender lens' has been inconsistently applied, creating a distorted picture of reality.

Notwithstanding Amnesty's claim, it is men—not women—who 'bear the brunt' of armed conflict. Both in uniform and out, men have been, and continue to be, killed, wounded and tortured in far greater numbers than women. Men are also, overwhelmingly, the major perpetrators of violence. Sexual violence is the area where women, not men, make up the majority of victims.

The World Health Organization (WHO) estimates that in 2002 approximately nine males were killed in armed conflicts around the world for every female.[45] WHO's annual estimates of the gender ratios of war victims vary considerably, but all its reports show that far greater numbers of males than females are killed in warfare.

WHO's global estimates are broadly in line with epidemiological case study evidence. For example, a 1999 survey of 1197 households in post-war Kosovo found that 75% of total deaths and 90% of war-related trauma deaths during the conflict were males.[46] Ratios vary from war to war, but the consistent pattern of far more male than female casualties is not surprising given that men make up the overwhelming majority of combatants. War is primarily an institution that pits males against other males.

Amnesty's claim that women 'bear the brunt' of collateral damage—civilians who get caught in the crossfire—is unsupported by any global data. In fact, case study evidence suggests that here again males, not females, are the primary victims.

One major epidemiological survey following the first Gulf War found that while men made up 51% of the Iraqi population they suffered an estimated 62% of the civilian deaths.[47] And a 2004 study of civilians who had been killed in the current Iraq conflict found that males were even more likely to be killed than in the first Gulf War. The study, which focused on individuals who could be identified by name, reported that for every female killed there were three male victims.[48] (One explanation for the difference may be that women had moved to safer locations.)

The gender breakdown of 'indirect deaths' from war-induced malnutrition and disease—particularly in refugee and internally displaced persons camps—is also at odds with the conventional wisdom. Amnesty's claim that in war 'it is women and children that are forced to leave their homes' is not borne out by the available evidence.[49] According to the UNHCR there are actually slightly more male refugees (51%) than female.[50]

The common assumption that women are more likely to be adversely affected by displacement than men has *some* supporting case study evidence,[51] but most of the case study data point in the other direction. A comprehensive review of 46 epidemiological surveys commissioned by the Human Security Centre for the *Human Security Report* found that the death rate for displaced males was generally higher than that for females.[52]

What about 'gender-based violence' in war—that is, violence that deliberately targets individuals or groups of individuals because of their gender? We know that women are far more likely to be the victims of rape and other sex crimes, but sexual violence is only one form of 'gender-based violence'.

Men, too, are targeted because of their gender. There is, for example, compelling evidence that non-combatant males, 'have been and continue to be the most frequent targets of mass killing and genocidal slaughter as well as a host of lesser atrocities and abuses'.[53]

Following the 1999 war in Kosovo, a report by the Organization for Security and Cooperation in Europe (OSCE) noted that the most systematic atrocities were inflicted disproportionately and overwhelmingly on non-combatant males.[54] The explanation? Part revenge and part bleak strategic logic: killing battle-age males minimises future threats to the victors.[55]

Men are also disproportionately victimised by violent state repression. One major study used census data to show that the population of the Soviet Union in 1959 was 'some 20 million lower than Western observers had expected *after* making allowance for war losses.'[56] The deaths that led to the lower-than-expected population total were the result of Stalin's purges in the 1930s. Most of the victims were men. Given that males constitute a more likely source of challenge to repressive regimes than females this is again not surprising.

A comprehensive gender analysis of human insecurity would examine how men as well as women are victimised because of their gender. And rather than presenting women primarily as passive victims of armed conflict, it would pay more attention to the growing role they play in fighting forces around the world.

In many countries women now make up between 5% and 15% of government armed service personnel. The ratios are even higher in some guerrilla organisations, especially those that espouse a commitment to gender equality. Women made up 30% of both soldiers and leaders in the Sandinista National Liberation Front in Nicaragua, for example.[57] Other rebel groups with a large female membership include Peru's Shining Path, the Revolutionary Armed Forces of Colombia (FARC) and Sri Lanka's Tamil Tigers.

Over the past 50 years women have also played important roles in terrorist organisations—from Germany's Red Army Faction and the Japanese Red Army to Chechnya's Black Widows. And according to *Jane's Intelligence Review*, there has been a dramatic upsurge in the number of women suicide bombers. For example, some 30% of suicide bombings by the Tamil Tigers have been carried out by women, as have most of the suicide missions perpetrated by Turkish terrorist groups.[58]

Finally, some 40% of child soldiers around the world are girls.[59] One recent study found that female child soldiers were involved in fighting forces in 55 countries between 1990 and 2003. They were involved in combat in 38 of them.[60]

Bringing a gender perspective to the study of armed conflict has provided many valuable insights and forced policymakers to focus on the unique threats that women and girls confront in conflict zones. But the huge costs that political violence imposes on males have been mostly ignored, while women's agency remains largely invisible and women themselves have been presented primarily as passive victims.

Unwanted children resulting from wartime rape are yet another burden for many survivors. Women may be stigmatised for bearing 'enemy' offspring—known as 'children of hate' in Rwanda. But the alternative—usually a backstreet abortion—poses grave health risks.

> In the past decade, there have been signs that the international community has begun to take war and sexual violence more seriously.

Rape victims are also prone to deep psychological harm—including depression, psychotic episodes and post-traumatic stress disorder.[61] For some, reliving and recounting the details of their trauma can trigger renewed feelings of vulnerability, humiliation and despair. Health workers in the former Yugoslavia reported that survivors of rape experienced severe clinical depression and acute psychotic episodes after they talked with journalists, human rights workers and medical personnel. Some attempted suicide.[62]

Humanitarian organisations have also reported high rates of suicide among rape victims. For some of Rwanda's genocide survivors, the mere sight of their persecutors—many of them neighbours and colleagues—going about their daily business with neither guilt nor fear of reprisal has been almost too much to bear. As one victim put it:

> Since the war has ended, I have not had my monthly period. My stomach swells up and is painful. I think about what happened to me all the time and I cannot sleep. I even see some of the Interahamwe who did these things to me and others around here. When I see them I think of committing suicide.[63]

Changing times?

During the past decade, there have been signs that the international community has begun to take the issue of war and sexual violence more seriously:

- In 1993 and 1994 the statutes of the International Criminal Tribunals for the former Yugoslavia and for Rwanda defined rape as a crime against humanity.[64]
- In September 1998 the International Criminal Tribunal for Rwanda convicted Rwandan mayor, Jean-Paul Akayesu, of committing rape as genocide and a crime against humanity.[65] This was the first such finding by an international tribunal.
- In February 2001 the International Criminal Tribunal for the former Yugoslavia convicted three Bosnian Serbs of rape, which it designated a crime against humanity.
- The statutes of the new International Criminal Court (ICC) stipulate that when rape is committed as part of a widespread attack against a civilian population it is both a war crime and a crime against humanity.[66]

On the political front, the UN and its agencies, the World Bank and most governments now routinely affirm the need to address the special needs of women and children in armed conflicts. Speeches are given, reports written and resolutions passed. But rhetorical affirmation of the need for change, while important, has yet to be matched by real commitment to act where action is most needed—on the ground in wartorn societies.

Giacomo Pirozzi / Panos Pictures

Child soldiers

In the many countries afflicted by violent conflict, child soldiers are doubly victimised—as vulnerable targets and as cannon fodder for armies devoid of conscience. But as in so many areas of human security, there is an absence of reliable global statistics from which to determine trends.

Throughout much of the world child soldiers play critically important, sometimes decisive, roles in government and rebel military forces—even in terrorist organisations. They serve as infantry shock troops, raiders, sentries, spies, sappers and porters.

> Children are recruited because they are plentiful, cheap, malleable and expendable—and because light and deadly modern weapons more than offset a child's lack of physical strength.

A 1996 UN report, *Impact of Armed Conflict on Children*, notes that 'Children as young as 8 years of age are being forcibly recruited, coerced and induced to become combatants. Manipulated by adults, children have been drawn into violence that they are too young to resist and with consequences they cannot imagine.'[67]

In a new study on child soldiers, Brookings Institution analyst Peter W. Singer argues that the norms of warfare that once provided a degree of protection for children have eroded dramatically—and with tragic consequences.[68]

> Not only have children become the new targets of violence and atrocities in war, but many have now become perpetrators.' Singer points out that 'of ongoing or recently ended conflicts, 68% (37 out of 55) have children under 18 serving as combatants' and '80% of these conflicts ... include fighters under the age of 15.[69]

Children are recruited because they are plentiful, cheap (often they are unpaid), malleable and expendable—and because light and deadly modern weapons more than offset their lack of physical strength.

The numbers of children under arms

Determining how many child soldiers serve in armed forces around the world is no easy task. The Coalition to Stop the Use of Child Soldiers, which defines child soldiers as persons under 18 years old associated with armed forces both in and outside conflict zones, puts the total at 300,000, with one-third serving in Africa.[70] But the reliability of this much-cited figure is highly questionable. The Coalition report simply notes that it dates back to 1998 and that it is 'believed to have remained relatively constant'.

It is estimated that there are more than 75,000 child soldiers in Burma, one of the highest numbers in any country in the world.

In fact, the 300,000 figure can be traced back to 1996. It has been endlessly repeated, but almost never questioned. It is unclear what evidence there was to support the original claim and it seems highly unlikely that the true number of child soldiers would have remained unchanged for nearly a decade while the number of wars declined significantly.

A worldwide problem

Children under arms can be found on every continent, but sub-Saharan Africa is the epicentre of the child soldier phenomenon:

- One of the worst affected countries is the Democratic Republic of the Congo. The 2005 Coalition to Stop the Use of Child Soldiers' report found that all parties in the long-running conflict 'recruited, abducted and used child soldiers, often on the front line'.[71] Children in armed political groups were sometimes abused by commanders and other soldiers and many were required to commit atrocities against civilians.[72] In 2003 approximately 30,000 children were awaiting demobilisation.[73]
- In Sierra Leone's 10-year civil war, as many as 70% of combatants were under the age of 18.[74] When the war ended in 2002, some of the children were recruited into armed groups fighting in neighbouring Liberia and the Côte d'Ivoire.
- When Charles Taylor seized power in Liberia in the early 1990s he did so at the head of a mainly youth rebel army. In 2003 Taylor was defeated by rival rebel groups that also relied heavily on child soldiers. An estimated 20,000 of the fighters in Liberia were children—some 70% of all combatants.[75]
- Northern Uganda's Lord's Resistance Army (LRA) has abducted an estimated 20,000 children during two decades of conflict, forcing them to wage war against government forces as well as civilians.[76] The LRA initiates children with beatings and forces them to kill other children who attempt to escape.[77] With a core of only 200 adult fighters, the bulk of its force consists of abducted children.[78] This child army has sustained a civil war that has killed thousands, displaced 1.5 million and been described by the UN as one of the worst humanitarian disasters in the world.[79] In October 2005 the International Criminal Court issued its first-ever arrest warrants, against LRA leader Joseph Kony and four others. Although the indictments are sealed, they are believed to include changes relating to child soldiers.

Sub-Saharan Africa is the epicentre of the child soldier phenomenon.

- In the Middle East and Central Asia children are or recently have been involved in combat in Algeria, Abzerbaijan, Egypt, Iran, Iraq, Lebanon, Palestine, Sudan, Tajikistan and Yemen.
- In the Iran-Iraq War, Iranian children were used in the first wave of attacks to help clear paths through minefields. An estimated 100,000 Iranian children were killed in the fighting. In the current conflict in Iraq children as young as 12 serve in the Mahdi Army of radical cleric Muqtada al-Sadr.[80]
- In Latin America Colombia has the dubious distinction of using more child soldiers than any other country in the region. In early 2004 as many as 14,000 children were serving in the country's paramilitary and rebel

groups.[81] Children have also been used by insurgent groups in Ecuador, El Salvador, Guatemala, Mexico, Nicaragua and Peru.

- In Asia children have served in rebel and/or government forces in Burma, Cambodia, East Timor, India, Indonesia, Laos, Nepal, Pakistan, Papua New Guinea, the Philippines, Sri Lanka and the Solomon Islands.[82]
- In Burma it is estimated that 'there are more than 75,000 child soldiers, one of the highest numbers of any country in the world'.[83] They serve in both government and rebel forces. One children's militia was led by 12-year-old twin brothers.[84]
- In Indonesia 'thousands of young Muslim and Christian boys have formed local paramilitary units' that take part in intercommunal violence.[85]
- In Europe child soldiers serve or have recently served in rebel military forces in Chechnya and other parts of the former Soviet Union, and in the Balkans.

Recruitment and indoctrination

Although many child soldiers are recruited at age 16 or 17, some are much younger. In one survey in Asia, the average age of recruitment of child soldiers was 13; an African study found that 60% of the children under arms were 14 or younger.[86]

Often separated from home and family, many child soldiers are recruited through offers of food, camaraderie and protection; some join rebel groups to seek revenge for government assaults on their families.[87] And as the HIV/AIDS crisis continues to generate millions of orphans, the pool of children susceptible to recruitment will inevitably grow.

The threats and privations that children confront in war zones are often so great that joining a rebel or official armed group may seem attractive by comparison. For example, in a 2003 International Labour Organization survey in Africa, researchers found that nearly 80% of child soldiers interviewed had witnessed some form of combat, 70% had seen their family home destroyed, and about 60% had lost a family member to war.[88] At least as combatants they are fed and provided with a measure of protection.

Once inducted into a military organisation, children are often subjected to threats, violence and psychological manipulation—all tactics designed to gain their unquestioning submission. To deter them from escaping and returning to their home communities, they may be forced to kill friends, neighbours or relatives.

The purpose of indoctrination is to detach children psychologically from their former lives, imbue them with a sense of group loyalty and, above all, to instill obedience. Some are given drugs to reduce their fear of combat, and their subsequent addiction provides their commanders with yet another level of control.

Often separated from home and family, many child soldiers are recruited through offers of food, camaraderie and protection; some join rebel groups to seek revenge for government assaults on their families.

The consequences of using children to fight wars are as predictable as they are tragic. Having less experience and training than adult fighters, children are more likely to be killed or injured. Seen as more expendable than adult fighters they are often given the most dangerous duties—including leading near-suicidal 'human wave' attacks and mine clearance missions. And because their inexperience puts them at a disadvantage against regular soldiers, they are more likely to be used to target civilians—including other children.

Signs of hope?

According to Amnesty International, 'increasing numbers of children are exposed to the brutalities of war'.[89] In a similar vein, the BBC has claimed that the child soldier numbers are increasing every year as 'more children are recruited for use in active combat'.[90]

Georges Gobet / Getty Images

Africa is the epicentre of the child soldier phenomenon. In Sierra Leone, Liberia, Uganda and elsewhere, children—most of them under 14 years old—have been turned into cheap and expendable killers.

These are common views, but they are not supported by any evidence. There is no doubt that new child soldiers are recruited every year, but, as this report has shown, the number of armed conflicts has been declining for more than a decade. And when wars end, soldiers—including child soldiers—are usually demobilised. So it is more likely that the number of child soldiers serving around the world has declined rather than increased in recent years.

In November 2004 the Coalition to Stop the Use of Child Soldiers reported that 'overall, the use of child soldiers ... appears marginally improved'.[91]

PART III

ENDNOTES

1. Global IDP Project, *Internal Displacement: Global Overview of Trends and Developments in 2004* (Geneva: Global IDP Project, 2005).
2. UN Development Fund for Women, 'A Portal on Women Peace & Security: Women, War, Peace and Displacement', www .womenwarpeace.org/issues/displacement/displacement.htm (accessed 19 April 2005).
3. UN High Commissioner for Refugees, '2003 Global Refugee Trends', 15 June 2004, http://www.unhcr.ch/cgi-bin/texis/vtx/statistics/opendoc.pdf?tbl=STATISTICS&id=40d015fb4 (accessed 20 April 2005).
4. The 70.5% figure is calculated by adding the 49% of 'persons of concern' who are female (children as well as adults) to the 21.5% who are male children.
5. This finding comes from a study commissioned by the Human Security Centre, the results of which will be published in the *Human Security Report 2006.*
6. This section relies on data that have been compiled by University of British Columbia researcher Philip Orchard from a variety of sources, including the Global IDP Survey/Norwegian Refugee Council, *Internally Displaced People: A Global Survey* (London: Earthscan Publications, 1998); UN High Commissioner for Refugees, *The State of the World's Refugees: Fifty Years of Humanitarian Action* (Oxford: Oxford University Press, 2000); UN High Commissioner for Refugees, *Statistical Yearbook 2001: Refugees, Asylum-seekers and Other Persons of Concern—Trends in Displacement, Protection and Solutions* (Geneva: UN High Commissioner for Refugees, 2002); 'The Global Response to Internal Displacement: Time to Close the Accountability Gap', Refugees International website, 11 February 2004, http://www.refugeesinternational.org/content/article/detail/936/ (accessed 13 September 2004); and US Committee for Refugees, *World Refugee Survey 2003* (Washington, DC: US Committee for Refugees, 2003).
7. The plight of the displaced is complicated by the fact that although the legal definition is quite clear, who gets defined—and counted—as a refugee is often both contested and highly politicised. For example, some 300,000 North Koreans have fled into neighbouring China. But the Chinese refuse to categorise them as refugees, claiming they are merely illegal economic migrants.
8. Data supplied by Philip Orchard, University of British Columbia, 2004.
9. Gil Loescher, *Beyond Charity: International Cooperation and the Global Refugee Crisis* (Oxford: Oxford University Press, 1993).
10. James C. Hathaway, 'Can International Refugee Law Be Made Relevant Again?' in James C. Hathaway, ed., *Reconceiving International Refugee Law* (The Hague: Martinus Nijhoff Publishers, 1997).
11. Bill Frelick, 'Evolution of the Term "Refugee"', US Committee for Refugees website, www.refugees.org/news/fact_sheets/refugee_definition.htm (accessed 6 September 2004; site discontinued).
12. Jeff Crisp, *Mind the Gap! UNHCR, Humanitarian Assistance and the Development Process,* New Issues in Refugee Research, working paper no. 43, May 2001 (Geneva: UN High Commissioner for Refugees, 2001).
13. Ibid.
14. Roberta Cohen and Francis Deng, *Masses in Flight: The Global Crisis of Internal Displacement* (Washington, DC: Brookings Institution, 1998); Asha Hans and Astri Suhrke, 'Responsibility Sharing', in James C. Hathaway, ed., *Reconceiving International Refugee Law* (Boston: Kluwer Law International, 1997).
15. James Bissett, 'Scrap the Refugee Board', *National Post* (Toronto), 3 March 2004. In fact, only 10 million of the 21 million 'refugees' referred to in the article were actually refugees; the rest were IDPs, asylum seekers and others.
16. Norwegian Refugee Council, 'Overview', Global IDP Project website, www.idpproject.org/global_overview.htm (accessed 6 September 2004).
17. Benjamin Valentino, Paul Huth and Dylan Balch-Lindsay, 'Draining the Sea: Mass Killing, Genocide and Guerrilla Warfare', *International Organization* vol. 58, 2 (Spring 2004): 375–407.

18. Fiona Terry, *Condemned to Repeat: The Paradox of Humanitarian Action* (Ithaca: Cornell University Press, 2002).

19. M. Sheik, M.I. Gutierrez, P. Bolton, P. Spiegel, M. Thieren and G. Burnham, 'Deaths Among Humanitarian Workers', *British Medical Journal* 321 (15 July 2000): 166–168.

20. Global IDP Project, '25m Internally Displaced by Conflict', press release, 23 September 2002, Global IDP Project website, http://www.idpproject.org/IDP_project/news23_9_02.pdf (accessed 6 September 2004).

21. Refugees International, 'The Global Response to Internal Displacement: Time to Close the Accountability Gap', Refugee International website, http://www.refugeesinternational.org/content/article/detail/936/ (accessed 9 April 2005).

22. World Health Organization, *World Health Report 2004: Changing History* (Geneva: World Health Organization, 2004). The WHO gender breakdown estimates are based on a relatively small sample of country data and should be taken as indicative of the small share of female war deaths rather than an exact figure.

23. The UN and the World Bank use the term 'gender-based violence', which includes violence against males. Most of the literature, however, is about violence against women.

24. Shana Swiss and Joan E. Giller, 'Rape as a Crime of War. A Medical Perspective', *Journal of the American Medical Association* 270, 5 (August 1993): 612–615.

25. Anthony Beevor, *The Fall of Berlin 1945* (New York: Penguin Books, 2002).

26. Gendercide Watch, 'Case Study: Genocide in Bangladesh, 1971', Gendercide Watch website, www.gendercide.org/case_bangladesh.html (accessed 8 March 2005).

27. Elisabeth Rehn and Ellen Johnson Sirleaf, *Women, War, and Peace* (New York: UN Development Fund for Women, 2002).

28. Peter Landesman, 'A Woman's Work', *New York Times Magazine,* 15 September 2002, http://www.jendajournal.com/vol2.1/landesman.pdf (accessed 25 September 2004).

29. Peter Gordon and Kate Crehan, 'Dying of Sadness: Gender, Sexual Violence and the HIV Epidemic', UN Development Programme website, http://www.undp.org/seped/publications/dyingofsadness.pdf (accessed 9 April 2005); Amnesty International UK, 'Amnesty International Launches Global Campaign to Stop Violence Against Women—A 'Cancer' and 'Human Rights Atrocity',' Amnesty International website, http://www.amnesty.org.uk/deliver/document/15231 (accessed 9 April 2005).

30. Betsy Apple and Veronika Martin, *No Safe Place: Burma's Army and the Rape of Ethnic Women* (Washington, DC: Refugees International, 2003).

31. United Nations, *Report of the International Commission of Inquiry on Darfur to the United Nations Secretary-General* (Geneva: United Nations, 2005).

32. Human Rights Watch, 'D.R. Congo: Tens of Thousands Raped, Few Prosecuted', 7 March 2005, http://www.hrw.org/english/docs/2005/03/07/congo10258.htm (accessed 8 March 2005).

33. Lynn L. Amowitz, Chen Reis, Kristina Hare Lyons, et al., 'Prevalence of War-Related Sexual Violence and Other Human Rights Abuses Among Internally Displaced Persons in Sierra Leone', *Journal of the American Medical Association* 287, 4 (23–30 January 2002): 520.

34. Ibid. The number of female IDPs in Sierra Leone was estimated at between 550,000 and 715,000.

35. UN High Commissioner for Refugees, and Save the Children UK, 'Note for implementing and operational partners by UNHCR and Save the Children UK on sexual violence and exploitation: The experience of refugee children in Guinea, Liberia, and Sierra Leone', 26 February 2002, http://www.savethechildren.org.uk/scuk_cache/scuk/cache/cmsattach/1550_unhcr-scuk%20wafrica%20report.pdf (accessed 8 March 2005).

36. United Nations, 'Investigation by the Office of Internal Oversight Services into Allegations of Sexual Exploitation and Abuse in the United Nations Organization Mission in the Democratic Republic of the Congo', 5 January 2005, http://www.monuc.org/downloads/0520055E.pdf (accessed 17 January 2005).
37. See Lynn L. Amowitz, Chen Reis, Kristina Hare Lyons, et al., 'Prevalence of War-Related Sexual Violence' for a discussion of the reasons that Sierra Leone rape victims did not report the crimes against them.
38. Human Rights Watch, 'Human Rights Watch Applauds Rwanda Rape Verdict', 2 September 1998, www.hrw.org/press98/sept/rrape902.htm (accessed 8 March 2005).
39. Elizabeth Wood, 'Sexual Violence During War: Explaining Variation', paper presented at the Order, Conflict and Violence Conference, Yale University, New Haven, CT, 30 April–1 May 2004.
40. Thomas Plümper and Eric Neumayer, 'The Unequal Burden of War: The Effect of Armed Conflict on the Gender Gap in Life Expectancy', Department of Political Science, University of Konstanz and London School of Economics, 2005.
41. Amnesty International, 'Sudan, Darfur: Rape as a Weapon of War: Sexual Violence and Its Consequences', 19 July 2004, http://web.amnesty.org/library/index/engafr540762004 (accessed 8 March 2005).
42. Peter Landesman, 'A Woman's Work', *New York Times Magazine,* 15 September 2002.
43. Human Rights Watch, *Federal Republic of Yugoslavia—Kosovo: Rape as a Weapon of 'Ethnic Cleansing'* (New York: Human Rights Watch, 2000).
44. Paul B. Spiegel and Peter Salama, 'War and Mortality in Kosovo, 1998–99: An Epidemiological Testimony', *Lancet* 355 (24 June 2000): 2204–2209.
45. World Health Organization, *World Health Report 2004.* WHO claims that there were 155,000 male direct deaths in wars in 2002, but only 17,000 female direct deaths. The ratio for 2001 is similar. It should be noted that the WHO estimates of male/female death ratios are based on a relatively small sample of countries and should be viewed with caution.
46. Paul B. Spiegel and Peter Salama, 'War and Mortality in Kosovo, 1998–99: An Epidemiological Testimony'.
47. Beth Osborne Daponte, 'A Case Study in Estimating Casualties from War and Its Aftermath: The 1991 Persian Gulf War', International Physicians for the Prevention of Nuclear War website, http://www.ippnw.org/MGS/PSRQV3N2Daponte.html (accessed 28 April 2005).
48. Iraq Body Count, 'Named and Identified Victims of the War in Iraq', September 2004, http://www.iraqbodycount.net/names.htm (accessed 2 May 2005). The study found that 2192 of the victims were male and just 630 were female.
49. Amnesty International, *Lives Blown Apart: Crimes Against Women in Times of Conflict* (London: Amnesty International Publications, 2004).
50. UN High Commissioner for Refugees, *2003 Global Refugee Trends.* UNHCR's data cover only a small percentage of internally displaced persons (IDPs), but a new study commissioned by the Human Security Centre for the *Human Security Report 2006* shows that the ratios are very similar for IDPs.
51. Michael J. Toole, 'Displaced Persons and War' in Barry S. Levy and Victor W. Sidel, eds., *War and Public Health* (New York: Oxford University Press, 1997); Thomas Plümper and Eric Neumayer, 'The Unequal Burden of War: The Effect of Armed Conflict on the Gender Gap in Life Expectancy'. The Plümper and Neumayer paper describes a new study that focuses on the impact of war on male and female life expectancy and finds that in the long term war has a greater negative impact on female than male life expectancy.
52. These findings will be released in the *Human Security Report 2006.* All of the surveys were by Médicins Sans Frontières and most involved displaced persons.
53. Adam Jones, who has undertaken an extensive study of 'gendercide', has presented a series of case studies that support this claim. See Adam Jones, *Gendercide and Genocide* (Nashville: Vanderbilt University Press 2004).

54. Adam Jones, *Gendercide and Genocide.*
55. Gendercide is analogous to genocide except that people are targeted because of their gender rather than their religion or ethnicity.
56. Adam Jones, *Gendercide and Genocide.*
57. Cited in Tsjeard Bouta, Georg Frercks and Ian Bannon, *Gender, Conflict and Development* (Washington, DC: World Bank, 2005).
58. Rohan Gunaratna, 'Suicide Terrorism: A Global Threat', *Jane's Intelligence Review,* 20 October 2000, www.janes.com/security/international_security/news/usscole/jir001020_1_n.shtml (accessed 5 May 2005).
59. Save the Children, 'Girls Are the Greatest Casualty of War', 24 April 2005, www.savethechildren.org.uk/scuk/jsp/resources/details.jsp?id=2746&group=resources§ion=news&subsection=details (accessed 5 May 2005).
60. Cited in Tsjeard Bouta, Georg Frercks and Ian Bannon, *Gender, Conflict and Development.*
61. World Health Organization, *World Report on Violence and Health* (Geneva: World Health Organization, 2002).
62. Shana Swiss and Joan E. Giller, 'Rape as a Crime of War. A Medical Perspective'.
63. Human Rights Watch, *Shattered Lives: Sexual Violence During the Rwandan Genocide and Its Aftermath* (New York: Human Rights Watch, 1996).
64. See Article 5 of the *Statute of the International Criminal Tribunal for the Former Yugoslavia at* http://www.un.org/icty/legaldoce/index.htm and Article 3 of the *Statute of the International Criminal Tribunal for Rwanda at* http://www.ictr.org/ENGLISH/basicdocs/statute.html.
65. International Criminal Tribunal for Rwanda, 'The Prosecutor versus Jean-Paul Akayesu', CHAMBER I, Case No. ICTR-96-4-T, http://www.ictr.org/ENGLISH/cases/Akayesu/judgement/akay001.htm#8 (accessed 25 April 2005).
66. International Criminal Court, 'Rome Statute of the International Criminal Court', International Criminal Court website, http://www.icc-cpi.int/library/about/officialjournal/Rome_Statute_120704-EN.pdf (accessed 8 March 2005).
67. Graça Machel, *Impact of Armed Conflict on Children* (New York: United Nations, 1996).
68. Peter W. Singer, *Children at War* (New York: Pantheon, 2005).
69. Ibid.
70. Coalition to Stop the Use of Child Soldiers, 'Child Soldiers: Some Facts', Coalition to Stop the Use of Child Soldiers website, http://www.child-soldiers.org/childsoldiers/some-facts.html (accessed 2 March 2005).
71. Coalition to Stop the Use of Child Soldiers, *Child Soldiers Global Report 2004* (London: Coalition to Stop the Use of Child Soldiers, 2004), 51, http://www.child-soldiers.org/resources/global-reports.html (accessed 1 March 2005).
72. Ibid.
73. Ibid.
74. Ibid.
75. Peter W. Singer, *Children at War.*
76. Coalition to Stop the Use of Child Soldiers, *Child Soldiers Global Report 2004.*
77. Ibid.
78. Martin Plaut, 'Profile: Uganda's LRA Rebels', *BBC News,* 6 February 2004, http://news.bbc.co.uk/1/hi/world/africa/3462901.stm (accessed 3 March 2005).
79. International Crisis Group, 'Northern Uganda: Understanding and Solving the Conflict', International Crisis Group website, http://www.crisisweb.org//library/documents/africa/central_africa/077_uganda_conflict.pdf (accessed 3 March 2005).
80. Peter W. Singer, *Children at War.*

81. Coalition to Stop the Use of Child Soldiers, *Child Soldiers Global Report 2004.*
82. Peter W. Singer, *Children at War.*
83. Ibid.
84. Ibid.
85. Ibid.
86. Ibid.
87. Coalition to Stop the Use of Child Soldiers, *Child Soldiers Global Report 2004.*
88. International Labour Organization, 'Wounded Childhood: The Use of Children in Armed Conflict in Central Africa', April 2003, http://www.ilo.org/public/english/standards/ipec/publ/childsoldiers/woundedchild.htm (accessed 25 May 2005).
89. Amnesty International, 'Child Soldiers: A Global Issue', Amnesty International website, http://web.amnesty.org/pages/childsoldiers-background-eng (accessed 25 May 2005).
90. BBC World Service, 'Children of Conflict: Child Soldiers', BBC World Service website, http://www.bbc.co.uk/worldservice/people/features/childrensrights/childrenofconflict/soldier.shtml (accessed 19 May 2005).
91. Coalition to Stop the Use of Child Soldiers, *Child Soldiers Global Report 2004.*

Andrew Testa / Panos Pictures

PART IV

COUNTING THE INDIRECT COSTS OF WAR

Part IV examines the impact of armed conflict on society. Battle-death counts are the commonly used indicators of the severity of conflicts. But while important, they measure only a small part of the real human cost of war.

PART IV

COUNTING THE INDIRECT COSTS OF WAR

Leo Erken / Panos Pictures

Introduction

The death toll from combat is an important, but incomplete, measure of the true costs of armed conflict. Warfare destroys infrastuctures, disrupts trade, causes capital flight and triggers economic crises. War-related diseases kill and disable far more people than bombs and bullets.

Battle-death numbers, as noted previously, are an inadequate measure of the total costs of war. In most wars far more people die from war-related disease and malnutrition than from combat.

Some idea of just how great the difference between total war deaths and battle-deaths can be is found in a recent study by Bethany Lacina and Nils Petter Gleditsch, which is briefly reviewed in the first section of Part IV.

The authors compare estimates of 'total war deaths' in nine major sub-Saharan African wars with their own count of battle-deaths in the same wars. The total war death estimates were drawn from a diverse variety of sources. They include battle-deaths, but also the far greater number of 'indirect' or 'excess' deaths from war-exacerbated disease and malnutrition.

Case study evidence suggests that the key determinants of excess deaths are the intensity and scope of political violence, the numbers of people displaced and the level of development—particularly with respect to health services. Poor countries, where most wars take place, are the worst affected.

Three ways of estimating the wider costs of war are examined in the sections that follow. First is a broad measure of the 'societal impact of war' developed by Monty G. Marshall. This measure uses a 10-interval scale to rank the severity of the societal impact of warfare in each country experiencing armed conflict. The societal impact trend data—like the armed conflict data—show a dramatic drop following the end of the Cold War.

A second approach uses epidemiological surveys to determine numbers of direct and indirect deaths in war-affected countries. The International Rescue Committee carried out a series of epidemiological surveys in the Democratic Republic of the Congo (DRC) between 1999 and 2002. The surveys estimated that some 3.3 million people died as a consequence of the civil war.

A third approach to estimating war-related indirect death rates has been pioneered by Yale University's Bruce Russett and colleagues. The Yale team used two datasets. The first was of battle-deaths in some 51 civil wars that took place between 1991 and 1997. The second was the

World Health Organization's 1999 dataset on mortality and disability rates from various causes—from disease to traffic accidents.

Controlling for other social and economic influences, the team sought to determine the association between the direct civil war fatalities from 1991 to 1997 and the death and disability rates reported by WHO in 1999.

The measure of the indirect impact of war wasn't simply the number of deaths, but rather the number of *healthy* years of life lost as a consequence of death, disease or other harmful conditions that develop as a consequence of war.

Using WHO data for 1999, the researchers found that for each civil war battle-death between 1991 and 1997 there were almost four additional years of healthy life lost in 1999.

As indicated in the earlier discussion of WHO's 'direct' war death data, there are many uncertainties associated with the organisation's mortality data. The measurement process is, in Professor Russett's words, an exercise 'subject to considerable approximation and speculation'.[1]

In the final section we examine the much-discussed relationship between security and HIV/AIDS, which Professor Russett's research found headed the list of diseases that are exacerbated by war.

The growing literature that deals with the AIDS-war nexus makes two important claims. First, that war is a major driver of HIV infections, and second, that the AIDS pandemic increases the risk of armed conflict by reducing state capacity.

However, the relationship is more complex than much of the literature suggests and challenges some of the assumptions of the new conventional wisdom on the AIDS-war nexus. Some long-duration wars are associated with very low levels of HIV infection, while some countries where HIV/AIDS is most prevalent are among the least prone to civil war.

Although the *Human Security Report 2005* offers one of the most comprehensive surveys of global political violence ever published, we are unable to do more than speculate about the true human costs of warfare. We know that indirect deaths in most wars greatly outnumber battle-deaths, but that is all.

Because the indirect human costs of war remain largely hidden and are under-researched and too often ignored, they will be a central theme of the *Human Security Report 2006.*

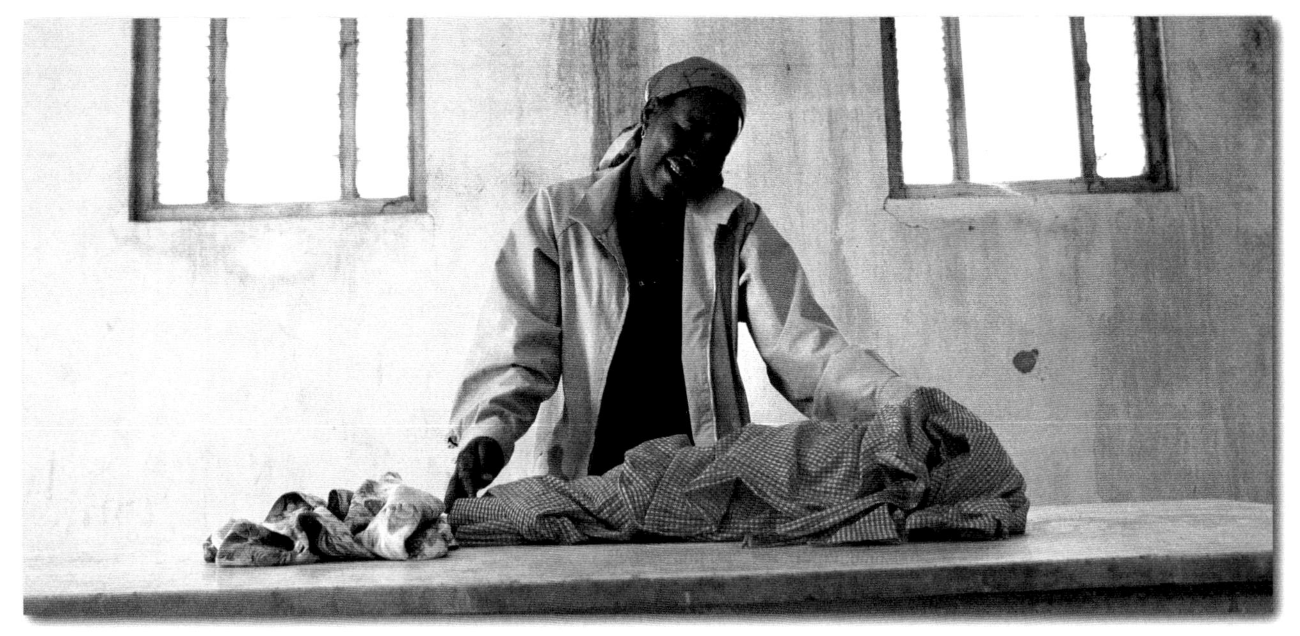

J.B. Russell / Panos Pictures

Beyond battle-deaths

Comparisons of battle-deaths and total war death tolls reveal that the latter often exceed the former by a huge margin. To determine the societal impact of armed conflict we need to look at a range of indicators.

Thus far this report has analysed battle-deaths—a relatively simple and straightforward measure. But as Figure 4.1 indicates, battle-deaths represent only a small fraction of the total number of people who die as a consequence of war.

Figure 4.1 presents some findings of a study by Bethany Lacina and Nils Petter Gleditsch, who compare battle-death totals with estimates of total war deaths in nine major conflicts in sub-Saharan Africa since the end of World War II.[2] The differences are sometimes huge—in Ethiopia, the extreme case, the number of battle-deaths was less than 2% of the total war death toll.

The 'total war death' figures include both battle-deaths and 'indirect' or 'excess' deaths. These figures come from a variety of sources—scholars, NGOs and journalists. Few can be considered reliable. They should be viewed as speculative 'guesstimates' rather than accurate measures. However, there is no doubt that far more people die from the indirect effects of political violence than are killed in battle.

The societal impact of war

Recognising the limitations of death tolls as indicators of the total cost of warfare, Monty G. Marshall of the University of Maryland developed a more inclusive yardstick. His 'societal impact of war' measure embraces not just war deaths but population dislocations, damage to 'societal networks', environmental and infrastructure damage, resource diversion and 'diminished quality of life'.

> The 'societal impact of war' measure embraces not just war deaths but population dislocations and damage to 'societal networks' as well.

Examining 291 cases of armed conflict from 1946 to 2004, the Maryland researchers scored each country in conflict on a scale of 1 to 10, with 1 indicating very low war costs, and 10 indicating total destruction.

The difference between each level on the scale is the same; two Level 4 conflicts, for example, will have the same

Figure 4.1 Battle-deaths versus total war deaths in selected sub-Saharan African conflicts

Country	Years	Estimates of total war deaths	Battle-deaths	Battle-deaths as a percentage of total war deaths
Sudan (Anya Nya rebellion)	1963–73	250,000–750,000	20,000	3–8%
Nigeria (Biafra rebellion)	1967–70	500,000–2 million	75,000	4–15%
Angola	1975–2002	1.5 million	160,475	11%
Ethiopia (not inc. Eritrean insurgency)	1976–91	1–2 million	16,000	<2%
Mozambique	1976–92	500,000–1 million	145,400	15–29%
Somalia	1981–96	250,000–350,000 (to mid-1990s)	66,750	19–27%
Sudan	1983–2002	2 million	55,000	3%
Liberia	1989–96	150,000–200,000	23,500	12–16%
Democratic Republic of the Congo	1998–2001	2.5 million	145,000	6%

Source: Lacina and Gleditsch, 2004[4]

The indirect impact of war in sub-Saharan Africa is revealed by the comparison of battle-deaths with estimates of war deaths from all causes—primarily disease and malnutrition.

societal impact as one Level 8 conflict or four Level 2 conflicts.[3] Because the difference between each consecutive level of conflict is assumed to have equal weight, it is possible to sum the impact-of-war scores for all countries to arrive at the annual global totals shown in Figure 4.2.

The trend data in Figure 4.2 reveal that since the end of the Cold War the societal costs of armed conflict have declined more rapidly than the number of armed conflicts, or battle-deaths per conflict.

This has important and encouraging implications for post-conflict recovery. All things being equal, the lower the societal costs of warfare, the greater the prospects for swift and successful recovery once a conflict ends.

Figure 4.2 The falling cost of armed conflict

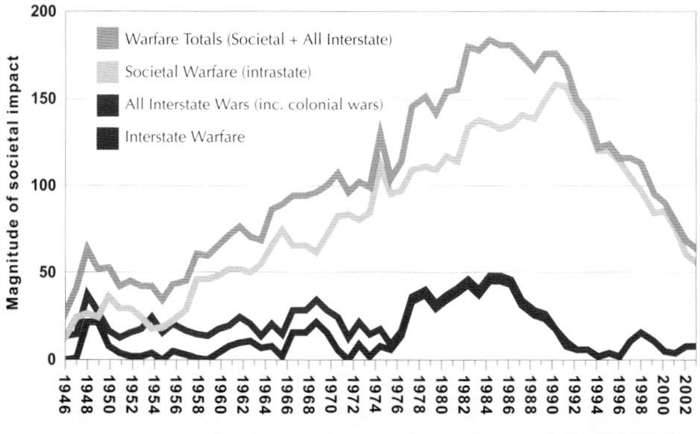

Source: Peace and Conflict 2005[5]

The global trend in the cost of conflict follows a similar pattern to the conflict numbers: several decades of increase then a sharp decline.

Eric Miller / Panos Pictures

Measuring the hidden costs of armed conflict

The greatest human costs of war are the 'indirect' deaths caused by disease and the lack of access to food, clean water and health care services. A recent study uses WHO mortality and morbidity data to estimate the impact of war on population health.

According to a recent study of battle-deaths around the world, some 134,000 people died as a direct and immediate consequence of armed conflicts in 1999.[6] These casualties are only the tip of the iceberg. Long after the shooting stops, wars continue to kill people indirectly.

Wars destroy property, disrupt economic activity, divert resources from health care and raise crime rates after the fighting has ended. Crowded into camps, susceptible refugees fall ill from infectious diseases and contribute to the further spread of these diseases.

Because many of these indirect effects may take years to manifest and are difficult to distinguish from the effects of diseases and conditions not attributable to war, they are often ignored in favour of immediate body counts. But disregarding indirect mortality and morbidity grossly underestimates both the human costs of war and the level of expenditure and effort needed to mitigate post-conflict suffering.

By using WHO data it is possible to estimate the long-term and indirect effects of wars, while holding constant other influences known to affect health outcomes. These include per capita income and health spending, type of political system, inequality of income distribution, urbanisation and women's education.

In a recent study, Hazem Ghobarah, Paul Huth and Bruce Russett considered 1999 data from selected formerly wartorn countries and their neighbours. They concluded that nearly twice as many years of healthy life were lost to indirectly caused death and disability as were lost from direct combat.[7]

Why does the misery last so long?

Wars increase exposure to conditions that, in turn, increase the risk of disease, injury and death. Prolonged and bloody civil wars usually displace large populations—either internally or across borders.

The Rwandan civil war, for example, generated 1.4 million internally displaced persons and sent some 1.5 million refugees fleeing into neighbouring Zaire (now known as the Democratic Republic of the Congo), Tanzania and Burundi.

Unable or unwilling to return home, refugees often stay in crowded makeshift camps for years. Bad food, contaminated water, poor sanitation and inadequate shelter can combine to transform camps into vectors for infectious disease—measles, respiratory disease and acute diarrhoea—while malnutrition and stress compromise people's immune systems. Diseases rampant in refugee camps easily spread to wider populations. Mortality rates among newly arrived refugees from countries ravaged by civil wars can be 5 to 12 times higher than normal.[8]

Prevention and treatment programs, already weakened by the wartime destruction of health care infrastructure, simply cannot cope with new threats posed by mass population displacements. In Africa, efforts to eradicate Guinea worm, river blindness and polio, successful in most countries, have been severely disrupted in states experiencing intense civil wars. Both soldiers and refugees are implicated in the spread of HIV/AIDS in Africa.

As well, murders, suicides and even accidental deaths often rise in the aftermath of civil war.[9] The widespread availability of small arms in most post-conflict situations makes violence difficult to control.

Civil wars typically have a severe short-term (approximately five-year) negative impact on economic growth following the end of hostilities.[10] Poor economic performance reduces tax revenues needed to finance public health care, while lower incomes mean people are less able to access the private health care sector. Civil wars also deplete the human and fixed capital of the health care system. Heavy fighting often destroys clinics, hospitals and laboratories, as well as water treatment and electrical systems.

> Mortality rates among newly arrived refugees from countries ravaged by civil wars can be 5 to 12 times higher than normal.

Even when funds are available, rebuilding health infrastructure takes a long time. Severe civil wars may also induce the flight of highly trained medical professionals, who may not return or be replaced until long after the war ends. Authorities are faced with many daunting challenges, including:

- Rebuilding infrastructure and repairing the environment.
- Reforming and rebuilding army and police forces, judicial systems and administrative capacity.
- Responding to continuing military and security threats. (Security threats may derive from domestic insurgent groups or from a powerful military force built up by a neighbouring state to fight its own civil war.)[11]

To meet these post-war demands, decision-makers must choose between competing priorities—with health care only one among many.

Measuring indirect health effects

WHO considers overall health achievement in any country by using the Health-Adjusted Life Expectancy index, which measures an individual's normal healthy life expectancy at birth. From this figure, WHO subtracts the number of years of healthy life an individual in a particular country loses through death, or through living with a major disability caused by either disease or injury.

This measure of lost years of healthy and productive life varies greatly by region and income level. In rich countries, most disabilities are associated with chronic conditions of old age—and, at that point, relatively short life expectancies.

By contrast, in poor tropical countries, infant mortality is much higher and more health problems arise from the burden of infectious diseases such as malaria and schistosomiasis. These costs are most often borne by children and young adults who may live a long time, but do so with seriously impaired health and quality of life.

Another useful indicator employed by WHO is the Disability-Adjusted Life Year or DALY, which measures the number of potentially healthy years of life lost to death and disability by gender and by age group. DALYs are also broken down according to 23 major disease categories and conditions.[12] A statistical model can then identify the 'normal' levels of death and disability from each disease in each country. This provides a baseline for measuring the 'excess' deaths and cases of disability caused by war, that is, those that would not have occurred had there been no war.

Thus, the WHO data can be used to determine whether war increases the burden of disease after the fighting has stopped. The data can also show how disease and other conditions arising from war affect a population differently according to age and gender.

Using the DALY measure

The following analysis focuses on civil wars. Not only are these conflicts 20 times more common than interstate wars, they are often far more deadly[13] in both their direct and indirect effects.

Following customary practice among conflict researchers, civil wars are defined here as armed conflicts challenging the sovereignty of an internationally recognised state, occurring within that state's boundary, and resulting in 1000 or more fatalities in at least one year.

The analysis covers civil wars during the years from 1991 to 1997 and uses immediate battle-related deaths as its key indicator of the intensity of the conflict in question.[14] (There are no reliable data on injuries for all countries.) To determine the intensity of civil war, war deaths per 100 people are measured in the country in question. For the 51 countries that experienced civil war during the period, mortality rates ranged from 0.001 to 9.420.

For most infectious diseases the time lag is usually short (less than five years), while the effects of damage to the health care system typically last five to ten years.

To determine the indirect effect of civil wars, war deaths between 1991 and 1997 are examined against DALY rates for 1999. It is assumed that the effects are not instantaneous, and the time lag used here is an approximation.

For most infectious diseases—the principal cause of indirect civil war deaths—the time lag is usually short (less than five years), while the effects of damage to infrastructure and the health care system typically last five to ten years. The delay preceding clinical manifestation of HIV/AIDS and many cancers can be even longer. In war zones in the developing world, borders are frequently porous and fighters can cross at will into neighbouring countries, often

Figure 4.3 The long-term impacts of civil wars by disease/condition

Disease/condition	Gender and age group affected
HIV/AIDS	Both genders about equal, and all age groups; greatest impact on children 0–4 years and men and women 15–59 years
Malaria	Both genders and all age groups; greatest impact on children 0–4 years
Tuberculosis, respiratory and other infections	Both genders, all age groups, but children 0–4 years particularly affected
Transportation accidents	Both genders, 15–59 years
Homicide	Girls, women and older boys and young men
Cervical cancer, maternal conditions	Older girls and women

Source: Bruce Russett, 2004

The indirect impacts of wars vary according to the age and gender of citizens.

spreading disease and causing disruption, death and injury. But the most significant health impact on border states comes from the floods of refugees seeking cross-border sanctuary from the fighting at home.

The effect of a civil war in a neighbouring country can be measured by the rate of immediate war deaths in that neighbouring country, adjusted for a measure of the border's permeability—the more porous the border, the easier it is for refugees to cross it.[15] If more than one contiguous state experiences civil war, their measures are added accordingly. The maximum value is for Zaire (now known as the Democratic Republic of the Congo), which borders seven countries that experienced civil war in this period and was affected by major wars in four of these countries—Rwanda, Angola, Sudan and Burundi.

These effects were identified by statistical (multiple regression) analysis of data from 165 countries during the late 1990s. The analysis holds constant the effects of several influences known to affect a country's average level of overall health. These include public and private sector health spending, educational levels (especially of women), rapid urbanisation and inequality of income. The last reduces average health levels by devoting more resources to a minority of wealthy households and substantially less to the poor majority.

By controlling for these social and economic influences, we can then ask what the additional effect of direct and immediate civil war fatalities in previous years is, and how these diminish healthy life expectancy below what would be expected in the absence of a war. The reduction in healthy life expectancy comes from diseases or conditions that develop—or increase—as a consequence of the war.

The multiple and long-lasting impacts of war

Inadequate health spending and lack of female education lead to a statistically significant loss of healthy years of life in countries that aren't at war, while rapid urbanisation and income inequality significantly increase that loss. When data analysts control for the impact of these influences, we see that civil wars result in additional loss. Countries experiencing civil war earlier in the 1990s subsequently suffered a significantly increased loss of healthy life in every age and gender category—amounting to almost 3.9 years of healthy life lost to death and disability for every direct and immediate civil war death.

Between 1991 and 1997 direct and immediate war deaths totalled approximately 3.1 million. This suggests that 12 million years of healthy life were lost indirectly from those previous wars in 1999 alone. In many age groups the impact was higher for females than for males. For some countries and some population subsets, the consequences were much worse. In the extreme case of Rwanda, where there were 9.4 civil war/genocide deaths per 100 people—most of them in 1994—subsequent losses amounted to 63 DALYs per 100 boys younger than five.

The implications become clearer in the impact of wars on the incidence of specific diseases and conditions (Figure 4.3).

> The most significant health impact on border states comes from refugees seeking cross-border sanctuary from the fighting at home.

Topping the list of diseases magnified by war is HIV/AIDS, hitting both genders hard in all age groups. The most devastating losses are concentrated in economically productive age groups (especially men aged 15 to 44, where the loss rate is more than two DALYs per 100 males) and on very young children (more than one DALY per 100 children). And this is the impact of just one disease out of many—the misery deepens with the accumulated losses wrought by other diseases and by an increase in injuries.

The next most damaging disease is malaria, which also affects all age and gender groups. Controlling for other factors, however, the greatest impact from malaria is reserved for the very young (1.75 years of healthy life lost per 100 boys younger than five). Three other major disease groups showing significant increases in the wake of civil wars are tuberculosis, acute respiratory infections and diarrhoeal infections—again, for both genders and most ages.

But infectious diseases are not the only killers. Included among the 23 categories of disease and other health-threatening conditions are 'transportation accidents', 'other unintentional injuries', 'homicides' and 'suicides'. Among young and middle-aged adults, a higher rate of transportation accidents may in part reflect the deterioration of roads and vehicles but is also consistent with greater stress and the breakdown of law and order. A more obvious indicator of breakdown in the social order is the increase in homicides—the victims being primarily women and younger men. Increases in other unintentional injuries within the same groups may also derive from stress and include unreported suicides.

Reports of elevated cervical cancer rates may seem surprising, given that cervical cancer usually develops too slowly to be seen in the fairly short time lag used in this analysis, but there are two possible connections to civil wars. First, the finding is consistent with the expectation of a breakdown in social norms—in this case, norms against forced sexual relations. Second, infection with some strains of the human papilloma virus (HPV) plays an important role in the development of cervical cancer,[16] and civil wars increase the incidence of many infectious diseases. In addition, in traditional societies, other sexually transmitted diseases may be recorded as cervical cancer.

Other threats to women's health in post-conflict situations include increased maternal mortality and morbidity—although some data may merely reflect the misreporting of sexually transmitted diseases.

Countries bordering on those that have been afflicted by civil war also experience rises in disease rates and other war-related health problems caused by military, refugee and other human traffic across borders during wartime. Once again, it is HIV/AIDS that exerts the greatest impact, with those most susceptible being young and middle-aged adults. Very young children make up the other major category of HIV/AIDS victims.

> Civil wars, in one's own country or a neighbouring country, produce damage to health and health care systems that extends well beyond the period of active warfare.

Malaria, tuberculosis, and respiratory or other infections are responsible for the other big post-war jumps in disease. Homicides of girls and younger women also increase sharply. Liver cancer increases in many age and gender groups, which probably represents the results of infectious hepatitis.

In sum, civil wars, in either one's own country or a neighbouring country, produce long-term damage to health and to health care systems that extends well beyond the period of active warfare. Women and children are most affected by these delayed war-induced negative health impacts.

Recall that some 12 million DALYs were lost in 1999 as a consequence of the delayed effects of the civil wars that took place between 1991 and 1997. If another 25% is added to take into account the estimated impact of these wars on neighbouring countries, the total number of DALYs lost becomes 15 million. These losses include only those incurred during a single year of a post-war process that lasts many years.

WAR AND DISEASE IN THE DEMOCRATIC REPUBLIC OF THE CONGO

Between August 1998 and November 2002, an estimated 3.3 million people died in the Democratic Republic of the Congo (DRC) as a consequence of civil war. The overwhelming majority of deaths did not result from violence, but from malnutrition and diseases associated with the war.

The shocking death toll in the Democratic Republic of the Congo made headlines only because researchers from the International Rescue Committee (IRC) had carried out a series of health surveys in the DRC during the war—and made major efforts to communicate their findings through the media. The 23 epidemiological surveys recorded crude mortality rates in rural areas of the DRC, and the causes of death.[17] Over the three years in which the surveys were carried out (1999–2002), the average crude mortality rate was 2.5 to 3.7 times the estimated pre-war rate of 1.5 deaths per 1000 per month. Knowing these ratios enabled the IRC researchers to estimate the total number of conflict-induced 'excess' deaths—that is, those that exceed the normal peacetime death rate. Of the 2223 civilian deaths reported from the surveys, only 8% resulted from violence. Infectious diseases caused most of the fatalities, with anemia and malnutrition being the most common other causes.

The surveys also revealed that the areas with the greatest rates of violence tended to experience the highest numbers of deaths from non-violent causes. This correlation is highlighted in the death rate in Kalonge, an administrative area within Sud-Kivu province. In November 1999, Rwandan government troops and their allies, the Congolese Rally for Democracy, withdrew from Kalonge, which led to an immediate takeover by rebels, including both Congolese Mayi-Mayi insurgents and former Rwandan soldiers who had fled to the DRC following the 1994 genocide. Killings of civilians were widespread and interviewees reported that virtually the entire population of 62,000 fled the area over a two-month period. The survey data showed that the rebel takeover was associated with a sixfold increase in the murder rate and a fourfold increase in the death rate from malaria and other febrile diseases. Lacking shelter, adequate clothing and access to health services, those who fled were highly susceptible to infectious diseases.

Two of the regions surveyed in 2001[18] were surveyed again in 2002[19] after a ceasefire agreement that sharply reduced the violence. Similar questions were asked in both surveys. In both districts violence-specific and crude mortality rates were initially exceptionally high, but following the troop withdrawals in 2002 the rate of violent death decreased by 96%, while the rate of excess deaths from other causes decreased by only 67%.[20]

The IRC conducted a repeat survey in the fall of 2004,[21] two years after the ceasefire and withdrawal of foreign troops, and found that the crude mortality rate was 2.3 per 1000 per month in the war-torn eastern provinces. This translates to approximately 31,000 deaths per month above the baseline rate that existed prior to the Rwandan and Ugandan invasion.

These surveys demonstrate how prolonged conflict can make a population extremely susceptible to death from diseases endemic in the population before the violence began. The link between violent death and death from infectious disease was strong, whether comparing the same populations at different times or different populations at the same time.

The interplay between violence and infectious diseases is complex and differs from year to year and country to country. But the evidence clearly suggests that the greater the wartime violence and the poorer and more vulnerable a country, the greater the number of excess deaths due to non-violent causes. The IRC's analysis of the first 11 studies undertaken when the fighting was at its peak between 1999 and 2001 found that for every violent civilian death there were six excess non-violent civilian deaths.

The IRC's surveys also clearly demonstrate that attempting to assess the impact of war by counting only those who die as a direct result of violence grossly underestimates the real human costs of conflict—particularly in poor countries.

Pep Bonet / Panos Pictures

HIV/AIDS and conflict

In both times of conflict and times of peace, the spread of HIV/AIDS depends on a complex range of factors. In some cases war contributes to the spread of the disease, in others it is associated with very low levels of infection. Claims that high rates of HIV/AIDS increase the risk of state failure appear to have little evidence to support them.

War and disease have been partners throughout history. The disruption of social structures, the mass movement of armies and refugees, and restricted access to food and clean water have always created conditions in which diseases flourish, often causing greater casualties than military action. In ancient Greece, Athens was ravaged by plague during its conflict with Sparta. In the 16th century Americas, severe outbreaks of smallpox, measles and typhus among Aboriginal peoples helped Europeans in their violent colonisation of the New World. In 1994 cholera and dysentery took the lives of almost 50,000 refugees in the first month after they fled from the Rwandan genocide.[22] Between 1998 and 2004, 3.8 million people are estimated to have died as the result of conflict in the Democratic Republic of the Congo; the vast majority were killed by disease, not violence.[23]

Rates of sexually transmitted infections (STIs) also rise in wartime. Men and women become more sexually active as uncertainty over the future reduces inhibitions among soldiers[24] and civilians; more people are encouraged by poverty or opportunism to sell sex; the incidence of rape often rises. Syphilis was first identified in the wake of the French invasion of Italy in 1494. In the 1960s, STI rates among US soldiers in Vietnam were nine times higher than among soldiers in the United States.[25]

Conflict can also lead to increased HIV infection. The virus probably first affected humans in central Africa in the 1930s in communities where patterns of sexual activity did not allow it to spread widely; in the late 1970s the many rapes committed during the Ugandan civil war and its spillover into Tanzania may have triggered the HIV epidemic in that part of the world.[26] HIV incidence in rural Rwanda, where approximately 95% of the population live, was considerably higher following the 1994 genocide—11% in 1997 compared to 1% prewar.[27] And reports from Sudan in 2004 showed HIV incidence rising to 21% in the conflict-ridden south, compared with 2.6% in the general adult population.[28]

HOW HIV SPREADS

HIV can be spread in many ways—from unprotected sex to drug injections. There is no cure for HIV/AIDS.

Human immunodeficiency virus (HIV) infection spreads primarily through sexual intercourse. It can also be transmitted through infected equipment used in recreational drug injection, through transfusion of infected blood products, through use of contaminated medical and other skin-piercing instruments (e.g., tattooing needles) and from infected mothers to their newborn children via the placenta and breast milk.

Although some soldiers, particularly in insurgent forces, inject drugs, sexual transmission alone is believed to play a major role in spreading HIV in times of conflict. Transmission can be prevented through consistent use of condoms.

Infection with HIV leads to a gradual breakdown of the immune system. The body becomes vulnerable to 'opportunistic' infections that it could normally overcome, such as pneumonia, fungal infections and long-term diarrhoea.

AIDS (acquired immune deficiency syndrome) is usually defined as the presence of one or more such infections and confirmation of HIV infection. Although AIDS is the most commonly used term, it only refers to the advanced stage of the disease.

Untreated, AIDS at present is invariably fatal. Antiretroviral therapy can keep HIV infection under control,but it is not widely available or affordable, and cannot cure the disease or prevent it from being transmitted to other people.

In both conflict and peacetime the extent to which HIV spreads depends on a combination of factors, including the following:

- Initial infection rates.
- Patterns of sexual behaviour (what percentage of the population changes partners and how often).
- The frequency of rape.
- Infectivity (individuals are more likely to pass the virus to others when they themselves have been recently infected).
- The presence or absence of other sexually transmitted infections which facilitate the transmission of HIV.
- The age of female partners (women under 25 are more vulnerable).
- The presence or absence of economic or social pressure on women to be sexually active, usually without the right to ensure condom use.
- The extent to which condoms are available, affordable and socio-culturally acceptable.
- Whether the male partner is circumcised (male circumcision reduces vulnerability) and whether, how often and with whom condoms are used.

The nature of a conflict also significantly influences the likelihood of an epidemic. Short wars that depend on 'distance' tactics such as aerial bombardment are less likely to spread HIV/AIDS than conflicts that lead to long-term fighting on the ground, to mass movements of soldiers and civilians, and to opportunities for soldiers and others to find new sexual partners.

The physical trauma of rape considerably heightens the risk of transmitting HIV, to the rapist as well as to the victim. Rape by individual soldiers acting alone and as a military tactic has always been a feature of warfare. The victims are usually women and girls, but rape of men and boys does occur. Reliable statistics are difficult to obtain, but estimates of mass rape in recent conflicts include 'thousands' in Sierra Leone[29] in the 1990s, at least 12,000 in Bosnia in 1992–93[30] and at least 250,000 in Rwanda.[31] Seventy percent of one group of victims in Rwanda later tested HIV-positive,[32] although it is not known how many contracted the virus during rape.

HIV infection may also rise in the aftermath of conflict. The rise in HIV incidence in Cambodia from 0% in 1990 to 2.6% by 2004 (the highest per capita incidence in Asia) has been attributed partly to the presence of peacekeepers in the early 1990s and partly to the re-emergence of sex workers after two decades of political and social repression. Peacekeepers have significant physical, moral and economic power, which frequently enables them to have sex with locals and sex workers, either consensually, in a short- or long-term relationship or through some form of coercion. That is not to argue that peacekeepers 'introduced' the virus to Cambodia or any other country—soldiers from many countries test HIV-negative before deployment and HIV-positive on return.

The nature of conflict influences the likelihood of an epidemic.

A rise in HIV infection is not inevitable in warfare. Where HIV incidence is minimal at the start of a conflict, as in several of the countries listed in Figure 4.4, rates do not rise significantly. Other factors may also reduce spread of the virus; it is believed that rates remained low during the Sierra Leone conflict because mass movement, including cross-border migration, became more difficult and impeded growth of the epidemic.[33] Similar factors may explain the relatively low rates of infection in Angola after three decades of war.[34]

HIV and the armed forces

Rates of sexually transmitted infection in the armed forces are usually higher than in the general population. Most soldiers are young men who spend long periods away from home and family and who are encouraged by peers, alcohol use and other factors to be sexually active. Military bases attract women who offer sexual services in return for money, gifts or accommodation, particularly in impoverished communities where soldiers have higher than average incomes. Where relatively few women have many soldiers as partners, infection can spread rapidly among both

Figure 4.4 Estimated HIV infection rates in the general population and the armed forces in sub-Saharan Africa

Country	HIV prevalence in 2001, 15–49 year-olds (%)	HIV prevalence in 1997–2002, armed forces personnel (%)
Angola	5.5	50 (1999)
Botswana	38.8	33 (1999)
DR Congo	4.8	50 (1999)
Lesotho	31.0	40 (1999)
Malawi	15.0	50 (1999)
Namibia	22.5	16 (1996)
South Africa	20.1	20–23 (2002)
Swaziland	33.4	48 (1997)
Zambia	21.5	60 (1998)
Zimbabwe	33.7	55 (1999)

Source: Heinecken, 2003[35]

Rates of HIV are generally higher in the armed forces than in the general population. Only Botswana and Namibia's armed forces recorded lower rates in the period studied.

groups and to their subsequent partners in both civilian and military life.

The extent of HIV infection in the world's armed forces is uncertain. Few in-depth surveys have been published, methodology is not always certain and some of the statistics regularly quoted may now be out of date. Where data are available, it is clear that soldiers in many countries have higher rates of infection than adults in the general population. The highest figures were recorded in Africa, as seen in Figure 4.4. Elsewhere, the highest figures came from Cambodia, where 7.1% of the armed forces were reported HIV-positive in 1997.[36]

The impact of widespread HIV on military preparedness can be severe. Soldiers lost through illness and death must be replaced, a process that costs time and money, particularly in the higher ranks. High turnover of personnel leads to potential disruptions in the chain of command and the loss of skills and institutional knowledge; it can also lead to increased absenteeism and reduced morale. So serious is the potential link between HIV rates and military preparedness that some militaries, such as Namibia's,[37] treat infection rates as classified information.

Since the 1990s many countries in Africa, Asia and the Americas have undertaken measures to minimise the incidence of HIV in the armed forces. These include rejecting recruits who test HIV-positive, educating soldiers and placing restrictions on their sexual behaviour (for example, making locations where sex workers are known to congregate out of bounds). A number of militaries have succeeded in maintaining or reaching low rates of infection. In 2000 only 2 in 100,000 soldiers were HIV-positive in Morocco, compared with 3 in 100,000 in the general population.[38] In Thailand, where a national campaign significantly increased the rate of condom use, HIV infection rates among new recruits fell from 12% to 3% between 1993 and 1998.[39]

Figure 4.5 HIV infection and the rise of conflict: Is there a correlation?

Country	HIV-positive (%)*	Intrastate armed conflict**	
		1990–2000	since 2000
Swaziland	38.8	no	no
Botswana	37.3	no	no
Lesotho	28.9	yes	no
Zimbabwe	24.6	no	no†
South Africa	21.5	yes	no
Namibia	21.3	yes	no
Zambia	16.5	no	no
Malawi	14.2	no	no
CAR	13.5	yes	yes
Mozambique	12.2	yes	no

Source: Martin Foreman, 2005

Of the 10 countries most affected by HIV only 5—the Central African Republic, Lesotho, Mozambique, Namibia and South Africa—have experienced armed conflict since 1990. In recent years only one country, the Central African Republic, has experienced armed conflict. In all cases the level of conflict has been relatively low.

* The estimated percentage of 15–49-year-olds living with HIV at the end of 2003.[40]
** The definition of armed conflict in this table is broader than that of the Uppsala/PRIO conflict database and includes non-state as well as state-based conflict.
† Since 2000 Zimbabwe has suffered from political violence and civil unrest but not at sufficiently high levels to be categorised as armed conflict.

Figure 4.6 HIV infection and fatalities from political violence: Is there a correlation?

Country/region	Battle-related deaths per 100,000 in 2003*	HIV-positive (%)**
Liberia	59.4	5.9
Iraq	35.1	<0.1
Burundi	16.2	6.5
Sudan	8.5	2.3
Uganda	6.5	4.1
Israel and the Palestinian Territories	5.8	Israel: 0.1; Palestine: n/a, believed very low
Nepal	4.4	0.5
DRC	4.2	4.2
Somalia	3.9	1.0–2.0 (1997–1999)
Colombia	1.6	0.7

Source: Martin Foreman, 2005[43]

In the 10 countries most affected by political violence, no more than 1 in 15 adults has contracted HIV, and in 4 countries fewer than 1 in a 100 adults is HIV-positive.

*From the Uppsala/Human Security Centre dataset 2005.

**The estimated percentage of 15–49-year-olds living with HIV at the end of 2003.

Other militaries, however, particularly insurgent forces, have no screening or education policies, or have policies that are poorly implemented. They may also have weaker discipline and may either turn a blind eye to soldiers' sexual activity or actively encourage it with partners who may or may not consent. In such situations, the rate of infection among soldiers and their partners is likely to be high compared with that of the general adult population.

HIV as a cause of conflict?

A strong argument has been put forward that HIV may not only be a consequence of conflict, but also a cause. In this scenario, whole nations would be affected, when high rates of infection among skilled labour, management and professional classes lead to lost productivity and high replacement costs and a smaller skill base. Increasing numbers of orphans grow up uneducated and unsocialised. Poor health correlates with distrust in local government and crime, reducing social cohesion. The impact on the military leads to lack of leadership, reduced competency and failure to modernise. Weakened in both civilian and military life, the nation becomes subject to internal disorder and more vulnerable to neighbouring states with aggressive intentions. Possible outcomes include destabilisation, civil conflict, war with neighbours and collapse of the state.[41] Currently, sub-Saharan Africa is at greatest risk, but countries in Central Asia and elsewhere may face similar problems in a few years.[42]

However, the actual evidence that HIV poses a current threat to national and international security is weak. Figure 4.5 indicates that, more than 20 years into the epidemic, there is no correlation between the intensity of HIV infection and the existence of conflict.

Figure 4.6 compares deaths from political violence with HIV infection, and again no clear correlation is shown. Other conflicts that have led to high death tolls in recent years also have relatively low rates of infection, including Algeria (0.1%) and Angola (3.9%). East Timor and the Solomon Islands witnessed the collapse of government functions but also had very low rates of HIV infection.

It is possible that the epidemic is at an early stage and a clear correlation between high infection rates and destabilisation will eventually be seen. In the absence of such evidence, however, a more appropriate analysis is that HIV is only one among many factors, including poverty, hunger, environmental degradation, ethnic and/or religious tensions and political ambition, that lead to destabilisation and conflict. As yet, the impact of the virus does not appear to play a primary role.

> The links between HIV and conflict are more complex than they appear.

An alternative view is that HIV may reduce rather than enhance the likelihood of combat. External threats may diminish when countries weakened by high rates of HIV infection have neighbours facing the same problem. Civil unrest may be less likely if individuals are increasingly preoccupied by their own health and that of their families. Furthermore, the conclusion to be drawn from Uganda and other countries where the virus has hit hardest may be that communities are resilient and although weakened are not overwhelmed by the epidemic.

In many countries awareness of HIV has led to a wide range of responses, from education programs for the military and increasing provision of antiretroviral therapies to involvement of the commercial sector in prevention and care activities. Such responses are often far from ideal and are sometimes missing where they are needed most, but they help to mitigate the worst impact of the epidemic. By doing so, they weaken the potential link between HIV and conflict both within and between nations.

The links between HIV and armed conflict are therefore more complex than they at first appear. While there is evidence that under certain conditions armed conflict can accelerate HIV epidemics, some conflicts appear to reduce the rate at which the virus spreads. Furthermore, the intuitive and widely quoted view that widespread HIV infection inevitably leads to conflict and other political violence is clearly not supported by the available evidence. More nuanced hypotheses, better data and more critical analyses are needed.

PART IV

ENDNOTES

1. Hazem Ghobarah, Paul Huth and Bruce Russett, 'The Postwar Public Health Effects of Civil Conflict', *Social Science and Medicine* 59 (2004): 869–884. These results refine those in Ghobarah, Huth and Russett, 'Civil Wars Kill and Maim People—Long after the Shooting Stops', *American Political Science Review* 97, 2 (May 2003): 189–202.
2. Bethany Lacina and Nils Petter Gleditsch, *Monitoring Trends in Global Combat: A New Dataset of Battle Deaths* (Oslo: Centre for the Study of Civil War, 2004), www.prio.no/cscw/cross/battledeaths (accessed 28 January 2005).
3. Note that this methodology relies, like that of the Political Terror Scale discussed earlier, on the subjective judgments of coders regarding the severity of the phenomenon in question. It is different from the much less subjective exercise of counting battle-related deaths to decide when episodes of political violence cross a threshold and become armed conflicts.
4. Bethany Lacina and Nils Petter Gleditsch, *Monitoring Trends in Global Combat: A New Dataset of Battle Deaths*.
5. Monty G. Marshall and Ted Robert Gurr, *Peace and Conflict 2005* (College Park, MD: Center for International Development and Conflict Management, 2005), http://www.cidcm.umd.edu/inscr/PC05print.pdf (accessed 31 May 2005).
6. Bethany Lacina and Nils Petter Gleditsch, *Monitoring Trends in Global Combat: A New Dataset of Battle Deaths*. The dataset from which this figure is taken relies heavily on Uppsala data. But the battle-death totals differ slightly from the battle-related death totals in the Uppsala/Human Security Centre dataset because the concept of 'battle-deaths' is defined somewhat more broadly. Note that this figure does *not* include conflicts in which the state is not a party.
7. Hazem Ghobarah, Paul Huth and Bruce Russett, 'The Postwar Public Health Effects of Civil Conflict'.
8. Michael J. Toole, 'Displaced Persons and War', in Barry S. Levy and Victor W. Sidel, eds., *War and Public Health*, updated edition (Washington, DC: American Public Health Association, 2000).
9. Duncan Pedersen, 'Political Violence, Ethnic Conflict, and Contemporary Wars: Broad Implications for Health and Well-Being', *Social Science and Medicine* 55, 2 (2002): 175–190.
10. James Murdoch and Todd Sandler, 'Economic Growth, Civil Wars, and Spatial Spillovers', *Journal of Conflict Resolution* 46, 1 (February 2002): 91–110.
11. Paul Collier, 'On the Economic Consequences of Civil War', *Oxford Economic Papers* 51 (1999): 168–183.
12. These data, though hardly perfect, are the best that have ever been available. See C. Murray, J. Salomon, J. Mathers, et al., eds., *Summary Measures of Population Health: Concepts, Ethics, Measurement, and Applications* (Geneva: World Health Organization, 2002).
13. Mikael Eriksson, Margareta Sollenberg and Peter Wallensteen, 'Patterns of Major Armed Conflicts, 1990–2002', in *SIPRI Yearbook 2003: Armaments, Disarmament, and International Security* (Oxford: Oxford University Press, 2003).
14. Michael Doyle and Nicholas Sambanis, *Making War and Building Peace: The United Nations after the Cold War* (Princeton, NJ: Princeton University Press, 2005).
15. An estimate of the permeability of borders is provided by Harvey Starr and G. Dale Thomas, 'The "Nature" of Contiguous Borders: Ease of Interaction, Salience, and the Analysis of Crisis', *International Interactions* 28, 3 (July–September 2002): 213–235.
16. See Anna-Barbara Moscicki, Nancy Hill, Steve Shiboski et al., 'Risks for Incident Human Papillomavirus and Low-Grade Squamous Intraepithelial Lesion Development in Young Females', *Journal of the American Medical Association* 285, 23 (2001): 2995–3002.
17. International Rescue Committee, *Mortality in the Democratic Republic of Congo: Results from a Nationwide Survey* (New York: International Rescue Committee, 2003), http://intranet.theirc.org/docs/drc_mortality_iii_full.pdf (accessed 5 April 2005).
18. International Rescue Committee, *Mortality in Eastern Democratic Republic of Congo: Results from Eleven Mortality Surveys* (New York: International Rescue Committee, 2001), http://intranet.theirc.org/docs/mortII_report.pdf (accessed 13 July 2004).

19. International Rescue Committee, *Mortality in the Democratic Republic of Congo: Results from a Nationwide Survey.*
20. Ibid.
21. Burnet Institute and International Rescue Committee, *Mortality in the Democratic Republic of Congo: Results of a Nationwide Survey* (New York: International Rescue Committee, 2004).
22. Goma Epidemiology Group, 'Public Health Impact of Rwandan Refugee Crisis: What Happened in Goma, Zaire, in July 1994?' *Lancet* 345, 8946 (1995): 339–344, www.ncbi.nlm.nih.gov/entrez/query.fcgi?cmd=Retrieve&db=PubMed&list_uids=7646638&dopt=Abstract (accessed 1 June 2005).
23. Burnet Institute and International Rescue Committee, *Mortality in the Democratic Republic of Congo: Results of a Nationwide Survey.*
24. In this essay 'soldiers' refers to men or women serving in any branch of the armed forces and includes armies, navies, air forces and insurgent forces.
25. Jerome Greenberg, 'Venereal Disease in the Armed Forces', *Medical Clinics of North America* 56, 5 (1972): 1087–1100.
26. M.R. Smallman-Raynor and A.D. Cliff, 'Civil War and the Spread of AIDS in Central Africa', *Epidemiology and Infection* 107, 1 (1991): 69–80.
27. Therese McGinn, Susan J. Purdin, Sandra Krause, et al., 'Forced Migration and Transmission of HIV and Other Sexually Transmitted Infections; Policy and Programmatic Responses', HIV InSite Knowledge Base Chapter, November 2001, HIV InSite website, http://hivinsite.ucsf.edu/InSite.jsp?page=kb-08-01-08 (accessed 30 May 2005).
28. 'Sudan: HIV/AIDS swell feared when refugees return—UNFPA', United Nations Office for the Coordination of Humanitarian Affairs and Integrated Regional Information Networks, 18 October 2004, UN Office for the Coordination of Humanitarian Affairs website, http://www.reliefweb.int/rw/rwb.nsf/AllDocsByUNID/36b1063f60c7402fc1256f3100242459 (accessed 22 November 2004).
29. Human Rights Watch, '"We'll kill you if you cry": Sexual Violence in the Sierra Leone Conflict', Vol. 15, No. 1(A), January 2003, http://hrw.org/reports/2003/sierraleone/ (accessed 22 November 2004). One study looking at displaced women suggests that the number 'sexually assaulted' (which is a broader category than rape) was 94,000 to 122,000. This estimate does not include women who remained in their homes. See Lynn L. Amowitz, Chen Reis, Kristina Hare Lyons, et al., 'Prevalence of War-Related Sexual Violence and Other Human Rights Abuses Among Internally Displaced Persons in Sierra Leone', *Journal of the American Medical Association* 287, 4 (2002): 513–520.
30. United Nations, 'Final Report of the United Nations Commission of Experts Established Pursuant to Security Council Resolution 780 (1992)', S/1994/674/Add.2 (Vol. I). Other estimates are considerably higher. See, for example, Peter Gordon and Kate Crehan, 'Dying of Sadness: Gender, Sexual Violence and the HIV Epidemic', UN Development Programme website, http://www.undp.org/seped/publications/dyingofsadness.pdf (accessed 9 April 2005); Amnesty International UK, 'Amnesty International Launches Global Campaign to Stop Violence Against Women—A "Cancer" and "Human Rights Atrocity"', Amnesty International website, http://www.amnesty.org.uk/deliver/document/15231 (accessed 9 April 2005).
31. UN Economic and Social Council, 'Report on the Situation of Human Rights in Rwanda Submitted by Mr. René Degni-Segui, Special Rapporteur of the Commission on Human Rights, Under Paragraph 20 of the Resolution S-3/1 of 25 May 1994', Office of the UN High Commissioner for Human Rights website, www.unhchr.ch/Huridocda/Huridoca.nsf/0/aee2ff8ad005e2f6802566f30040a95a?Opendocument (accessed 30 May 2005).
32. This is according to a study of 1125 rape survivors undertaken by the AVEGA-AGAHOZA Association of Genocide Widows. See AVEGA-AGAHOZA Association of Genocide Widows, 'Background', AVEGA-AGAHOZA website, www.avega.org.rw/background.htm (accessed 10 June 2005).
33. Joint UN Programme on HIV/AIDS, *2004 Report on the Global AIDS Epidemic* (Geneva: Joint UN Programme on HIV/AIDS, 2004).

34. Paul B. Spiegel and Esmee de Jong, *HIV/AIDS and refugees/returnees: mission to Angola* (Luanda: UN High Commissioner for Refugees, 2003).
35. Lindy Heinecken, 'Facing a Merciless Enemy: HIV/AIDS and the South African Armed Forces', *Armed Forces & Society* 29 (Winter 2003): 281–300.
36. Asia-Pacific Military Medicine Conference XIII, 'Asia-Pacific Military Medicine Conference XIII HIV/AIDS Report', Bangkok, 12–16 May 2003, http://coe-dmha.org/Media/HIV/APMMC_AAR.pdf (accessed 10 September 2005).
37. Maggi Barnard, 'AIDS "An Intelligence Issue"', *The Namibian,* 13 February 2001, http://www.namibian.com.na/2001/February/news/01D3168B4F.html (accessed 30 May 2005).
38. S. Nejmi, A. Sekkat, M. Oualine et al., 'Preventing STI HIV/AIDS Through Extensive IEC Among the Royal Armed Forces of the Kingdom of Morocco', Abstracts of XIII International AIDS Conference, Durban, South Africa, 2000.
39. 'Condoms, Education Dramatically Reduce Spread of HIV in Thailand', *The Gazette Online, The Newspaper of the Johns Hopkins University*, 1 April 2002, www.jhu.edu/~gazette/2002/01apr02/01condom.html (accessed 30 May 2005).
40. Based on data derived from the Joint UN Programme on HIV/AIDS, 'Table of Country-Specific HIV/AIDS Estimates and Data, End 2003', *2004 Report on the Global AIDS Epidemic*.
41. Randy B. Cheek, 'Playing God with HIV: Rationing HIV Treatment in Southern Africa', *African Security Review* 10, 4 (2001).
42. Peter W. Singer, 'AIDS and International Security', *Survival* 44, 1 (Spring 2002): 145–158.
43. Based on data derived from the Joint UN Programme on HIV/AIDS, 'Table of Country-Specific HIV/AIDS Estimates and Data, End 2003', *2004 Report on the Global AIDS Epidemic*.

Sven Torfinn / Panos Pictures

PART V

WHY THE DRAMATIC DECLINE IN ARMED CONFLICT?

There has been a great deal of research on the causes of war, but very little on the causes of peace. Since the end of the colonial era there have been fewer and fewer international wars, while the last 15 years have seen a dramatic decline in civil wars. Why?

PART V

WHY THE DRAMATIC DECLINE IN ARMED CONFLICT?

Paul Smith / Panos Pictures

Introduction

The post–World War II era witnessed an extraordinary increase in the number of wars—most of them civil wars. This was followed by a steep decline after the end of the Cold War.

Part V of this report reviews some of the findings that will be presented in greater detail in the *Human Security Report 2006*. It focuses on the causes of the recent decline in global conflict, and addresses two key questions:

- How do we explain the decline in the use of force in relations *between* states since the end of the colonial era?
- What brought about the remarkable post–Cold War decline in wars *within* states?

Strangely, neither of these important trends has been the subject of much scholarly investigation. 'For every thousand pages on the causes of war,' historian Geoffrey Blainey has noted, 'there is less than one page directly on the causes of peace.'[1]

Blainey may have overstated his case, but there is no doubt that scholars have generally been more interested in explaining the drivers of war than the determinants of peace. This is particularly true with respect to the remarkable post–Cold War decline in civil wars.

In the past 30 years three remarkable changes in international politics have had a major—and mostly positive—impact on global security.

First, by the early 1980s, wars of liberation from colonial rule, which had made up between 60% and 100% of the international wars occurring in any one year from the beginning of the 1950s to the end of the 1970s, had virtually ceased.[2]

The security import of this change is as profound as it is rarely acknowledged. Between 1816 and 2002 there were some 81 wars of colonial conquest and subsequent struggles for independence from colonial rule.[3] With the demise of colonialism one of the major drivers of international conflict had simply disappeared.

By the early 1980s, wars of liberation from colonial rule had virtually ceased.

Second, the end of the Cold War removed another major cause of armed conflict from the international system. Approximately one-third of all wars in the post–World War II period had been driven wholly, or in part, by the geopolitics of the Cold War.[4]

The end of the political confrontation between East and West in the late 1980s not only removed the only real threat of war between the major powers, but also meant that Washington and Moscow stopped supporting 'proxy wars' in the developing world. Denied the external assistance that had long sustained them, many of these conflicts simply petered out, or were ended by negotiated settlements.

Third, the end of the Cold War set off an explosion of international activism directed toward stopping ongoing wars and preventing wars that had ended from starting up again. This little-analysed but critically important development appears to offer the most compelling explanation for the steep decline in warfare that started in 1992.

Part V uses a different dataset from those reviewed earlier in this report. The dataset is based on information going back nearly 200 years and deals only with wars.[5] It does not include data on the less deadly 'minor' armed conflicts that are part of the Uppsala/PRIO dataset featured in Part I of this report. Despite the differences, the post–World War II conflict trends are very similar in both datasets.

The decline of international war

A newly revised dataset tracks the number of wars since the Congress of Vienna ended the Napoleonic era in 1815. The decline of international war that began in the 1980s is associated with the end of wars of liberation from colonial rule and the end of the Cold War.

Between 1816 and 2002 there were 199 international wars (including wars of colonial conquest and liberation)[6] and 251 civil wars—one international war on average for every 1.3 civil wars over the entire period.[7]

International wars accounted for one-fifth to three-quarters of all wars being waged in the 1950s, 1960s and 1970s. As Figure 5.1 shows, the anti-colonial struggles and then the conflicts related to the Cold War came to an end,[8] the total number of international wars declined both absolutely and relatively.

From the early 1980s to the early 1990s the number of international wars declined. For the rest of the 1990s and the early years of the 21st century there have been almost no international wars. The one exception was 1999, when there were three wars—two of which, Kosovo and India-Pakistan, had relatively small death tolls.[9]

How do we explain this drop in the number of international wars? Much of the research on the causes of international peace over the past 20 years has used large datasets and statistical inference models to examine the 'correlates of war'—the economic, political and sociological factors associated with interstate war—and peace. This research points to a number of long-term global trends that are associated with reduced risks of international conflict:

- **A dramatic increase in the number of democracies.** In 1946, there were 20 democracies in the world; in 2005, there were 88.[10] Many scholars argue that

Figure 5.1 International wars, 1816–2002

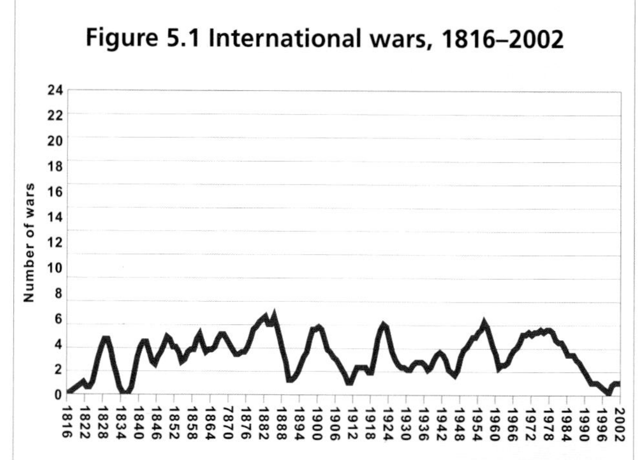

Source: Human Security Centre, 2005[11]

There is no obvious trend in the number of international wars until the end of the 1970s. But following the end of colonialism and then the Cold War, the number declined dramatically.

(The graph shows the annual number of wars expressed as a five-year moving average.)[12]

this trend has reduced the likelihood of international war because democratic states almost never fight each other.

- **An increase in economic interdependence.** Greater global economic interdependence has increased the costs of cross-border aggression while significantly reducing its benefits.[13]
- **A decline in the economic utility of war.** The most effective path to prosperity in modern economies is through increasing productivity and international trade, not through seizing land and raw materials. In addition, the existence of an open global trading regime means it is nearly always cheaper to buy resources from overseas than to use force to acquire them.
- **Growth in international institutions.** The greatly increased involvement by governments in international institutions can help reduce the incidence of conflict. Such institutions play an important direct role in building global norms that encourage the peaceful settlement of disputes. They can also benefit security indirectly by helping promote democratisation and interdependence.

Greater global economic interdependence has increased the costs of cross-border aggression while reducing its benefits.

These interrelated and mutually reinforcing trends have given rise to what is often referred to as the 'liberal peace'—a transnational security system that is credited with having created an unprecedented 60 years of peace within Western Europe, indeed between all the liberal democracies.[14]

The liberal peace thesis is challenged by many traditional strategic analysts who believe that security is achieved through credible deterrence, effective war-fighting capabilities and—especially for smaller powers—membership of alliances.[15] From this perspective the unprecedented period without war between the European powers that followed the end of World War II had more to do with mutual solidarity against a common communist threat than with democracy or economic interdependence.

Anti-violence norms are often transgressed and they are more entrenched in some regions than in others, but they play an important role in constraining behaviour.

In fact, the long period without war between the major powers since World War II is likely a function of *both* the growth of the institutions and processes stressed by the liberal peace theorists, *and* the impact of traditional 'peace through strength' deterrence policies—in particular the caution-inducing effect that nuclear weapons had on relations between East and West.

The power of ideas: A war-averse world

A quite different explanation for the decline in interstate war stresses neither the role of liberal economic and political institutions, nor military deterrence, but a gradual normative shift against the use of violence in human relationships.[16]

Among the key indicators of this general shift in attitudes, one that has been underway for several centuries, are the outlawing of human sacrifice, witch-burning, lynching, slavery, vigilantism, duelling, war crimes, crimes against humanity and genocide.

These anti-violence norms are often transgressed, of course, and they are more entrenched in some regions than others, but they play an important role in constraining behaviour. They also inform the creation of laws and institutions—which in turn can provide the monitoring and enforcement mechanisms to help encourage compliance.

Nowhere is this normative shift more evident than in changing public attitudes toward war. Prior to the

20th century, warfare was a normal part of human existence. For governments, war was simply an instrument of statecraft.

Today the forcible acquisition of territory is universally perceived as a blatant transgression of international law, and resort to force against another country is only permissible in self-defence, or with the sanction of the UN Security Council.

There has been a similar change in attitudes to colonialism. While colonial subjugation is now universally abhorred, such conquests were once accepted as a normal part of empire and were often depicted as morally justified, in that they brought the benefits of civilisation to the colonised.

Ideologies that glorify violence and see war as a noble and virtuous endeavour are today notable mostly by their absence. Insofar as similar ideologies still exist they are mainly found not in governments but in small, fanatical, terrorist organisations, such as those associated with al-Qaeda. In addition, the sort of hyper-nationalism that drove Nazi German and Imperial Japanese aggression in the 1930s and 1940s is now extremely rare.

Some scholars argue that the rise of war-averse sentiment in the industrialised countries has been the critical factor in the worldwide decline in international war.[17]

The reason that liberal democracies live in peace, according to this view, is not because they have democratic modes of government, but because their leaders and peoples have become more averse to war.

From this perspective, interdependence and the rapid growth of membership in international institutions are a *consequence* of the peace achieved by increased war-aversion, not its causes.[18]

While the rival merits of the different explanations of the decline in international conflict are subject to intense debate within the scholarly community, they are not necessarily contradictory. The problem with them all is that while they surely point to changes that are likely to enhance security in the long run, none can account for the steep decline in international wars between 1980 and 2002.

Countries didn't become dramatically more interdependent in this period; war didn't suddenly become more costly; nor was there a huge increase in membership in international institutions. And a global increase in anti-war sentiment around the world can't explain the decline, for while *international* wars declined from 1980 to the beginning of the 1990s, *civil* wars increased dramatically during this period (Figure 5.2).

The evidence suggests that the end of colonialism triggered the decline in international wars that started in the early 1980s, and that the end of the Cold War ensured that it continued.

The rise and decline of civil war

Civil wars were rare in the immediate aftermath of World War II, but over the next four decades they increased in number at an unprecedented rate. This increase was followed by a more rapid decline. The Cold War—and its ending—was a critical determinant of the changes.

The most dramatic changes in the incidence of warfare in the past two centuries have taken place in the last 60 years and relate to changes in civil war (also known as intrastate war).

The number of civil wars taking place around the world increased from two in 1946 to 25 in 1991.[19] Prior to World War II the maximum number of civil wars in the world in any one year had never exceeded 10. (Note that because Figure 5.2 shows five-year moving averages the highest totals for particular years will not be shown.)

As Figure 5.2 shows, the escalation in the number of civil wars from 1946 to 1991 was by far the largest in the entire 1816 to 2002 period. This remarkable increase was due mainly to the rise in Cold War–related conflicts and to struggles for control over the new states created by the end of colonialism.

The *decline* in civil war numbers that began after 1992 was steeper than the considerable increase from

1946 to 1992. In just 10 years, the number of civil wars fell by 80%.[20]

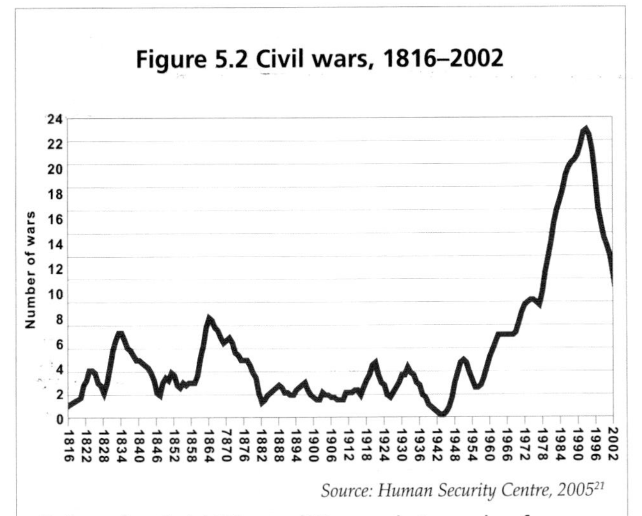

Driven by Cold War politics and struggles for control of the post-colonial state, civil wars soared after World War II, then declined even more rapidly after the end of the Cold War.

(The graph shows the annual number of wars expressed as a five-year moving average.)

The decline in civil wars is due in large part to changes wrought by the end of the Cold War. But before discussing these changes in detail, four other potential explanations are considered.

> The end of colonialism contributed to an increase in civil wars.

The end of colonialism

The often violent demise of colonial rule around the world removed a major driver of war from the international system. However, this change did not reduce the number of *civil* wars. These continued to rise rapidly in number throughout the 1980s. Part of the reason for this was that in many newly independent countries the stuggle against colonialism was replaced by wars over who should control the post-colonial state.

The end of colonialism contributed to an increase rather than a decrease in the number of civil wars. But not only were new post-colonial stuggles being waged, throughout the 1980s many civil wars were being prolonged by continued support from the superpowers and their allies.

Democratisation

Established democratic states almost never go to war against each other; they also have a very low risk of succumbing to civil war.

The number of democracies increased by nearly half between 1990 and 2003 (Figure 5.3),[22] while the number of civil conflicts declined sharply over the same period. Can the surge in democratisation explain the decline? The evidence suggests that this is unlikely.

The risk of civil war is indeed low in stable and inclusive democracies, but countries with governments that are partly democratic and partly authoritarian—dubbed 'anocracies' by political scientists—are *more* prone to civil war than either democracies or autocracies.[23]

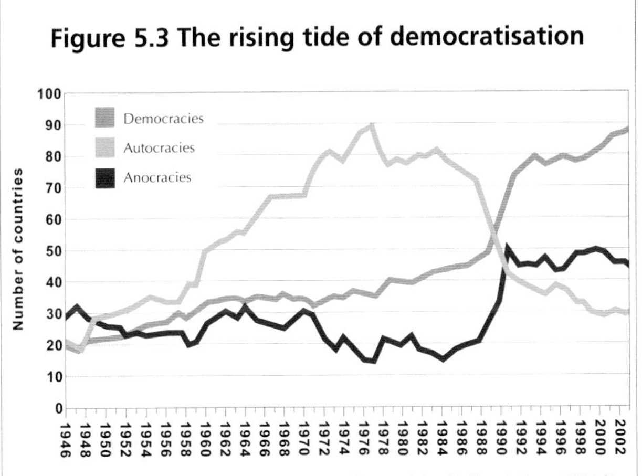

The number of democratic regimes increased consistently in the 1990s. But any security benefits from this change were likely offset by the increase in the number of 'anocracies'—regimes that are neither democratic nor autocratic, and which are associated with a higher risk of civil war.

This finding is important. While the number of inclusive democracies increased dramatically as the Cold War wound down, so too did the number of anocracies. So it is likely that the positive impact on global security of more democracies was offset by the negative impact of the increase in risk-prone anocracies.

State capacity

Levels of economic development and the risk of war are strongly related (Figure 5.4). Indeed, one of the most striking findings to emerge from conflict research is that most wars take place in poor countries, and that as per capita income increases, the risk of war declines.

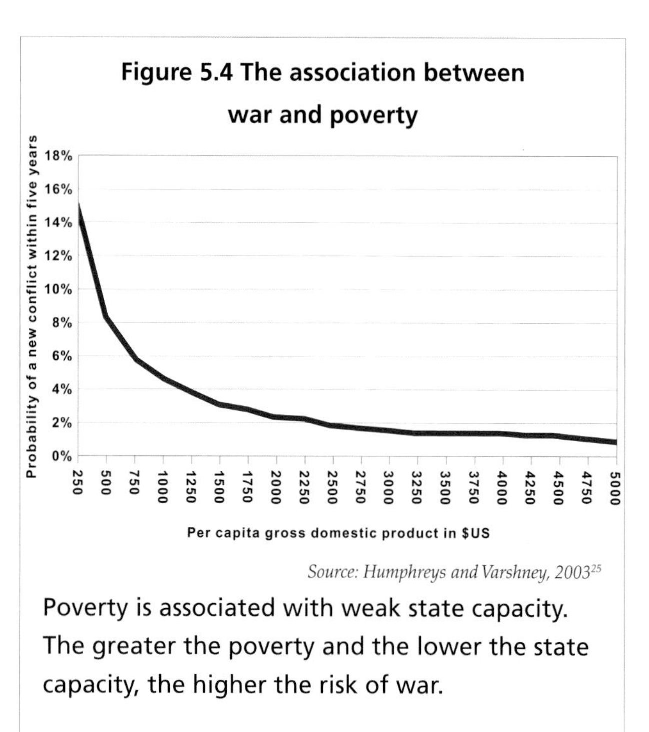

Figure 5.4 The association between war and poverty

Source: Humphreys and Varshney, 2003[25]

Poverty is associated with weak state capacity. The greater the poverty and the lower the state capacity, the higher the risk of war.

This doesn't, of course, mean that the poor are inherently more violent than the rich. Indeed, the key factor here does not appear to be per capita income as much as state capacity. Other things being equal, the higher the per capita income a country has, the stronger and more capable its government. This in turn means more state resources to crush rebels and to redress grievances.

The pursuit of equitable economic growth would thus appear to be an effective long-term strategy for enhancing security, in addition to being a necessary condition for sustainable human development.

But while there is no doubt that growth in state income and capacity is associated with a reduced risk of armed conflict *in the long term,* neither factor can explain the major decline in civil wars since the early 1990s. The rate of economic growth in this period is simply too slow to account for such a rapid drop in conflict numbers.

Ethnic discrimination and conflict

Ethnic conflict has been the subject of intense scholarly scrutiny in recent years. A new analysis by the Minorities at Risk project at the University of Maryland argues that 'high levels of political discrimination are a key cause of violent ethnic conflict' and that there has been a steady decline in political discrimination by governments around the world since 1950.[26]

In 1950, some 45% of governments around the world actively discriminated against ethnic groups; by 2003, that share had shrunk to 25%. Economic discrimination by governments followed a similar trend.[27]

The decline in official discrimination has also been paralleled by a long-term rise in government-sponsored *positive* discrimination/affirmative action programs for ethnic minorities around the world. This appears to be part of a broader normative shift toward greater recognition of minority rights and away from seeking to resolve political conflicts by force.

Other things being equal, the higher the per capita income a country has, the stronger and more capable its government. This in turn means more state resources to crush rebels and to redress grievances.

But while this is clearly a trend that enhances security in the long term, it cannot explain the sharp decline in armed conflicts—including ethnic conflicts—in the 1990s.[28]

The security-enhancing effect of the steady reduction of political and economic discrimination was not strong enough to offset the rapid increase in civil wars from the 1950s to the early 1990s. And there is no evidence to suggest that after the end of the Cold War the reduction in discrimination suddenly became a powerful enough force to account for the decline in conflict numbers.[29]

The explanation for the dramatic drop in political violence in the 1990s has to be related to other changes that took place during, or immediately preceding, this period.

The end of the Cold War

The most persuasive explanation for the decline in civil conflict is found in the far-reaching political changes wrought by the end of the Cold War.

What were the forces that drove the decline?

First, as already noted, the end of the Cold War removed a major driver of ideological hostility from the international system. This affected civil wars as well as international wars.

Second, the end of the Cold War meant that the two superpowers largely stopped supporting their clients in proxy wars in the developing world. Denied this support, many of these conflicts died out, or the parties sued for peace. But less than 20% of the post–Cold War decline in conflict numbers appears to be attributable to this factor.[30]

Third, and most important, the end of the Cold War liberated the UN, allowing it for the first time to play an effective global security role—and indeed to do far more than its founders had originally envisaged.[31] The impact of this wave of post–Cold War activism on the global security front—which went well beyond the UN—has been both profound and the subject of extraordinarily little study.

The upsurge of international activism

Since the end of the 1980s, the UN has spearheaded a remarkable, if often inchoate, upsurge in conflict management, conflict prevention and post-conflict peacebuilding activities by the international community. The World Bank, donor states and a number of regional security organisations, as well as literally thousands of NGOs, have both complemented UN activities and played independent prevention and peacebuilding roles of their own.

The extent of the changes that have taken place over the last 15 years[32] is as remarkable as it is under-reported:

- **A dramatic increase in preventive diplomacy and peacemaking activities.** UN preventive diplomacy missions (those that seek to prevent wars from breaking out in the first place) increased from one in 1990 to six in 2002.[33]

  UN peacemaking activities (those that seek to stop ongoing conflicts) also increased nearly fourfold—from four in 1990 to 15 in 2002 (Figure 5.5).

Figure 5.5 UN peacemaking activities, 1989–2002

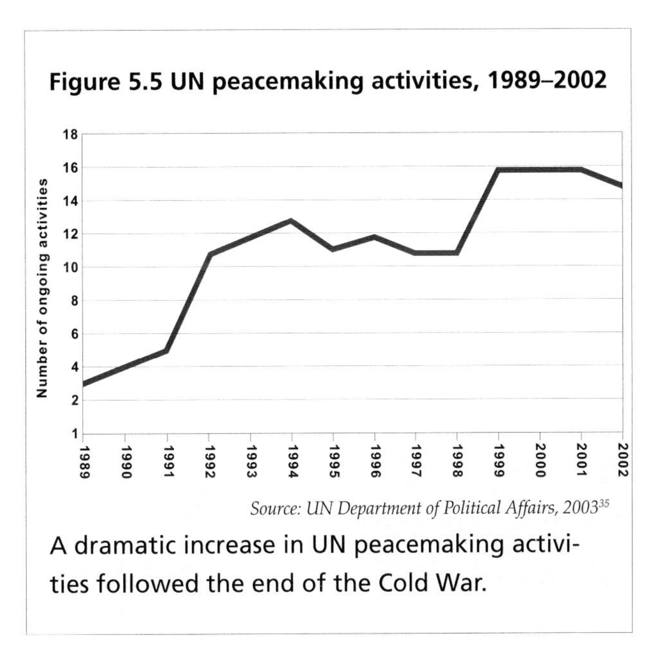

Source: UN Department of Political Affairs, 2003[35]

A dramatic increase in UN peacemaking activities followed the end of the Cold War.

The increase in preventive diplomacy helped prevent a number of latent conflicts from crossing the threshold into warfare, while the rise in peacemaking activities has been associated with a major increase in negotiated peace settlements. Approximately half of all the peace settlements negotiated between 1946 and 2003 have been signed since the end of the Cold War.[34] The average number of conflicts terminated per year in the 1990s was more than twice the average of all previous decades from 1946 onwards.

- **An increase in international support for UN peacemaking.** The number of 'Friends of the Secretary-

General', 'Contact Groups' and other mechanisms created by governments to support UN peacemaking activities and peace operations in countries in—or emerging from—conflict increased from 4 in 1990 to more than 28 in 2003, a sevenfold increase.[36]

- **An increase in post-conflict peace operations.** There has been a major increase in complex peace operations, not just UN missions, but those of regional organisations as well. These have involved an ever-growing range of peacebuilding activities that are designed in part to prevent the recurrence of conflict. Since 40% of post-conflict countries relapse into political violence within five years,[37] any policy initiatives that can minimise this risk will in turn reduce the risk of future wars.

The number of UN peacekeeping operations more than doubled between 1988 and 2004—from 7 to 16 (Figure 5.6).

Figure 5.6 UN peacekeeping operations, 1948–2004

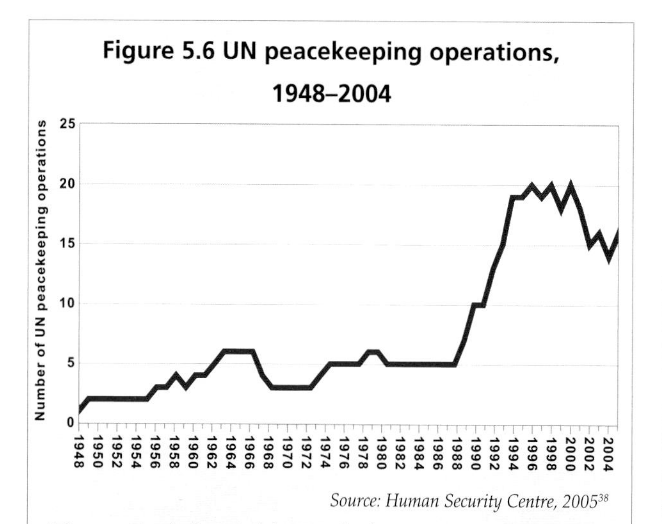

Source: Human Security Centre, 2005[38]

The end of the Cold War led to a steep increase in UN peacekeeping operations. Peace operations now play a critical role in rebuilding war-shattered societies and in preventing peace agreements from breaking down.

The peace operations of the post–Cold War era are not merely larger and more numerous than Cold War peacekeeping missions, they are also far more ambitious. Whereas the Cold War missions typically involved little more than monitoring ceasefires, many of today's operations are more akin to nation building.

A recent RAND Corporation study found that despite the much-publicised failures, two-thirds of UN nation-building missions examined were successful. This compared with a 50% success rate for comparable US missions.[39]

- **A much greater willingness to use force.** The Security Council has been increasingly willing to authorise the use of force to deter 'spoilers' from undermining peace agreements and in so doing to restart old conflicts. UN peace operations are now routinely mandated to use force to protect the peace, not just their own personnel.[40]
- **An increased resort to economic coercion.** Since the end of the Cold War the Security Council has been increasingly willing to impose economic sanctions—the other coercive instrument in the council's armoury. The number of UN sanctions on regimes increased more than fivefold between 1990 and 2000.[41] Sanctions can help deny warring parties access to arms and can pressure recalcitrant regimes—and rebel groups—to enter peace negotiations.
- **An assault on the culture of impunity.** In addition to the establishment of the International Criminal Court and the various UN and ad hoc tribunals, the number

Figure 5.7 Numbers of international tribunals and countries prosecuting grave human rights abuses, 1970–2004

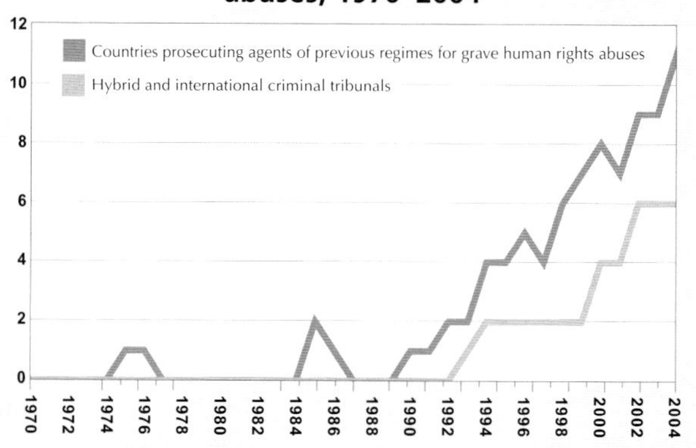

Source: Human Security Centre, 2005[42]

The ending of the Cold War was associated with an increase in national and international prosecutions of perpetrators of grave human rights abuses.

of governments prosecuting agents of former regimes for grave human rights abuses increased from 1 to 11 between 1990 and 2004 (Figure 5.7). If would-be perpetrators of gross human rights abuses believe there is a real prospect that they will be brought to justice they may be deterred from acting in the first place.[43]

- **A greater emphasis on reconciliation.** The number of truth and reconciliation commissions in operation in any one year has more than doubled since the end of the Cold War—from one in 1989 to seven in 2003.[44] Pursuing reconciliation rather than revenge in post-conflict societies reduces the risk of renewed violence. Reconciliation is also a major aim of most peacebuilding programs.
- **Addressing the root causes of conflict.** The UN, the World Bank along with other international agencies and donor governments are increasingly designing development and aid policies that address what are perceived to be the root causes of political violence.

Individually, none of these policies has had a great impact on global security. Most have achieved only modest success in terms of their own goals. But taken together, their impact has been highly significant.

Overall, this surge of international activism provides the single best explanation for the extraordinary decrease in civil wars around the world since the 1990s.

Conclusion

The evidence and analysis briefly reviewed here support the following conclusions:

- International wars are extremely rare today and are likely to remain so for the foreseeable future. The reasons for this include the factors identified by proponents of the liberal peace, the caution-inducing existence of nuclear weapons, the spread of the norm of war-aversion and the growing acceptance of norms prohibiting the use of force except in self-defence or when authorised by the Security Council.
- The sharp decline in international wars since the end of the 1970s is best explained not by institutions, structures and processes, which change slowly, but by the two dramatic shifts in global politics during this period—namely the demise of colonialism and the end of the Cold War.
- The civil war story is quite different. Over the long term, the evidence suggests that the risk of civil conflict is reduced by equitable economic growth, good governance and inclusive democracy. Development, in other words, appears to be a necessary condition for security, just as security is a necessary condition for development.

The 80% decline in the most deadly civil conflicts numbers that has taken place since the early 1990s owes little to any of the above factors, however.[45] Here the evidence suggests the main driver of change has been the extraordinary upsurge of activism by the international community that has been directed toward conflict prevention, peacemaking and peacebuilding.

This last point is both the most surprising and the least examined.[46] The evidence that international activism has been the main cause of the post–Cold War decline in armed conflict is persuasive, but thus far it is mostly circumstantial. A lot more research is required to determine which specific activities and mechanisms have been most effective in bringing about the recent improvement in global security—and under what conditions.

The *Human Security Report 2006* will provide a more detailed analysis of these trends and the data that support them. It will also examine the counter-trends that, if not addressed, may pose a major threat to global security in the long term.

PART V

ENDNOTES

1. Geoffrey Blainey, *The Causes of War*, 3rd ed. (New York: Free Press, 1988).
2. Because colonial wars are not between states, but between an external state and an indigenous liberation army, they are referred to by many scholars as 'extra-systemic' conflicts.
3. This estimate is drawn from tables in Kristian Gleditsch, 'A Revised List of Wars Between and Within Independent States, 1816–2002', *International Interactions* 30 (2004): 231–262. The Gleditsch dataset is a revised version of the Correlates of War dataset.
4. Ibid.
5. Wars are defined in this dataset as conflicts that result in 1000 or more battle-deaths and in which at least one of the warring parties is a government.
6. Kristian Gleditsch, 'A Revised List of Wars Between and Within Independent States, 1816–2002'. The term 'international war' as opposed to 'interstate war' is used because the dataset includes anti-colonial struggles which do not, strictly speaking, involve two or more governments.
7. Ibid.
8. Some anti-colonial conflicts were, of course, related to the Cold War.
9. The third war in 1999 was that between Eritrea and Ethiopia.
10. Monty G. Marshall and Ted Robert Gurr, *Peace and Conflict 2005*, Center for International Development and Conflict Management (College Park, MD: University of Maryland, May 2005), http://www.cidcm.umd.edu/inscr/PC05print.pdf (accessed 20 July 2005).
11. Based on data in Kristian Gleditsch, 'A Revised List of Wars Between and Within Independent States, 1816–2002'.
12. Note that while five-year moving average graphs show trends more clearly than single-year graphs, they tend to obscure some annual changes.
13. Bruce Russett and John O'Neal, *Triangulating Peace: Democracy, Interdependence and International Organizations* (New York: WW Norton, 2001). Some critics object to this argument noting (correctly) that pre-war relationships between Germany and the countries it attacked were characterised by a high degree of economic interdependence, but that this did not prevent German aggression. This sort of criticism misses the point. The fact that *some* incentives for going to war have been reduced does not mean other drivers may not, on occasion, impel countries into war. Reducing the risk of war is not the same as eliminating it.
14. Ibid.
15. John Mearsheimer and Christopher Layne in Michael E. Brown et al., eds., *Theories of War and Peace* (Cambridge, MA: MIT Press, 1998).
16. John Mueller, *The Remnants of War* (Ithaca: Cornell Univeristy Press, September 2004).
17. Ibid.
18. Ibid.
19. Kristian Gleditsch, 'A Revised List of Wars Between and Within Independent States, 1816–2002'. Note that while these figures refer only to civil (or intrastate) *wars*, the patterns are very similar to the intrastate conflict trends seen in the Uppsala/PRIO dataset discussed in Part I.
20. Ibid. If *all* civil conflicts involving a state are considered—that is, all civil conflicts resulting in at least 25 battle-related deaths per year as opposed to only those resulting in at least 1000 battle-deaths—there is nearly a 40% decline over the same period.
21. Based on data in Kristian Gleditsch, 'A Revised List of Wars Between and Within Independent States, 1816–2002'.
22. Monty G. Marshall and Ted Robert Gurr, *Peace and Conflict 2005*.

23. See Håvard Hegre, Scott Gates, Nils Petter Gleditsch, et al.,'Toward a Democratic Civil Peace? Democracy, Political Change, and Civil War, 1816–1992', *American Political Science Review* 95, 1 (March 2001): 16–33, http://www.prio.no/page/Publication_details/CSCW_Staff_alpha_ALL/9429/38020.html (accessed 27 July 2005).
24. Monty G. Marshall and Teb Robert Gurr, *Peace and Conflict 2005.*
25. Macartan Humphreys and Ashutosh Varshney,'Violent Conflict and the Millennium Development Goals: Diagnosis and Recommendations', 1st draft, background paper prepared for the meeting of the Millennium Development Goals Poverty Task Force Workshop, Bangkok, June 2004, http://www.columbia.edu/~mh2245/papers1/HV.pdf (accessed 27 July 2005).
26. Victor Asal and Amy Pate,'The Decline of Ethnic Political Discrimination, 1950–2003' in Monty G. Marshall and Ted Robert Gurr, *Peace and Conflict 2005.*
27. Ibid.
28. For data on the increase and subsequent decline in ethnic conflicts see Monty G. Marshall, Ted Robert Gurr and Deepa Khosla, *Peace and Conflict 2001*, Center for International Development and Conflict Management (College Park, MD: University of Maryland, 2000), 10–11, http://www.cidcm.umd.edu/peaceconflict.pdf (accessed 27 July 2005).
29. Clearly, not all conflicts are ethnic conflicts.
30. This approximate percentage was established by a review conducted by the Human Security Centre of all the conflicts that have ended since 1989. About half these conflict terminations started *after* the Cold War was over.
31. The UN was established in an era when civil conflict was extremely rare. This is reflected in the language of the Charter which assigns to the Security Council the primary responsibility for maintaining *international* peace and security but contains no provisions for dealing with civil war. Indeed, Article 2.7 of the UN Charter precludes UN intervention in 'matters which are essentially within the domestic jurisdiction of any state'. The Charter also contains no reference to peacekeeping, let alone peacebuilding. However, since 1989 the UN has become increasingly involved in activities that address conflicts *within* states.
32. References for these figures will be presented in the *Human Security Report 2006.*
33. Data provided by the UN Department of Political Affairs.
34. This finding comes from a new dataset on conflict termination created by the Uppsala Conflict Data Program that was commissioned by the Human Security Centre and will be reviewed in detail in the *Human Security Report 2006.*
35. Data provided by the UN Department of Political Affairs.
36. Calculations based on data in Teresa Whitfield,'A Crowded Field: Groups of Friends, the United Nations and the Resolution of Conflict', a paper reflecting work in progress for an upcoming book, New York, April 2005.
37. Paul Collier and Anke Hoeffler, 'The Challenge of Reducing the Global Incidence of Civil War', Copenhagen Consensus Challenge Paper, March 2004, www.copenhagenconsensus.com/Files/Filer/CC/Papers/Conflicts_230404.pdf (accessed 27 July 2004).
38. Based on data from the UN Department of Peacekeeping Operations, http://www.un.org/Depts/dpko/dpko/index.asp (accessed 22 July 2005).
39. Rand Corporation, 'Rand Study Says UN Nation Building Record Compares Favourably with the US in Some Respects', press release, 18 February 2005, http://www.rand.org/news/press.05/02.18.html (accessed 26 July 2005).
40. Data provided by Peter Wallensteen and Patrik Johansson, Department of Peace and Conflict Research, Uppsala University, 2003.
41. United Nations, 'Use of sanctions under Chapter VII of the UN Charter', Office of the Spokesman for the Secretary-General website January 2005, http://www.un.org/News/ossg/sanction.htm (Accessed 23 August 2005).
42. Data compiled by the Human Security Centre, from a wide variety of print and online sources.

43. However, some argue that threats of prosecution mean that those responsible for the crimes in question will be less likely to give up power.

44. Data compiled by the Human Security Centre, from a wide variety of print and online sources. Note that some commissions are truth commissions while others are both truth *and* reconciliation commissions.

45. Kristian Gleditsch, 'A Revised List of Wars Between and Within Independent States, 1816–2002'.

46. Notable exceptions are found in the work of Ted Robert Gurr and Monty G. Marshall of the University of Maryland and Peter Wallensteen of Uppsala University.